GOVERNANCE UNDER ISLAM

Governance Under Islam

B.D. USMANI

ANMOL PUBLICATIONS PVT. LTD.
NEW DELHI - 110 002 (INDIA)

ANMOL PUBLICATIONS PVT. LTD.
4374/4B, Ansari Road, Daryaganj
New Delhi - 110 002
Ph.: 23261597, 23278000
Visit us at: www.anmolpublications.com

Governance Under Islam

First Published, 2004
ISBN 81-261-2011-8

PRINTED IN INDIA

Published by J.L. Kumar for Anmol Publications Pvt. Ltd., New Delhi - 110 002 and Printed at Mehra Offset Press, Delhi.

Contents

Preface

Islam is not a philosophical faith alone. It is a practical religion and a perfect way of life, covering all areas. Hence, it has given the world a flawless system of governance.

Islam does not separate religion from the wordly affairs. The tenets of Islam instruct about a cohesive system, which combines spiritual, social and political systems. In true spirit of faith, the sovereignty lies in Almighty only. Under Him, His deputy, the chief of the community *Ameer-ul-Momineen* is the religious head also. He is supposed to lead *Ummah* (Muslim Community) in all fields. He is the Head of State, Commander-in-Chief and spiritual guide, all rolled into one. However, practically, this institution could not continue beyond four pious caliphs. The later caliphs turned themselves into monarchs and made the position hereditory, which was un-Islamic and undemocratic.

In Islam, the political system is based on democracy. All decisions are to be taken on the basis of consensus or by majority opinion, in case of disagreement. As a progressive and democratic religion Islam bestows the right of opinion (vote) upon all the members of community and right to protest and oppose any decision of even the top functionary. In fact, Islamic system is the only system of governance, which allows any individual to challenge any decision of the Head of State in an open assembly. This is one privilege, which perhaps, no modern constitutional system can offer, in actual practice.

This research based work covers all the issues concerning the governance under Islam in historical context and explores all inherent angles of theoretical and practical aspects of Islamic Political System, which flourished under Holy Prophet himself.

The undersigned feels honoured in presenting an authentic and exhaustive book on a subject, which has attained new significance in the context of some recent developments on the horizon of the world. Expectedly, this sincere effort should invite due recognition.

—Editor

1

Introduction

We have had a brief appraisal of Constitutional Charter of Madina from the point of view of seeing how its clauses affected the Believers and Jews and the importance given to the task of defending the state, created as a consequence of this Document. Every document, however detailed it may be, creates a number of questions. A perusal of the document does raise a few questions which need further explanation. The Charter clearly lays down in Clauses 28 and 47 that the final decision or in other words, the Sovereignty belongs to Allah. Modern trend is that sovereignty belongs to the elected representatives of the people known as the Parliament. In the case of British as pointed out earlier, "The law assumes that Parliament is omnipotent and paramount. It can make or unmake laws on any matter whatsoever."[1]

Why do people in the Western world desire to grant sovereignty to their elected representatives and have after great struggle freed themselves of the sovereign power which the Church had held. The reason appears to be that the so-called Divine Laws enforced by the Church were in actual fact not of Divine origin, with the result that they did not meet the needs and demands of the people. As has been said, "Sovereignty is not an end in itself; it is a means to government, just as government is not an end but a means to the good life."When laws given by the Church failed to provide good life, they were discarded. The result of twisted and moulded laws of pseudo-Divine origin resulted in a disturbed society in which people tried to find Saviors from among philosophers. "Before the end of the seventeenth century there had been a revulsion in the West not merely against religious fanatism but against religion itself in consequence of the West's weariness of its own domestic wars of religion." The search to find freedom from the philosophers led them to seek the help of politicians which after a time transferred sovereignty from the Church and the rulers annointed by the Church to the representatives of the people.

Muslim societies have gone through nearly the same process. An outsider has observed that, "The growth of royalty and the emergence of a priesthood to twist and mould the Scriptures to a required pattern has been the main influence that led to the ultimate destruction of the tremendous influence of Islam." This may not be a completely correct analysis but it is correct to a large extent.

The sovereignty of the people is evident from nearly all Western Constitutions. Article I of the Constitution of the United States of America (1787), on the lines of the British Constitution lays down that, "All legislative power herein granted shall be vested in a Congress of the United States, which shall consist of a Senate and House of Representatives. This constitution assumes that the Congress shall be omnipotent and paramount as any parliament in any other part of the world."

The Muslim countries have also established parliaments, whose members are elected as in other countries of the world. The question, however arises as to the correct limit of paramountcy of these parliaments, if the Muslims wish to act on their belief that Sovereignty belongs to Allah.

Theoretically speaking, the answer is simple. The Muslims have to obey the Laws of the Quran and the Sunnah. The limit of the paramountcy of their Parliaments would, therefore, be confined to problems which have not been dealt with by the Quran and the Sunnah. As a guide it can be said that the Quran and the Sunnah have avoided laying down laws pertaining to problems which are subject to changes resulting from difference in time and place.

The first Constitutional Charter of the first Islamic state provides clear guidelines in this manner that it avoids giving details of the form and shape of the government and the functions of the various organs and personalities of the state, except the question of declaration of war by the head of the state.

The modern constitutions, as referred to earlier, "aspire to regulate the allocation of functions, powers, and duties among the various agencies and offices of the government, and define the relationship between these and the public." All these aspects of the functions of a state are not of permanent nature, and are subject to changes in time and place. The Constitutional Charter of Madina does not touch any of these aspects. These are to be decided by the people. They have, in this process, to observe the Commandment:-

> "And consult with them upon the conduct of affairs."
> 3: 159

And that is why Allah says that one of the characteristics of Believer is that:-

> "And whose affairs are a matter of counsel." 42: 38

The modern constitutions lay down, as a check, on members of their Parliaments, on the lines given in the Constitution of Federal Republic of Germany, which says, that the members will be "Conscious of their responsibility before God and man." They, however, do not place any definite demands or limits placed by the God of their imagination. The Charter of Madina had laid down such a limit before the future generations. It was in the shape of Laws Revealed to Muhammad (PBUH) as the Last Prophet of Allah. The difference between the West and Islam has appeared because of the false idea about God which had crept in before the appearance of Muhammad (PBUH), and which alters the very process of thought. "False idea of God means a false idea of our own inner selves of our relations to the world around us, and of our duties to our fellow creatures." The result of this false idea of God has been the flouting of the moral and ethical Code given by Him, through His Prophets. Islam has reminded mankind of what earlier Prophets had brought from Allah. "The originality of Islam lies in the fact that it has taught the world what the world had forgotten or perverted.... It has reminded humanity that there is only One Omnipotent, Just and Merciful, Creator and Sustainer,..." His attributes and His Sovereignty cannot be usurped by His creatures, without resulting in the loss of happiness and contentment in this world itself and grave consequences in the next. The Muslims, themselves, however, forgot this truth.

The principle of Sovereignty of Allah, through organizing the society according to the Revealed Law of Allah has not been given enough attention. The fault lies with the Muslims, who enamoured of establishing themselves over vast areas, forgot that their supremacy lay in the observance of the Revealed Law and not in the qualities which they acquired through the faithful observance of this law. Law of Quran, as explained earlier, does not permit aggression, which means that war as such is prohibited in Islam. It goes further. The Revealed Law of Allah, lays down that the moment the aggressor leans towards peace the Muslims must also do so.

"If they incline to peace, incline thou also to it". 8: 61

This means that the Law promulgated through the Constitutional Charter (Clauses 28, 47 and 54) does not permit the continuance of fighting even against the aggressor, the moment the aggressor wishes to lay down weapons. This emphasis on "Peace," is not found in any man-made law, because, law as visualised, "represents the policy of the master or the leading class (in a country). It (law) is the tool of such a policy...." If all nations were subject to the Revealed Law of Islam, which does not permit war in the national or any other interests, war would be eliminated. The entire world being subject to the same Law, will, in practice amount to one state.

"In a state which is practically capable of embracing the world and has its law laid down by a Supreme Legislator, territorial limitations are irrelevant. The allegiance of men would be to a symbol of unity, not to territorial divisions." The fault of Muslims is, that they have failed to bring into existence such conditions, as would amount to only one state. If they had continued to adhere to Clause 19 of The Charter, and not divided their peace, they would have virtually been members of a super-state, composed of administrative units, known as countries, in the same way as they have to-day provinces, divisions, districts and counties. They would thus have attracted the rest of humanity to join this mighty confederacy of Muslim states, each independent in itself, but all of them following the same Divine Law.

This picture of humanity, standing on one platform, was shattered by the Jews of Madina, whose petty-minded aloofness resulting from their false notion of being the chosen people has brought them to the position of self-appointed untouchables of humanity. The position offered to them was unique and unprecedented in human history, in view of the inferior position they held, all the world over, particularly in Arabia. The Jews were told that no harm will come to them, because of their being Jews. They were also assured that their allies abroad will be given the same status as they chose for themselves and no help of any kind will be given to their enemies. These concessions did not carry any responsibilities. If, however, they followed the Believers and fought Jehad alongside them, they were to be given an equal status and would have formed ONE UMMAH with the Believers, but, they would have retained their Jewish identity." These were very generous terms. They accepted them but on second thought they seem to have come to the conclusion that they could not accept the principle of Sovereignty of Allah and His Prophet (PBUH). They had already discarded the Divine Law, in total. They were not prepared to subject themselves to a Divine Law being revealed to Muhammad (PBUH).

The Jews, however, true to their traditions, were not united among themselves and although of the same mind did not decide to take concerted action. The first Jewish tribe to take steps to start opposition to the Prophet (PBUH) in Yathrib, appear to be Banu Qainqa. There is not enough material available to determine the exact time when they established contact with the Quraysh of Makkah. It must have been even before the battle of Badr. This is evident from the activities of Quraysh and their allies soon after Badr. The raid by Abu Sufian at a time when their allies the Banu Ghatfan were also preparing to attack Yathrib, and the rebellion of Qainqa, all taking place, during the space of just over one month leads us to the conclusion that they are parts of a single plan. They could not be synchronized because events took place in an unexpected manner. Ka'ab bin Ashraf, of whom mention has been made, appears to be the key figure who left Yathrib soon after Badr and when in Makkah wrote poetry inciting the Quraysh to avenge themselves without loss of time. The plan did not succeed because the Banu Ghatfan were dispersed by the Prophet (PBUH) before they could concentrate for the march against Yathrib. The Jews of Banu Qainqa were over -confident and they started their rebellion too soon, when neither the Makkans, were yet ready nor had they co-ordinated with Banu Ghatfan. The information conveyed by Ka'ab bin Ashraf to Makkah about the ability of Banu Qainqa to withstand the siege was wrong, and they had to surrender before Abu Sufian could reach the outskirts of Yathrib. Abu Sufian, when on arrival outside Yathrib, found that the Banu Ghatfan had been made to disperse by the Prophet and the Banu Qainqa had surrendered and left Yathrib only a few days before his arrival, he realised that he was alone. As a result he undertook a hurried retreat and found himself in so precarious a position that he and his contingent of 200 had to throw away their bags of rations, to lighten the burden of their camels, in order to avoid being overtaken by the Prophet (PBUH). The part played by Ka'ab bin Ashraf and the treacherous behavior of Banu Qainqa, so soon after Badr, in contravening the Clauses of the Charter, clarifies the situation in Madina during the post Meethaq-e-Madina period. Banu Qainqa had sown the seeds of treacherous rebellion, at the most critical period of Muslim history. These seeds were to sprout and continue creating mischief for Muslims in later days.

The rebellion of Banu Nadhir immediately after the battle of Ohud, in which the Believers had suffered losses was the result of the Prophet (PBUH) calling upon this Jewish tribe, to contribute towards defraying the expenses resulting from the payment of blood money to Banu Nadhir. This demand had been under Clause 43 of the Charter. They, like Banu Qainqa were allowed to migrate from Madina with all their possessions and wealth, except weapons.

The third large Jewish tribe was Banu Quraiza. They joined the invaders, at the time of Ghazwa-e-Ahzab. After the dispersal of the besieging confederate forces they were besieged. They surrendered after a few days and chose Sa'ad bin Ma'adh the chief of the tribe of Aus, as the judge. He chose the Jewish practice of punishment in such cases, which, in the days of King David had decided.

"The conquered Ammonite be treated with even greater ferocity, tearing and having some of them in pieces with harrows, axis, and pbuhs and roasting others in the brick kilns."

The Banu Quraiza were not treated with in the manner in which Jewish custom demanded.

The reason for the Charter to have lost importance in the eyes of historians, is obvious. The "others," who were expected to "work under the leadership of Believers," were no more. The Muhajirs and Ansars had become one body and there was no need to refer to the Charter with regard to relations between them. Obedience to Allah and His Messenger (PBUH) was being practiced in all walks of life. The Hypocrites, even though sizeable, dared not to be counted among "The Others," or anything but "Believers". Hence the Quran and the Sunnah were the Normal Law of the state. The Fundamental Law was being acted upon in all its Clauses. Unless one of its clauses was challenged there was no need to refer to it. As a result of the fact that after the departure of Jews there was no need to refer to this Document, the mistaken view received strength that it lost its importance, because there were no Jews left. Years later the view gained strength that it was a Document laying down terms of agreement between the Prophet (PBUH) and the Jews. It was natural for the Orientalist and later Muslim writers to refer to it as a treaty between the Jews and the Prophet (PBUH).

The Charter, however, needs to be studied afresh. It holds the position of written orders issued by the Prophet (PBUH), which have not been cancelled by any other document. They hold the position of confirmed Sunnah. The invitation in it to "others," to accept leadership of Believers, holds the position of a precedent. Hence if Believers issue similar invitations to others, who agree to live as Constitutional Muslims, there would be no breach of a Sunnah of the Prophet (PBUH). The Charter gives guarantee of safe and unmolested life to minorities. Muslim countries must afford full protection to the lives, property and honour of their minorities.

The relations to be maintained between the Head of State and the Armed Forces of Muslim States, need to be studied in the light of this Document, which would also include the place to be held by the Armed Forces, within their respective states.

Clause 24 laying down that "Peace of Believers is indivisible," needs a great deal of study. Its implications are:-

1. Believers cannot go to war against one another.

2. If the land of one Muslim country is invaded it amounts to an act of war against all Muslim countries.

3. Peace treaties with non-Muslim countries must be executed after consultation with all other Muslim countries.

The implication of this Clause are of great significance and amount to planning for the setting up of a Joint Defence Organization. At the present moment, although there exists the Organization for Islamic Countries it has inadequate staff for undertaking the planning of a Joint Defence Organization.

Joint Defence cannot be undertaken until information of present and possible future enemies and there capabilities is collected, collated and analysed at a central place. It would, at the same time, be necessary to determine the present capabilities and future potential of the Muslim States desiring to share defence responsibilities. Collection and collation of information about the Muslim States and likely enemies will be a time consuming undertaking. A library will have to be established and research worker from all Muslim countries, possessing knowledge of their countries and having defence background will be needed. Muslim World is spread out along the major part of the Globe, so are its enemies. Therefore "Any research organization supporting a total war of this magnitude must be capable of furnishing the latest and most authentic information on all aspects of life of entire humanity spread throughout the surface of the Globe."

"The Believers, because they fear Allah, are better in showing steadfastness and as a result receive Guidance."

This is not a mere statement of fact. The Charter would not contain a mere statement of fact. There has to be some action which needs being taken as a result of such a categorical statement. Could it not be that apart from depicting the difference between the mental and spiritual build up of Believers and un-Believers, it lays down that Muslim States need to keep this fact in mind and not to omit the task of continuous motivation of their people, and thus fulfil the task which is the responsibility of the leaders of the Ummah contained in the following Verse of the Quran:-

> "And urge on the believers. Peradventure Allah will restrain the might of those who disbelieve." 4: 84

It has been said that the source of wisdom and its highest point lie in inculcating "Fear of Allah'". Arrangements must be made to educate the youth of Muslim countries in the Philosophy of Life which is the result of Belief in the Unity and Sovereignty of Allah. The life led by the Prophet (PBUH) as a result of this Philosophy needs to be kept as a model for all Muslims.

The heading of the Document and Clause 30 need very detailed objective study, keeping in view the teachings of the Quran and the Sunnah of the Prophet (PBUH). The Prophet (PBUH) never in his life gave an undertaking which he did not fulfil. To have promised un-Believers equality and membership of the Ummah if they performed two things:-

1. They followed the Believers.

2. They fought alongside the Believers, when the Believers were engaged in battle in the Path of Allah.

It needs determining as to what is meant by the words "if they followed the Believers." Following the Believers could only be in respect of:-

(a) The type of communal life which was led by the Believers and when it was also adopted by them.

(b) All undertakings in respect of Internal Security of the Society were observed by them.

(c) All decisions in respect of relations with other states were approved and observed by them in equally the same manner as adopted by the Believers.

(d) They did not interfere in defence preparations.

(e) They fulfilled defence responsibilities in the manner decided and directed by the state in which they resided.

This Document can form the basis of rules, regulations and directions issued in relations to minorities residing in Muslim countries. In this respect the following Clauses also need being considered.

Clause 34 lays down that "those in alliance with the Jews will be given the same treatment as the Jews."

It can now be interpreted as helping the co-religionists of minorities living in Muslim lands.

Clause 26 which lays down that "No un-Believer will intervene in favour of Quraysh."

This means that minorities in Muslim lands will have to sever relations with the enemies of the state they reside in. Those who were desirous of receiving equal treatment and being considered as part of the Ummah, would have had to conduct themselves like the Believers. The others realised that the state was being established by the Believers, who were the ruling party, forming the government of the country. They could, therefore, dictate the terms for accepting "others," as a part of the government.

There is a mistaken notion that prior to the arrival of the Prophet (PBUH) in Yathrib, it was a city state in exactly the same sense of that of Makkah, or the city states of Greece. In Makkah life was organized as best as it was anywhere else in the world. They had a Council of Elders which held proper meetings whenever any important problem arose. They had allotted subjects to individuals. No such arrangement existed in Yathrib.

The establishment of a state and the decision to run the affairs of the state and particularly its defence in accordance with a written Document was a momentous step forward. It was, as a result, a point of honour and prestige to be associated with the people who had the foresight to establish a state and administer it not on the dictatorial pattern of neighbouring states of Byzantium and Iran but on democratic lines in which the rights of even hitherto protected. People like Jews were to be considered on the same level as those of the ruling party forming the government. It was an unprecedented offer of a people who had been told by Allah, their Creator, Sustainer and Master of the Day of Judgement that they are the best Ummah. (Aal-e-Imran 3: 110)

To rub shoulders with an Ummah which was to conquer the Qaisars and Khusroes of the world would have been a unique experience for these others but in the words of Iqbal, the philosopher poet of Pakistan.

It amounts to entering the field of martyrs.

People, somehow, thinks that it is easy to become a Muslim.

They approached this ground which those alone, who were in search of martyrdom could tread, and when within sight of eternal bliss they turned back and started hatching plots to destroy the only state which, in their entire history, had offered to them the elevated position of co-rulers.

In the end we would like to invite the modern Western thinkers to study the Constitutional Charter of Madina, a little more objectively than in the past. This is a Document which belongs to the earliest period of organized Islam. This was the time when the central core of Believers had just managed to free themselves from thirteen years of persecution at the hands of a ruling party which was composed of their own kith and kin. They themselves had volunteered to form a government and defend the territory which had become their heaven. The memories of the period of persecution through which they had passed were still fresh in their minds. It seems a miracle of humane behavior to have promised equality as rulers of a state and emancipation to "the others," including the Jews, to whom they owed nothing.

This Document, as pointed out earlier on a number of occasions, is the Fundamental Law of the very first state of Muslims. It was promulgated by Prophet Muhammad (PBUH) himself, whose Commands have to be obeyed by Muslims until the end of time. The scare in Western World against the trend of Muslim countries towards Fundamentalism, cannot be justified in the light of the

Fundamental Law for Muslim states, that we have briefly studied in these pages.

The Western intellectuals have lately been holding international seminars to find out whether the Muslims are likely to get united in the near future. They have undertaken studies to pin point those points in their history which have resulted in diversity among Muslims. No Western scholar has taken pains to throw light on areas of unity among Muslims. The subject of Unity and Diversity among Muslims should have been undertaken by Muslim scholars long before it occurred to the Western scholars. Their approach would have been with a positive objective as opposed to the negative approach shown by the scholars of Western countries.

At times it becomes difficult for Muslim observers to understand unanimity among the policies of Western and Eastern blocks, when they both go to great lengths and try to root out Fundamentalism in a Muslim country. Fundamentalism is a term coined by Western intellectuals to denote their fears of a Muslim country adopting Islamic Shariat. The present writer has yet to come across a single work of scholarship, by either Western critics or Muslim modernists, which has spelled out the Laws of the Quran and the Sunnah which are not applicable in the twentieth century or which are derogatory to the smooth functioning of a modern society. To merely generalise and say that Laws meant for a undeveloped land and a young semi-civilised society cannot be implemented in an advanced society of twentieth century. It becomes necessary, for such critics, if they are sincere and honest in their approach to mention those laws specifically, and explain how they are likely to hinder progress in the setting of twentieth or twenty first century. The laws deduced from the Quran and the Sunnah, during the 12th or 13th century as a result of Ijtehad, do not justify opposition to the imposition of Shariat, which should be based on the Quran and the Sunnah and should be free to differ with the learned jurists of subsequent periods. If different versions have been accepted as a result of independent studies by men like Abu Hanifa and

Shafi'ee, then similar efforts of modern Muslim scholars should not be opposed on the supposed fear of such an effort becoming a retrograde step. Could it not be that the opposition to Islamic Shariat has been opposed, under the fictitious label of Fundamentalism, as a result of similar fears as those of the Quraysh of Makkah, and the two super powers of that age. The basic principle of Sovereignty of Allah and social and economic equality which becomes the right of every individual, in Muslim State, resulting from the practical application of the principle of Sovereignty of Allah seems to be the real cause of opposition to Fundamentalism.

If the intellectuals of today, whether Muslims or non-Muslims, desire to lead the world to complete and total peace then they should encourage the Muslim States to speed up their Fundamentalism and impose Shariat as soon as possible. What better Code of Law could there be, than the Divine Law which conveys the Commands from Almighty Allah that you will under no circumstances, spread the Way of Life, I have given to you by force or through social and economic pressures.

There is no Compulsion in Deen (Islamic Way of Life).

And then He has Ordained that you who Believe in my Sovereignty will neither be the aggressor by attacking some one, nor act as a transgressor when some one else has attacked you.

> Fight those who fight you and do not be the aggressor, (nor the transgressor).

Even when some one has been the aggressor against you and has invaded your territory but due to change of heart or fear of reprisals from your wishes to gain time and gives a hint of seeking peace, you must, at once, agree to the acceptance of peace, without putting any pre-conditions.

"If they incline to peace, incline thou also to it". 8: 61

The present writer, in compliance of the Dictates of the Quran and the Sunnah, invites the non-Muslims World to forget differences and agree to implement the points common amongst us so far.

> "Say, O Peoples of the Scriptures come to an agreement between us and you: that we shall worship none but Allah." 3: 64

As a result of mutual efforts towards peace, it is certain that other venues of co-operation and peaceful co-existence will gradually emerge. Let us prove the high qualities of "Man," the most upright creation of Allah, before the day when the curtain will drop and all else will vanish except the countenance of the Lord.

2

The Backdrop

Muhammad (PBUH) son of Abdullah and grandson of Abdul Muttalib of the well-known tribe of Quraysh was born at Makkah, on Monday the 12th of Rabiul Awwal, during the Year of Elephant, corresponding to 22nd of April 571 A.C., 53 years before Hijrah.' It was an event of great rejoicing in the house of Abdul Muttalib, a venerated old chief amongst the Quraysh. Abdullah, father of the child, had died, a few months earlier, during a visit to Yathrib. The child was named Muhammad, 'The Praised one,' by the grandfather. It was a name unusual in Arabia, but the old chief liked to have his grandson grow up as a person worthy of praise and honour. The mother Amina, also gave the child a name. It was Ahmad, 'worthy of praise.'

The Native Place

According to the prevailing custom, among the Quraysh, the child was handed over to Halima Saadiya, of a branch of the tribe of Huwaizan, after a few days, to be brought up, in the desert. Although the Quraysh were a city people and tradesmen who were acquainted with international markets from Aden to Istanbul yet they liked their male children to grow up in the free atmosphere and clean air of the desert, so that they grew up as bold and upright men who could defend their honour.

The desert of Arabia seems to have a charm of its own. An English poet has paid tribute to Arabia in touching words. He sings thus:-

Far are the shades of Arabia
Where the princes ride at noon.
Sweet is the music of Arabia
In my heart when out of dreams
Descry her gliding streams
Hear her strange lutes on the green banks
Ring loud with the grief and delight.
They haunt me—her lutes and her forests
Still eyes look upon me
Cold voices whisper and say—
He is crazed with the spell of Arabia
Walter De La Mare
Such is the charm of the Arabian desert

The period of Muhammad (PBUH) with the Huwaizan turned out to be longer than usual. At the end of the stipulated period he was brought back but due to some epidemic in Makkah, Amina, the mother asked Haleema Saadiya to look after him a little longer. This allowed him to live close to nature a little longer and develop a liking for the desert so dear to an Arab. He was five years old when he started living with his mother. Some sources place this event when he was six years of age. We are not told how relations developed, between mother and son, but the affection with which Muhammad (PBUH) remembered his mother in after life shows that relations must have developed fairly quickly between the two. The mother decided to visit Yathrib and show her young son the grave of his father. While journey to Yathrib and the period of stay there must have further developed the much needed affection between the two but maternal love was not destined to shape the character of "Mercy to Mankind." The mother died during the return journey at Abwaa, a small halting place, which he visited specially after Hijrah. This journey must have further brought him closer to nature but the loss of mother to an orphan child of a little over six years of age, alone in a caravan, developed in him the fortitude and patience so needed to face the turbulence of the world at large.

None can tell the chain of thought which was generated by the loss of the only person so close to him in this vast world. The caravan marching towards Makkah, the desert on all sides, the maid servant Umm Aiman, sitting in the litter on the other side of camel, were all that could distract from the acute sense of loss suffered by him. He never spoke of those days in his later years. In what manner Umm Aiman, herself a young girl conveyed the news and meaning of death to her ward, is not known. How she consoled him is a secret and will remain so for ever. What was his reaction and how patiently he bore the loss has not been narrated by Umm Aiman. He had been deprived of a "father figure" from birth. A normal man looks to his early days and takes guidance from the memories of his father, and the manner in which his father used to meet various situations. An average person considers his father as the wisest human being. Muhammad (PBUH) had been denied this most valuable source of inspiration because Allah desired that he should not be guided by the behaviour of any human source. Allah had shaped events in a manner that Muhammad (PBUH) had to remain in the desert for a much longer period than was the usual custom. If he had come back to the city at the age of three years, it was possible that he might have been sent to a learned person to learn how to read and write, but Allah had wished that he should remain Ummi—illiterate, and thus avoid all sources of human learning and wisdom prevailing at that time and in that age.

At Abwaa he was denied the benefit of the guidance which a cultured lady of that period could provide for him. His mother a kind lady could have, in a practical way, demonstrated to him, even though, in an imperceptable manner, what love, compassion, mercy and kindness mean. "Mercy to Mankind" was to learn these lessons from Almighty Allah Himself. On return to Makkah Umm Aiman delivered the trust to the venerable old man, Abdul Muttalib, a chief of the Quraysh, the grandfather of the child. He was respected and could have taught his beloved intelligent grandson the secrets of leadership of men. This was not to be. Allah had decreed that He had his own plans to teach him Wisdom, Leadership and all that would be needed to guide mankind for all times to come, in His Own Way, and remove from him all those influences and practices learnt from wisdom resulting from human endeavours. Very soon the grandfather also died and young Muhammad (PBUH) hardly eight years of age, went to the household of his uncle Abu Talib, who loved him greatly but was not very well off as far as worldly means were concerned. Muhammad (PBUH), as a result had to become a shepherd very early in life. The herd included goats of neighbours also and what they paid helped in defraying expenses of Abu Talib's household.

Travels Abroad

Abu Talib, like other members of the tribe, went out with caravans for purposes of trade. Muhammad (PBUH) was twelve when, on his insistence, he was taken out on a trade journey to Syria. There are hints by Orientalists that during this journey, his meeting a Christian hermit taught him the stories in Bible and he repeated these stories after declaring his prophethood. This suggestion is so illogical that it need not even be discussed. A boy of twelve does not become a learned man after meeting a philosopher, during his short stay at a caravan serai.

There must have been other journeys. He started trading on his own account very early in life. It was the prevailing custom that those members of the tribe who did not wish to undertake long journeys would entrust their goods to other members of the tribe. Muhammad, very soon, became popular among such members of the tribe, for his honest dealings, and giving better dividends to people, he earned the rare title of Al-Ameen—The Trustworthy.

It was a time when boundaries of states and areas of tribal sovereignty were not very clearly demarcated and merchants ran the risk of having their goods confiscated if they ventured into areas where disputes between rival claimants had not been settled. Knowledge of geography, alternative routes, political affiliations of tribes, social customs, cultural differences and religious practices along various trade routes were to be learnt by merchants regularly visiting these trade routes and markets. It was also necessary to know a great deal about lands from where the items of trade in these markets commenced their journeys. Knowledge of the details of supply and demand of particular commodities in various countries had to be gathered by these merchants. The knowledge of the habits of the merchants of Middle East and Europe who were dependent on trade through Arabia were no less important. Goods to be carried to Syria had to be those which would find ready market in the Middle East, for onward despatch to Turkey, Greece and farther west in Europe. International markets are not easy to understand. Supply and demand graphs keep changing overnight and not all those involved in supply or purchase of goods from abraod can forecast the trends of market correctly. Wires, cables, telephone calls and air journeys have made a great difference to international trade and commerce. How much more intricate it must have been in his time can be imagined correctly with difficulty. Goods exchanged at these trading centres had travelled thousands of miles over land and sea, and at times making use of both means of transport. Their sources were too distant to know of the vagaries of weather and other natural calamities. A merchant purchasing silk of a particular pattern in China, or spices in Jakarta and selling them in the market at Aden or Yenbo could never be sure that, if, after many hazards, he reached safely at these sea-ports, there would be merchants to lift his goods and there would be enough load of goods available there which would be in demand in his home market.

Muhammad (PBUH), as was natural must have studied the minds of men from distant lands of east and west, and, as was natural for a young man of reserved and contemplating nature to have thought of the secrets of nature and the power behind the sun, the moon, the stars and how these celestial bodies have influence over the rising and falling of the vast expanses of water of numerous oceans.

This period of his life, however, has not been reported upon as fully as later part of his life. It may be so, because, as a young man he was quiet, did not drink or join other young men in their social and cultural activities and pursuits of pleasure. His search for the ultimate Reality, the Truth could have been the result of his deliberations during these journeys. Allah has referred to his search for Truth in the following Words:-

> "Did He not find thee wandering and direct (thee)"? 93: 7

> "And may perfect His favour unto thee, and may guide thee on a right path." 48: 2

We are told that after the war of Fajjar, a number of young men joined together and formed a society which swore that they would try their best to get the rights of weaker members of society, restored to them. The group was called, "members of Half-al-Fudhool—"People of Pact of Justice." When relating how much he was impressed by the idea of helping the weak to get his rights he is reported to have said, "If there was a group of this nature today I would join it." When he said this he was the head of the State of Madina. It probably meant that he would join a similar group formed of other heads of neighbouring states, because, within the State of Madina he had already succeeded in creating a society in which fullest possible justice was being administered. The world at large was being denied justice at that time. A group of states, of the nature of Half-al-Fudhool, would see that justice was done in problems connected with the rights of small nations. If a council of the heads of rulers of Middle East had been possible, how different would the world have been today. His letters, as the head of State of Madina and the Last Prophet of Allah to the rulers of neighbouring states need to be studied from this point of view.

He had travelled in these lands as a merchant and he must have known the conditions under which a common man lived and toiled to look after his needs and those of his family. When writing letters, inviting these rulers to embrace Islam, he had kept their people in mind. He had said in his letter to the Roman Emperor, "If you do not accept, then the responsibility of the sins of people of the land will be on you."

The rulers of these states would have earned double reward if their people had led a freer and a happier life as a result of their rulers embracing Islam. International markets of those days, when there were no visas and no restrictions on entry into foreign lands, except the hazards of journey, gave a greater international look, than at present although travel facilities have increased many times.

A mind which had been introduced to life under the vast expanse of desert sky and the limited approach to life on the other hand must have reacted in a mixed manner to the varied scenes and strange ideas of men from different lands. We have very little evidence to fall back upon, to guide us to the shaping of his ideas during this period. We, however, know, as we are told, that he was respected by all as a result of his honesty, sincerity and readiness to help the needy. When rebuilding of Ka'aba was taken in hand, and the question of placing in its proper place the sacred "Black Stone" came up every branch of the Quraysh desired that this honour should be bestowed on its members alone. "Matters reached the stage where bloodshed appeared imminent and the work stopped for a few days, Umayyah bin Mugheera, an elderly person advised of leaving the matter to Allah. Whoever entered the precincts of Ka'aba, through Bani Shaiba gate, should be appointed as the arbitrator."

The elders of various branches assembled at the appointed time to see who would enter first from Bani Shaiba gate. It happened that Muhammad (PBUH) was the first to emerge from behind the hill of Safa and enter the Haram. Someone shouted, "It is the Ameen, The Trustworthy." The problem was at once placed before him. His decision was prompt and such that none would be offended. He proposed that the four large branches of Quraysh must nominate a representative. When this was done, he spread his mantle on the ground, placed the Sacred Black Stone on the mantle and asked the four representatives to lift the mantle from its four corners and take it gently to the corner of the Ka'aba, where it was to be fixed. When they arrived with the stone at the spot, he lifted it up and with the help of all four representatives fixed it in its proper place. This issue was thus solved amicably and bloodshed was avoided.

His reputation for honesty was so well founded and well known that it reached the ears of Khadija, a rich widow, who had substantial business abroad. She entrusted her merchandise to him during one of the trading seasons. The profits that he brought were far more than used to be, in the case of earlier trading activities. This business partnership only ended when, after usual enquiries, Khadija sent word that if marriage was acceptable to him, he should arrange through his uncle, Abu Talib, and ask for her hand. Apart from being a widow her father was dead and one of her uncles acted as her guardian during the Nikah ceremonies.

It was an ideal of a happy life. Her age at the time of marriage with the Prophet (PBUH) is said to be forty years. Dr. Hamidullah, however, on the strength of Muhammad bin Habib Baghdadi's book Kitab-ul-Muhabbar says that it was 28 years. The fact that they had eight children, four sons and four daughters, of whom three have left children behind,appears to support this view. It, however, needs further study. After forty years of age the remaining span of middle age is too short to have more than three or four children.

Some time after marriage he is known to have turned towards contemplation and meditation. His journeys to various international markets, travelling through hundreds of miles of sandy deserts, barren hills and thick forests must have inclined his thoughts to the Creator of all those. He must have met thousands of people both good and bad, pious and inclined towards evil, powerful and weak and must have thought of finding out the truth for himself. It is only natural for a man of his reserved and sober nature to turn towards the Creator. It is not that the Arabs did not believe in a Supreme Being. They had the concept of Allah but He had been relegated to an inactive position. The three hundred and sixty odd gods with names like Lat, Uzza and Manat according to their belief, had all the power, which helped human beings. Allah was there, but did not interfere or direct the affairs of mankind. He was to them just a Name and no more. These and other thoughts, not possible of being defined by a layman, like the present writer, must have appeared to him and he would have started searching for the Turth in right earnest. He chose the cave of Hera on Jabal-e-Noor, as his usual venue for contemplation. The word Hera means 'one that is found after searching'. He used to spend days there. He would take water and some provision for three or four days. If he did not return on the stipulated day, we are told, that, Khadija would take food and water for him and thus enable him to prolong his stay in Hera. We know nothing of the subjects that he addressed to himself during this entire period. He was alone with nature and that was enough for him. If the mind of man, the most balanced Creation of Allah can be turned to the Supreme Will, could any mundane thought remain in the tiny mind of man which is supported by His Spirit. Allah Himself was preparing him, though not known to him, in a manner that his mind should be ready to receive The Final Divine Message for the guidance of mankind. This Last and Final Message to mankind was to terminate and end for all time the system of Divine Revelation which had been in vogue from the days of Adam and Noah. There was a purpose in this ending of Allah's Message, which had always been a Blessing of Allah but it had, throughout the ages, tied the mind of man to get directions from Him, through His chosen Messengers. This had resulted in numerous schisms and innumerable denominations under the umbrella of a number of so-called religions. This was hindering the physical and spiritual progress of man, which in itself was a barrier to the ultimate achievements of mankind—The conquest of elements and of nature itself.

Hidden Force

Man has been bestowed with a mind which has inherent powers of innovation the heights of which have not yet been scaled and which is still in the process of developing. Allah's Messages through the ages have been commensurate with the progress made by the mind of man. The Final Message which was to be beyond Time and Space, was not sent until such time that mind of man had not reached the requisite maturity. His mind—the mind of Muhammad (PBUH) was being prepared in the cave of Hera to develop to a standard which will be needed by the mass of humanity near the Dooms Day, to unravel all the secrets of nature. Mankind by then would have practically "put to service what-so-ever is in the heavens and what-so-ever is in the earth," and the Sun, the Moon, the countless heavenly bodies and their constellations would have floated through the Cosmos, and arrived at the final destination.'

To reach that stage of mental development, where man will be able to master and benefit from all that is in nature, he needs knowledge far in excess of what his mind can imagine today. As long as man is divided in ethical, linguistic, and geographical groups and on the basis of faith and religion, he will never be able to conquer that limit of knowledge. He needs peace for such great heights of mental excellence and gain scientific and philosophical knowledge and truth. To overcome all these differences man had to be given an ideology which would surpass all such minor differences and prejudices that keep mankind divided. Allah in

His Mercy and Benevolence, closed the door of all religions and gave to mankind One Last and Final Way of Life, and did not even call it a religion. This Way of Life, which can contain all modes of thought was named by Allah Himself as The Way of Life of Peace.

> "This day have I perfected your religion for you, and completed My favour unto you, and have chosen for you as religion AL-ISLAM." 5: 3

Mankind was invited, for this very reason, to forget all minor differences and join to work together to give Peace to humanity through cooperation on those parts of Belief which were common to all schools of thought or whatever denomination people wished to be given to themselves. Muhammad was Ordered by Allah to:-

> "Say O People of the Scripture! Come to an agreement between us and you that we shall worship none but Allah, and that we shall ascribe no partner unto Him, and that none of us shall take others for lords beside Allah." 3: 64

We shall come to that part later on, as to how Muhammad (PBUH) the last Prophet of Allah whose Mission was to live and demonstrate the manner in which mankind had to be brought on to the same platform, acted on this Verse, and invited People of The Book to join with him and more towards the ultimate objective of unity and peace of mankind. He did this through this Document which we have undertaken to study. Mankind which had been bestowed with knowledge at the time of his Creation, and Commanded to read, recite, study and absorb all possible knowledge through the pen will, one day, climb the platform of Islam and will seek knowledge even when available in far off China.

The Last Message, for unity and peace of mankind, in the very Words of Allah, was conveyed to mankind as a Trust from

Him. Every word that was Revealed was dictated to scribes and was written down on paper, wood, bone, skin, stone or whatever material was available. Men were encouraged to remember it word for word, a practice which is even today being carried on all over the world.

A message through words is like the theory of a problem. For mankind, particularly those generations which were not in existence at the time, the words were like a written desire, to be translated into action at a later stage. The Prophet (PBUH) lived his life in accordance with the Words of the Quran. Every action of his has been recorded meticulously. No life whether ancient or modern has been passed down containing so accurate details of it as his life has been recorded. The wonder is, that from the space of one life time, particularly the period at Madina, all aspects of life of an average human being can receive guidance from it. Whether a man lived during the first century after his death or the fourteenth century after him, and whether he was in Arabia then or is in Japan or United States of America today, whether it be a merchant, a husband, a neighbour, a politician, a statesman, a ruler of state or the supreme commander of a victorious army, he can receive the most moral, the most ethical and the most profitable guidance from the Sunnah of the Prophet (PBUH).

God's Reward

Allah had promised, that he will protect the Quran from all kinds of adulterations and will retain it in its original form for ever. He has been Most Kind. Not only that. He has looked after the details of His Messenger's Sunnah as well. Praise be to Allah, the Mighty, the Kind, to The Most Compassionate.

An unseen hand, unknown to him, had been guiding him to fulfil the destiny of mankind. At the appropriate time when the heart and mind were well tuned and all senses were awake and in harmony with the All Pervading, Mighty, All Knowing, Allah's

Mercy, the man, Muhammad son of Abdullah, an orphan child of Amina, was elevated to the highest pedastal that mortal man could conceive of occupying—the pedestal of Mercy to Mankind. It was mercy to entire mankind because the life he led, the laws which were promulgated by him, and the collective communal life, of which he was to give practical demonstration, was to benefit millions after millions in every age. They were to copy his laws, make slogans of his actions, like liberty, freedom, equality, fraternity, justice for all, education, social service and untold number of minor and major acts, which, he initiated and mankind was to emulate, even though denying him the credit and the status of a guide from Allah.

Liberty, equality, and fraternity have been practiced by Muslim societies all the world over. The West copied these phrases during the closing years of eighteenth century. It was first in France that "equality" became a slogan. The impressions of these slogans created on Englishmen are vividly described by an Englishman while he was travelling in the East where he had come across Muslims who really practiced equality. He writes:-

> "Our demagogues have translated the French words 'liberte, egalite, fraternite,.... by the English words, liberty, equality, fraternity, and because there is much resemblance in the sounds, they would persuade the people that there is also a resemblance in the ideas. Facts teach us that liberty signifies the most horrible tyranny, silencing all low, and violating all property; that egalite (equality) signifies murdering foreigners and the higher classes, and pulling over the people men of the most low, ignorant, and wicked.... Fraternite, in France, signifies being a Frenchman; applied to other nations, it signifies, forcing on them a government, plundering their property, and taking their wives and daughters."

Allah, The Most Powerful, has powerful means at His disposal to speak to mortal man. When He sends His Angels (if we may call his messengers by this name) which convey His Commands to mankind are powerful beings, even though they may be ethereal, and they have spoken Allah's Words to His Prophets. Adam, Noah, Abraham, Moses, Jesus, to name a few, they all received Allah's Commands through Angel Gabriel—Jibraeel—the most powerful source of conveying Messages to His Servants.

> "That this is in truth the word of an honoured messenger. Mighty, established in the Presence of the Lord of the Throne, (One) to be obeyed, and trustworthy."
>
> 81: 19-21

He had to be obeyed.

He appeared before Muhammad and passed on the Command of Allah. "Read."

The Ameen, who had been the trustworthy, the truthful, throughout his life replied, "I cannot read."

The mighty messenger of Mighty Allah pressed him in an embrace which he could hardly bear and Allah's Command was repeated again "Read."

Muhammad son of Abdullah gave the same answer. "I cannot read."

The pressure was felt and borne again and the Command from Almighty Allah was repeated third time.

"Read."

The unlettered became learned, wise and knowledgeable with the Grace of Allah, and from this moment onward Muhammad son of Abdullah became Muhammad The Prophet of Allah (PBUH).

> "O ye who believe. Ask blessings on him and salute him with a worthy salutation." 33: 56

> Because "Allah and His Angels shower blessings on the Prophet."

The experience had exhausted him. All spiritual experiences are trying, tiring and exhausting in the extreme— so say the - knowledgeable. Man is the sum total of the spiritual and the material. Allah, having made him out of clay, granted life to him through the action of water and when He had given him his beautiful shape He infused a little of His Spirit into Him and then granted a little of His Own Knowledge, because He had destined him to be His Vicegerent on earth.

Muhammad was a man in his feelings and reactions to unusual incidents like all other men. He had long been in search of Truth but not having had a single lesson or guidance from any other man or woman, he got worried to the extreme. The experience of being face to face with Jibraeel and being embraced by him, infused into his heart mighty feelings, he was un-nerved. He could not help it.

> "And lo! thy Lord! He is indeed the Mighty, the Merciful. And lo! it is a Revelation of the Lord of the Worlds, Which the True Spirit has brought down Upon thy heart, that thou mayest be (one) of the warners. In plain Arabic Speech." 26: 191-195

We are told that he was very worried. Allah brought him to normal mental and spiritual condition. His prayers, his meditations and his search of The Truth was for the sake of Truth and not for material or other gain. He had not been a pupil to any learned or to any other-worldly person. If he had known what Revelation is, he would have, at once, realised that his efforts of years of meditation had borne fruit and there would have been no cause, in his mind, to have worried about his unusual experience. He went home and took solace from Khadija, the "Pure," a great lady from all standards.

He told her to cover him with a blanket. She obeyed and when he had calmed down he told her of the whole incident and said, "I am afraid of my life."

She had known him for years. She replied

> "Allah will not treat you thus because he knows your truthfulness, your great trustworthiness, your fine character, and your kindness."

Khadija's words were good and comforting and must have reassured him a great deal but the matter was not such that it could be disposed off in a little while or even in a day or two. The experience was unique, in that, the Voice had originated from the Conscious Will of the Creator of man and universe. He knew or must have known, that He had spoken to Prophets before but he had never desired, imagined or dreamed that he will be called upon to join the company of the chosen ones. If he had desired any such thing it would have been shown in his words or deeds. It never did and Allah was later on to remind him to tell people, and

> "Say, If Allah had so willed I should not have recited it to you nor would He have made it known to you. I dwelt among you a whole lifetime before it (came to me). Have ye then no sense"? 10: 17

If he had ever desired to become a saintly person, those around or near him and particularly those who had remained in close contact with him during trade journeys would have known of his inclinations and would have said so.

Khadija had a cousin, Warqah bin Noufal, who was a man well versed in Scriptures but had become blind due to old age. She visited him and told him the story. He reassured her and told her that there had come unto Muhammad the greatest Namus, the same that came to Moses. He assured her that Muhammad was a Prophet of Allah. He asked her to tell her husband that he should rest assured of Allah's help.

She returned home and repeated the words of Warqah to Muhammad (PBUH) but he could not believe it just because a wise old man had said so. Belief in Allah and belief in himself as the Prophet of Allah had to be bestowed and repeatedly drawn attention to the extent of duties and responsibilities attached with such a high office. As said earlier, he had laboured for years to know The Truth, but he had never aspired for any personal elevation. Warqah may be right but he had to await and see what Allah had decreed and what exactly was expected of him.

It is difficult, and in point of fact, impossible to mark out the stages through which Muhammad (PBUH) may have passed to Believe that he really was the Prophet of Almighty Allah, to whom he had been praying for Guidance for years.

To be His prophet was the greatest honour. He had never dreamed of it and yet the Verses Revealed on Jabal al-Noor, in the cave of Hera, were meaningful and of great significance. A man who had travelled abroad, met and had done business with people of many nationalities and lands, had been respected in society and had been spending days contemplating on the sun, the moon, the stars, the way they moved, through different seasons, but yet according to a fixed plan and at a fixed speed, cutting across each others path and yet not colliding. These and other tokens of the Master Mind of all Powerful Allah were not for nothing. All these must fit into some plan, a plan which would also have a special place for man, the only rational creature he had come across in his numerous journeys. His mind must have gone to the Words Revealed during the first encounter with the Angel Jibraeel. These Words were to be repeated, nay read, recited and deliberated upon by him again and again.

"Read:"

"In the Name of the Lord Who Createth."

He would have stopped to think. That henceforth he had to read and contemplate, in the Name of the Lord of all these floating constellations, the earth, the moon and all there is in them all, and to Read. Yes, to read and to think and deliberate on the greatness of his Lord. He is Great. There is no doubt. His Creation, which the eye can see is vast beyond imagination. To prove that man is His slave and servant he must study His creation. Yes! man must see things logically, rationally and systematically.

And then his mind would go towards his responsibility. He had been told to read, recite and ... Could it not be that he had to tell men and women to read and study His Creations. And his mind would go to strange things and to man himself as a Creation of Allah. And the following Words of the Revelation must have boomed large before his mind:

"Createth man from a clot."

Man, the beautiful, the knowledgeable, the learned, the scientist, the preacher of religion, the wealthy merchant, the ministers, courtiers and rulers of other men; they all were created from a clot. They must be told this, so that they humble themselves and prostrate themselves before their Lord. What secrets could be unveiled and steps taken to improve conditions for man if he was to know exactly what processes his life went through from the stage of a clot to a healthy human child. He would not have guessed it then but history records that his insistence on learning and acquiring knowledge would take man out of the orbit of earth and not only land him on to a distant planet but this knowledge would bring him back safely to his present abode, the earth, which itself needs further probing into it. And He has repeated the Command, "Read." It is no doubt to emphasis but also because "It" goes on to say:-

And thy Lord is the Most Bountiful, because He had placed His entire Universe at the service of man—His Viceroy on earth. And these bounties of Allah, The Most Merciful can be made use of only through knowledge, the result of "reading, reciting, deliberating and examining." Allah's bounties pile up when the 'pen' is used. Man's memory is limited. If knowledge was to be passed on from memory to memory it would remain limited and eventually stagnate. It has been through the use of pen that the knowledge acquired by numerous generations has been preserved. It goes on accumulating generation after generation. Acquisition and then preservation of the wealth acquired through pen has made human life more pleasant after every generation and has brought mankind to the doorstep of the unchartered expanse of this universe. Allah gave to man the use of pen. Pen has recorded knowledge of hundreds of generations and Allah has to be praised for teaching man the use of pen. Through "Pen," Allah

> "Teacheth man what he knew not." 96: 5.

How long he must have thought on the Words Revealed to him in the very first Revelation cannot be known. It must have, however, brought him nearer to his "Belief in himself as the Messenger of Allah..." He had always believed in Allah and Allah had now commanded him to read, recite and think so that he should, from then onwards, believe in himself as the Messenger of Allah. Without, his own belief in himself as the Prophet, Allah's Command could not be communicated to mankind.

He was given Revelations on subsequent occasions in which reference was drawn to himself, because it was essential that his belief in himself must be firm and without any flaw. Some of the opening Verses of Makki Suras are of interest in this respect.

> "Alif. Lam. Ra.
>
> These are verses of the wise Scripture. Is it a wonder for mankind that We have Inspired a man among them."
>
> 10: 1-3.

This Wisdom of the New Philosophy of Life based on the unshared Sovereignty of Allah is destined to lead mankind to Eternal Bliss. This Book is not only full of Wisdom, it is also "Plain" and easy to understand.

> "These are Verses of the Scripture that maketh plain. Lo! We have revealed it, a Lecture in Arabic, that ye may understand." 12: 1-2

This fact, that this Book of Wisdom has been Revealed to Muhammad (PBUH) has to be kept in mind all the time. Initially it had to be kept in mind by Muhammad (PBUH) himself, for instance, the following Verse:-

> "These are Verses of the Scripture. That which is Revealed unto thee from thy Lord is the TRUTH (and you were, for years searching TRUTH) but most of mankind believe not. Allah it is who raised the heavens without visible support, then mounted the THRONE, and compelled the sun and the moon to be of service." 13: 1-2

Truth had been revealed to His chosen men in all ages:-

> "There is no God save Him, the Alive, the Eternal. He hath revealed unto thee (O Muhammad) the Scripture with truth. Confirming that which was (revealed) before it, even as He Revealed the Torah and the Gospel."
> 3: 2-3

The object of the Book being revealed to him was also being explained to him.

> "(This is) a Scripture which We have Revealed unto thee (O Muhammad) that thereby you mayst bring forth mankind from darkness to light, by the permission of your Lord." 14: 1

The treatment of this subject in this forthright manner is not confined to opening Verses of Surahs only. It has been emphasized elsewhere as well. For instance: -

> "Lo! We, even We, have revealed unto thee the Quran, a revelation; So submit patiently to thy Lord's command, and obey not of them any guilty one or disbeliever."
>
> 76: 23-24

When studying any incident of Muhammad's life it must be borne in mind all the time that previous to his enlightenment in the cave named Hera, he had no knowledge of those Divine subjects, which were being Revealed to him. When Prophethood was conferred on him the dis-believers were all the time using all means at their disposal to dissuade him from embarking on this great Mission from Allah. He was, therefore, every moment in danger of exposure to the misleading of others. Allah warned him of such moments:-

> "But for the grace of Allah upon thee (O Muhammad), and His Mercy, a party of them had resolved to mislead thee but they will mislead only themselves and they will hurt thee not at all. Allah Revealeth unto the Scripture and Wisdom, and teacheth thee that which thou knewest not. The grace of Allah toward thee hath been infinite."
>
> 4: 113

Revelation of the Eternal Message, a message which will be applicable for all lands, for all people and until the end of Time, is a Miracle from Allah, which needs to be studied with great care and sincerity. A message surpassing Time and Space is being put before humanity of all ages by a man who never sat at the feet of any teacher, any sage, or philosopher is a phenomenon demanding attention from all those who have regard for truth. The wonder and the miracle, on his part, is that from the time he was given this Mission of conveying Allah's Message to mankind, he translated the theory into practice, and demonstrated to his generation, and the coming generations of mankind, the leadership of an Ideal Society, who believe in the New Way of Life.

> "Blessed is He Who hath revealed Unto His slave the Criterion (of right and wrong), that he may be a warner to the people." 25: 1

But there is, in reality, nothing to be surprised at, because the Revelation is from Allah. He says:-

> "The revelation of the Scripture is from Allah, the Mighty, The Wise. Lo! in the heavens and the earth are portents for believers." 45: 2-3

Man's mind must be satisfied. Satan was there and is still there to whisper doubts. Allah has, therefore, brought home to mankind that there should remain no doubt regarding the issue of a man rising to hitherto such unsealed heights of Wisdom, as Muhammad demonstrated. He says:-

> "The Revelation of the Scripture is from Allah the Mighty, the Knower, The Forgiver of sins, the Accepter of repentance, the Stern in punishment, the Bountiful. There is no God save Him, Unto Him is the journeying." 40: 2-3

Because the conveying of good tidings to the righteous and warning of punishment to the evil doers are tasks both equally necessary, the Prophet (PBUH) has been adjudged as the final witness on the Day of Judgement. Allah has said:-

> "O Prophet! Lo! We have sent thee as a witness and a bringer of good tidings and a warner. And as a summoner Unto Allah by His Permission, and as a lamp that giveth light." 33: 45-46

And:-

> "Lo! (O Muhammad) We have sent thee with the truth, a bringer of glad tidings and a warner. And thou wilt not be asked about the owners of hell fire." 2: 119

Muhammad (PBUH) was the first and the direct recipient of Allah's Commands contained in the Quran. He had to be the first Believer and he became the first Believer. Allah in His Wisdom has confirmed the superb belief of Muhammad (PBUH).

> "The messenger believeth in that which hath been revealed unto him from his Lord And (so do) the believers." 2: 285

It was this unflinching Belief in Allah and His Words that carried him through the hard days of persecution, by his own people, against him and his Companions, the Believers, about whose Belief Allah has testified in the Verse given above. It was this rock like belief in Allah and His promise, at a time, when he and his Companions were being attacked by Makkan superior forces and Allah had said:-

> "Faint not, nor grieve, for ye will overcome them if ye are (indeed) believers." 3: 139

They proved that they were true Believers and Allah kept His promise to the minutest detail.

> "It is a promise of Allah. Allah faileth not His Promise, but most of mankind know not." 30: 6

Muhammad (PBUH) and his Companions knew this and believed in it. His proclamation of his being Allah's Messenger was to be conveyed to all mankind. The emphasis which was being laid on this fact, of addressing entire humanity, was to remind that both the Quran and the Sunnah had to be kept alive for all times:-

> "Say (O Muhammad) O mankind! Lo! I am the messenger of Allah to you all--(the messenger of) Him unto whom belongeth the Sovereignty of the heavens and the earth. There is no God save Him. He quickeneth and He giveth death. So Believe in Allah's messenger, the Prophet who can neither read nor write, who believeth in Allah and in His Words, And follow him, that hoply ye may be led aright." 7: 158

The Mission progressed slowly. He announced it to the members of his family and then to the people of Makkah.

Khadija was the first to accept his Prophethood. Zaid must have been next but, somehow, history books relegate him to the third or fourth position. Ali is said to be the second but the occasion when he announced it was at a feast which took place sometimes after the original announcement. He is said to be twelve years of age. According to the version given about Abu Bakr's embracing Islam, it appears that he was the first person outside the family to have entered the fold of Islam.

He may have felt that the progress of Islam was not as it could have been. This thought may have depressed him. Allah who knows the innermost thoughts of man, at once, consoled him by saying:-

> "Ta Ha. We have not revealed unto thee (O Muhammad) this Qur'an, that you should be distressed, but as a reminder unto him who fearth, A revelation from Him Who created the earth and the high heavens." 20: 1-4

His task was confined to conveying the Message but the acceptance by people depended on their decision whether they desired to remain in darkness or wished to see light.

> "(This is) a Scripture Which We have revealed unto thee (O Muhammad) that thereby thou mayst bring forth mankind from darkness unto light, by the Permission of their Lord unto the Path of the Mighty, the Owner of Praise." 14: 1

> "O Messenger! Make known that which hath been revealed unto thee from thy Lord for if thou do it not, thou will not have conveyed His Message. Allah will protect thee from mankind Lo! Allah guideth not the disbelieving folk." 5: 67

After this Verse was Revealed, the guarding of his residence, at night, was discarded. This is a Surah of Madina, and, belongs, to the early days after Hijrah, when the Makkans had started invading the territories of Madina.

The Makkan period is conspicuous for persecution of his Companions. The weaker among the Muslims were the main target. Abu Bakr used to purchase the Persecuted slaves and set them free. Bilal the first Muazzan of Islam, a venerated African Muslim, was one of these freed slaves, who used to be spoken of by Omar, as "our master."

We are told that one of the usual complaints of the Quraysh, against the Prophet (PBUH) was that he "insults our religion and mocks our way of life." They approached his uncle Abu Talib and wanted him, "to stop him or you must let us get at him, for, you yourself are in the same position as we are in opposition to him and we will rid you of him." Things had reached the stage where the Quraysh had decided to kill the Prophet (PBUH) and thus save their cherished 'Way of Life'. They were afraid that if he continued propagating the New Way of Life, which Islam offered, then their own religion and their cherished way of life would vanish. They were the established leaders of the existing Way of Life which was followed by the whole of Arabia. It gave them social, economic and religious prerogatives and preferences which would be no more, if their way of life disappeared. As opposed to their way of life, Islam, brought in equality of men and treated the free citizen and a slave on equal footing, in all fields, social, cultural and economic. Their established customs, rules, prerogatives of certain sections and even the philosophy of life on which their way of life was based, were all at stake. They had to do something to save their vested interests.

They made one more effort at conciliation but on their peculiar terms. They took a young man of martial bearing, and offered him for adoption by Abu Talib. In return they wanted Muhammad (PBUH) to be killed at the altar of one of their gods. They argued that they were giving to Abu Talib a young man of excellent physique, who would be an asset to him in all respects. In exchange they were asking Abu Talib for a man who "has severed the unity of your people and mocked our way of life. Either you must stop him or let us get at him."

If the question is examined a little more in detail it becomes clear that the objection of the Makkans was not that a new religion was being introduced in their society or they were afraid of sectarian disturbances. This could not be the reason. They, already, had people who belonged to various religions and they were all living peacefully. The Arabs did not take religion very seriously. They were tolerant of all modes of worship, as long as religion was a matter of personal views and did not disturb the existing social structure. There were in Makkah, at that time, Christians, Jews, Sabians and the Quraysh had excellent relations with them. There was a picture of Jesus Christ inside Ka'aba itself. It appears that the Quraysh were like the Brahmins of India, who were ever-ready to accept under the umbrella of their spiritual leadership any and every mode of worship as long as they were accepted as the supreme religious and spiritual authority.

Their objection to Islam resembled the criticism of Nehru and Gandhi of India, who maintained that the basis of Millah had to be geographical loyalties and not ideological commitments. This objection stemmed from the fundamental belief of Islam in the Sovereignty of Allah. Allah being the sole Sovereign in the universe, He was to be obeyed above all other forces and persons. In practice, it means the supremacy of the Law given by Allah through His Prophets. Those who accepted this Divine Law formed ONE UMMAH to the exclusion of others.

This Law included the principle of equality of mankind. Allah has created mankind as equals. Therefore, there should be no difference between an Arab and an Ajami or between a ruler and the ruled. Equality of men and brotherhood within Islam were principles, which had been highly abhorrent to the Jews, the Quraysh and the Brahmins alike. Abu Talib, a soft spoken person, was able to postpone the final rift between Quraysh and himself.

He called Muhammad (PBUH) one day and having told him what the Quraysh had wanted, he said to him, "Do not put a burden on me greater than I can bear." The Prophet (PBUH) thought that his uncle wanted to abandon him and he would lose his support and protection completely. He reflected for a moment and replied, "O my uncle, by Allah, if they put the sun in my right hand and the moon in my left hand, on condition that I abandon this course, until Allah has made me victorious, or I perish therein, I will not abandon it."

The realisation, that those who were entering the brotherhood of Islam were a people apart, was mutual. He knew that he was creating a new Millah which would follow its own Way of Life known as Islam and, therefore, he and his Millah will be opposed by any and every people that they came in contact with. He realised the intensity of struggle that lay before him. He was, in view of this, prepared to be completely wiped out. He believed in the Sovereignty of Allah, and that His Will was supreme in the Universe and He had said, that he, Muhammad, had been appointed by Him to bring mankind out of darkness of unequality and iniquity into light:-

> "He it is Who sendeth down clear revelations unto His slave, that he may bring you forth from darkness unto light, and lo! for you Allah is Full of Pity, Merciful."
>
> 57: 9

Allah would not have delegated such high responsibilities to him if the eventual salvation, through Islam, was not the scheme of things. He was confident of his success with the permission and help of Allah. His whole life was a witness to it. His prayer to his Lord, at the time of Badr was:-

> "O Allah if this little group of Believers is wiped out today there will be none left to obey Your Commands (live according to the Way of Life given by you) until the Day of Judgement."

His answer to his uncle, Abu Talib, and his prayer to his Lord, Almighty Allah, are symbolic of the Truth that he stood by. He was the Last Prophet. Islam was the final Way of Life based on the Last Revelations. If, therefore, he, and his Companions, the few that were there, were wiped out in the life and death struggle, then there would have been none left to obey and worship Allah as Dictated by Him in the final Message, He was sending through Muhammad (PBUH). He was, therefore, confident that Allah would make him victorious. This confidence in the Truth of his Mission and in Him Who had assigned to him. This Mission is evident throughout the period of the struggle. The other important point uppermost from the beginning was to organize all those who embraced Islam into a separate Millah, in relation to the rest of the world. These two points, the struggle to the last i.e. the fight unto martyrdom and Believers being an Ummah by themselves, form two most important objectives of the Prophet (PBUH). Islam has held the" uppermost position whenever these two Sunnahs of the Prophet (PBUH), both based on logical explanation of Quranic Verses, have been observed by Muslims".

The Makkans did not give up their opposition because Abu Talib had not withdrawn his support of the Prophet (PBUH). "When the Quraysh became distressed by the enmity between them and the Prophet (PBUH) they stirred up against him foolish men who called him a liar, insulted him and accused him of being a poet, a sorcerer, a diviner, and of being possessed...they said that they had never known anything like the trouble they had endured from him, he had declared their mode of life foolish, insulted their forefathers, reviled their religion, divided their community, and cursed their gods." Matters reached the stage when due to the constant persecution of his Companions and persistent opposition to himself, he was forced to say, "Will you listen to me O Quraysh? By Him Who holds my life in His hands, I bring to you slaughter." One of them replied, "Depart, O Abul Qasim, for by Allah you are not violent."

They often consulted one another in connection with finding of the best way to get rid of him. After one such discussion Utbah bin Rabiyah went, on behalf of the leaders of Quraysh, to the Prophet (PBUH) and said to him, "O son of my friend, you belong to us, although by insulting our religion, and traditions of our fathers, you have embroiled us, I have come to you to put an end to this great misfortune. Give an ear to my proposals. May be they find a place of grace in your sight." "Speak, I am listening," said the Prophet.

"O son of my friend! If you hope that your undertaking will make you wealthy, each of us is willing to sacrifice a part of his fortune in order that you should become the richest man among us. If you seek honours, we will set you up lord over us all and come to no decision without consulting you. If you dream of royal privileges, we will make you our king. If on the contrary, the thoughts that inspire you arise from some malady which you are powerless to resist, we will fetch, at any cost, from any country, the most celebrated doctors, so that you may be cured. Choose, therefore."

The Prophet (PBUH) had listened unmoved. "Have you finished?" he answered. He then recited the Surah of the Quran, Haameem Al Sajdah XLI. Muhammad (PBUH) after prostrating himself, rose up and turned to Utbah, saying, "You have heard me, O Utbah? Now it is for you to choose."

"Utbah bewildered went back to his companions. He told them, "I have just listened to Words. By our gods, I have never heard anything like it before. It is neither poetry, nor sorcery, nor magic. O Quraysh men assembled! believe me and let this man fulfil his Mission among the Arabs, for his words are full of surprising prophesies. If harm comes to him by the fault of Arabs, you will be freed from anxiety. If on the other hand, he succeeds and conquers the Arabs, his empire will be your empire and thanks to him you will attain the highest pinnacle."

As mentioned earlier, a few points are clear. It was understood by the Makkans that Islam was a complete New Way of Life. As a result it created a new Ummah, which due to its peculiar nature, had to have its own separate communal life. The Prophet (PBUH), from the beginning was convinced, in his own mind of the role Islam had to play and that either Allah will make Islam victorious or he himself will perish in the fulfilment of the duty entrusted to him by Allah. As time passed, this state of affairs became gradually more and more clear. They went so far as to say to him, "By Allah, we will not leave you and our treatment of you, until either we destroy you or you destroy us." They had gone to his uncle and failed to win him over to their side. They had tried to bribe him by offering riches, kingship and chieftainship and he had not accepted either wealth, honour or supreme power over Arabs. They had threatened him and had failed to intimidate him. If he had wanted any of these honours, here was a chance to get it among a society which he knew and understood. He was the grandson of a chief who held the leadership of entire Quraysh. He would have inherited it.

The incidence of Utbah bin Rabiyah, leaves no doubt that the desire to achieve power and wealth, never passed through his mind. Riches, power and dominance had been offered to him under the existing mode of life which was not unknown or foreign to him. He had turned away from them in youth. He could not have done so in hazy imagination of power which may or may not have been within a mortal's reach. During his whole life, not even during the period of his success when entire Arabia lay at his feet, did any ambitious thought pass his mind. The idea of his having had "day dreams of power and domination," in his young days, is, to say the least, dishonest scholarship.

The leaders of Quraysh widened their plan of persecution and pressurization of those who embraced Islam. Their families were told to put pressure on them to abrogate Islam. The slaves were the worse hit. Abu Bakr purchased a few and set them free, including Bilal the first Muazzan of Islam. "A stage arrived when people were afraid that they may be forced to renounce Islam. When the Prophet (PBUH) saw the affliction of his Companions... and that he could not protect them, he said to them, 'If you were to go to Abyssinia it would be better for you, for the king will not tolerate injustice and it is a friendly country, until such time as Allah shall relieve you from distress."

As a result of this a number of Companions, eighty three in number, according to Ibn-e Ishaq, went to Abyssinia. The Makkans did not like their going away. They were afraid that, if Muslim were able to establish themselves, away from Makkah, they will get strong and become a threat to the Quraysh. They sent a party after them to stop them from sailing. When they came to know of the sailing of the boat they organised a delegation which among others was composed of Abdullah bin abu Rabiya and Amr ibn al Aas, and sent them to the king of Abyssinia, loaded with presents for the courtiers, generals and the king himself.

The emigration to Abyssinia was successful. The king gave them permission to reside in the capital and they settled there. But soon the delegation from Makkah arrived and requested for their extradition. The king asked for the reason and was told that the refugees had left the religion of their forefathers and thereby committed the sin of weakening the religion so dear to the rest of them. They also told him that the Muslims held adverse views about Jesus Christ. He sent for the Muslims. Jaffer Ibn-e Abi Talib went as head of the delegation. He asked him of his views about Jesus Christ. Jaffer recited Verses of Surahn Mairyam. The king was impressed by the passage and refused to hand over the Muslims to the delegation. He promised the Muslims protection and a fair and just treatment. This is the first Hijrah of Islam and can be termed as the first instance of a group of people having been provided political asylum by the government of a neighbouring state. The king and his government stood by their promise and the refugees passed their time peacefully as long as they stayed there.

The failure of the delegation at the court of Negus embittered the Quraysh more than ever before. The idea of establishing himself out of Makkah but within Arabia seems to have taken root at this time. The chiefs of Banu Thaqeef, inhabiting Taef and the surrounding hills were powerful. He decided to approach them.

He went to Taef, but the chiefs there did not listen and instead employed young men to throw stones at him. He received wounds and returned without any success.

On his return to Makkah he found that the intensity of Quraysh opposition had increased further. He realised that the only course open to him and his Companions was to find protection with some tribe at a considerable distance from Makkah. We are told that, "The Prophet (PBUH) offered himself to the tribes of Arabs, telling them that he was a Prophet who had been sent (i.e. had not declared prophethood on his own accord). He used to ask them to believe in him until Allah should make clear to them the Message with which He had charged the Prophet."

Bayhara bin Firas of Banu Aamir bin Sahsaa understood the Prophet (PBUH) and the likely impact of his Message better than others. He is reported to have said, "By Allah, if I could take this man from Quraysh I could eat up the Arabs with him." His conception of Allah, however, was limited and although he had visualised the importance of the New Way of Life preached by the Prophet (PBUH), he was limited in his imagination of the life that could lived, by a people who feared Allah and were prepared to sacrifice every thing on the Path of Allah. He asked the Prophet (PBUH), "If we actually give allegiance to you, and Allah gives you victory over your opponents, shall we have authority after you? The Prophet (PBUH) replied, "Authority is a matter which Allah places where He places." Bayhara in his reply showed his lack of breadth of vision and quickly said, "I suppose you want us to protect you from the Arabs with our breasts and then if Allah gives you victory some one else will reap the benefit. "Thank you. No." They had missed the opportunity and were told so by one of their elders when they went back to their tribal territory.

A question may be asked, at this stage, as to why did he not go to Habsha, where the ruler had given asylum to a number of Muslims already and who had even refused to hand over these political refugees to the high powered delegation sent by the elders of Quraysh. The answer is that, he could not go to Habsha because his object was not that he or his Companions or the Muslim Ummah should remain safe and sound under a society or a government which did not conduct its collective communal life on principles of the Sovereignty of Allah. Habsha may have been acceptable to a few Muslims where they were permitted to live as a minority but Habsha could not be made a centre for him, unless it accepted the Sovereignty of Allah and his Prophethood. Sovereignty of Allah can be established only through the Rule of Law given by Allah. Sovereignty, in every case, belongs to the power, institution or person whose law is being enforced. If a parliament exercise these functions, then the joint will of the people, through their parliament, possesses Sovereignty. If, on the other hand, Laws Ordained by Allah are Supreme in a land, then it can be said that

Sovereignty of Allah is recognised in that land. No land can claim to be a Muslim land, unless it recognises the Sovereignty of Allah, through the implementation of Laws based on the Quran and the Sunnah. When an early historian records, on the authority of contemporary evidence that "He used to ask them to believe in him and protect him until Allah the Message with which He had charged His Prophet (PBUH)," it means that he is not asking them merely to protect him but he is warning them of the ultimate purpose, the imposition of The Shariah by Allah which would then have to be implemented. It has to be kept in mind that Quranic Law had not yet been Revealed, in full, and, he, therefore, could only refer them to it by saying, "until Allah should make clear the Message with which He had charged His Prophet." The Vahee, Revelation which is referred to in the Quran'. -

> "And Lo! it is a revelation of the Lord of the Worlds, Which the True Spirit hath brought down upon thy heart, that thou mayst be (one) of the warners."
>
> 26: 192-194

The details of such Revelations were known to the Prophet (PBUH) and he announced them in his own way, at the appropriate time. Revelations which form the text of the Quran were spoken Words which were later dictated by the Prophet (PBUH); however, he consigned these words to his memory. Allah has referred to these Revelations in these Words:-

> "Stir not thy tongue herewith to hasten it. Lo! upon Us (resteth) the putting together thereof and the reading thereof and when We Read it, follow thou the reading."
>
> 75: 16-18

To believe in him was to believe in Allah:-

> "Say, (O Muhammad, to mankind) If you love Allah, follow me; Allah will love you and forgive you your sins. Allah is Forgiving, Merciful." 3: 31

To believe in him meant to believe in him as The Messenger of Allah. As such belief in him could not be complete without first having believed in Allah. He was certain that when they believed in him and Allah as the only Sovereign Power in Universe, then they would be only too ready to lay down their lives to bring about justice through the Rule of Law which was due to be Ordained by Allah.

The Sovereignty of Allah was essential to be established in some piece of land. Unless the Shariah of Islam was practically brought into force, the benefits of Islam to the masses in social, economic, educational and political fields could not be demonstrated. Islam has three levels at which it effects and the effect of its application is visible. At the individual level belief in Allah grants peace of mind, contentment and courage to face the world far better than in other faiths. At the level of society its laws afford justice, fairplay, equal status, freedom of speech and thought a great deal more than humanity has experienced under any organized system of society. The third and the last level is the international level. It is unfortunate to admit that after the era of the guided four Khalifas, even Muslim states have not dealt with other nations in the light of the Quranic Laws on Jehad and Foreign Relations. Space does not permit of an exhaustive treatment of the subject. Suffice to say that in view of Quranic injunctions Muslims cannot use force unless it is first used against them.

> "Fight in the way of Allah against those who fight against you, but being not hostilities. Lo! Allah loveth not aggressors." 2: 190

And

> "There is no compulsion in religion." 2: 256

And even when the aggressor having initiated hostilities and having occupied Muslim territory leans towards cease fire, Muslim must do likewise:-

> "And if they incline to peace, incline thou also to it, and trust in Allah. Lo! He is the Hearer, the Knower. And if they would deceive thee, then lo! Allah is sufficient for thee. He it is Who supporteth thee with His help and with the believers." 8: 61-62

In view of certainty of peace being attained at individual, society and international levels through the Rule of Law based on the Sovereignty of Allah and His Prophet, the stage has reached that mankind is directed towards the implementation of the Quran and the Sunnah. When the Prophet (PBUH) referred to "Sovereignty being in Allah's hands" he meant to draw their attention to the fact that the sovereignty which he desired and aimed at was the Sovereignty of Allah through the implementation of His Laws.

At the time of Hajj some men from Yathrib visited Makkah. They were members of the tribe of Khazraj. The Prophet (PBUH) spoke to them about Islam and recited to them Verses from Quran. They told him that they were "allies" of Jews and they had heard from them that according to their books it was clear from certain passages that "a prophet will soon come." His day is at hand. We shall follow him and kill you with his aid." As a result of this meeting they were convinced that he was the prophet about whom the Jews had been telling. These men of the tribe of Khazraj from Yathrib "accepted his teachings and became Muslims." They spoke to him about their tribal affairs, saying that they were a very disunited tribe and expressed their hope that they would be able to live as a united people through him. They said, "Perhaps Allah will unite them through you. So let us go to them (their people) and invite them to this Deen of yours." Having become Muslims, they returned to Yathrib. This was the beginning of an era, which has expanded beyond imagination.

Among them was a man named Asaad bin Zurara of Najjar tribe, who returned next year with eleven others and took part in the First Bayah of Al-Aqba. Their Bayah, in the words of Ubada bin al-Samit, of allegiance to the Prophet (PBUH) said: "We will associate nothing with Allah, will not steal, not commit fornication, not kill our offsprings, not slander our neighbour, not disobey him in what is right; if we fulfil this, paradise will be ours; and if we commit any of these sins we will be punished in this world and this will serve as an expiation; if the sins are concealed till the Day of Resurrection, then it will be for Allah to decide.

The Prophet (PBUH) sent Musab bin Umayr bin Hashim with them, to teach them Quran and other thing in Islam. He was to lead Congregational prayers in Yathrib until the arrival of the Prophet (PBUH). Musab lodged with Asaad bin Zurara in Yathrib. The spread of Islam, however, was not an easy affair. Opposition soon appeared in the form of the leaders of tribes who were losing their authority, because Musab had started deciding the problems arising among Muslims. Usayd spoke on behalf of the others and wanted Musab to leave Yathrib, saying, "Leave us if you value your life." Musab asked him to sit down for a while and listen to what he had to say. He was won over by Musab as a result of this friendly discourse and he went and recommended Islam to Saad bin Muaz. He also was furious at first, but having listened to the recitation of the Quran he also entered Islam. His conversion opened the door to Islam still wider, as he was not only the chief of his tribe but was effectively influential and universally popular.

As a result of these influential persons Islam started spreading quickly in Yathrib, until very soon every household had one or two members, who had embraced Islam. Yathrib, thus became a city of mixed beliefs, as nearly every house contained both Believers and un-believers, living together. This fact had influence on the dictation of some of the Clauses of the Document, which we hope to study in this brief essay. When going into the details of the Charter we may have to refer to this fact of the social life of Yathrib, during that early period, following immediately after Hijrah.

The next event of importance, in the life of the Prophet (PBUH) is the second Bayah of Aqba, which took place during the next Hajj season. On this occasion, the party from Yathrib numbered 73 men and 2 women. Due to Makkan opposition, they had to go, "arriving softly like sandgrouse to our appointment with the Prophet (PBUH), as far as the narrow valley of Aqaba."

At the meeting, Abbas, uncle of the Prophet (PBUH), was also present. Addressing the Believers from Yathrib, he said, "O people of Khazraj you know, what position Muhammad (PBUH) holds among us. We have protected him from our own people, who think, as we do about him, but he will turn to you and join you. If you think that you can be faithful to what you have promised him and protect him from his opponents, then assume the burden you have undertaken. But if you think that you may betray and abandon him after he has gone out with you, then leave him now. For he is safe where he is now."

The reply of the Believers from Yathrib was, "We have heard what you have said." Then addressing the Prophet (PBUH) they said, "O Prophet, chose for yourself and for your Lord what you wish."

It may be realised that the conversation was between forthright outspoken but sincere people. They were honest and were trusted men of honour among their people. Some words and phrases of this conversation need being kept in mind, when studying the Constitutional Charter. For instance, Abbas the uncle of the Prophet (PBUH) had said:-

"We have protected him."

In spite of hardships resulting from consistent persecution he was still propagating Islam. Abbas meant that, his family had prevented his enemies from killing him. He was not able, while in Makkah, to establish Sovereignty of Allah. The main object of his Mission had not been achieved. Abbas, however, could not understand the implications of the Mission remaining unfulfilled.

"If you think that you can be faithful to him."

Fear of treachery and unfaithfulness was natural, particularly when an old established Way of Life was being threatened.

"Protect him from his enemies."

Coming events prove that his fears were justified.

The reply of Believers from Yathrib was brief and meaningful. They had said, "Choose for yourself and for your Lord," which shows that Believers from Yathrib had studied Islam carefully and they knew the importance given by the Prophet (PBUH) to the desires and commands of Allah, because of the Revelations he was receiving constantly.

The Prophet (PBUH) had said, "I invite your allegiance on the basis that you will protect me as you would your wives and children." The words, "I invite your allegiance", are to be kept in mind because later on, "allegiance" was expected from all those to whom the Constitutional Charter was given. He is "inviting allegiance for protection," but allegiance to him as The Prophet of Allah is the main point. The protection was to be given to a superior to whom allegiance had been submitted. The 'Bayah' was and is a promise, a word of honour, an undertaking of complete loyalty, as if it was being sworn in the presence of Allah. This fact will have to be kept in mind when studying the Charter.

The Believers from Yathrib had, however, one worry. They said, "O Prophet of Allah! We have ties with other people, and if we sever these, and, later when Allah brings you with victory, perhaps you will return to your own people and abandon us."

He smiled and said:-

"No! blood is blood. If blood is not to be paid for, then it is not to be paid for. I am of you, you are of me. I will at war against those, at war against you and be at peace with those that are at peace with you."

This answer of the Prophet (PBUH) is reproduced in the Charter in the form of a Commandment for Believers, for all times to come. We will be examining it a little more minutely when studying the appropriate Clause.

Before the Believers from Yathrib left Makkah, the Prophet (PBUH) appointed twelve leaders from amongst them "that they may take charge of their people's affairs." Of those given leadership, nine of them were from Khazraj and the remaining three were from the tribe of Aus. The organization of the Ummah, as a socio-political entity, and a full fledged Deen had started. These twelve formed the government of Believers, without being called a government. The men appointed were known as Amirs and no more. Even when the Prophet (PBUH) moved to Yathrib and the Constitutional Charter was issued, there was no mention of a government being formed or a state being established. It was Deen of Islam, which was being fully operated and "the affairs of the people were being taken charge of." Even when Abu Bakr took over these responsibilities, he was an Amir over the people in order "to arrange the affairs of the people."

A careful look at this episode makes it evident that every one was certain that the Quraysh of Makkah will go to war against the Prophet (PBUH) and those who gave protection to him. The fear of Yathribite was that after Allah will have given him victory, he will return to his people, could mean only that the victory would be against those enemies who forced him to leave his people, and when these enemies—the Quraysh—were defeated, he might decide to return to his people in Makkah. A number of post-Hijrah incidents need to be examined in the light of this remark. The man from Banu Aamir bin Sasaa was also cognisant of this possibility and expressed similar ideas, but not so clearly.

During the conversation prior to the Bayah being taken there was mention of 'fear', 'the need for loyalty' and care taken to guarantee that 'treachery' will not be permitted to occur. All these ideas go to describe the element of uncertainty resulting from the efforts of Quraysh, over a number of years, to spread rumours against the Prophet (PBUH) among visiting tribes, at the time of Hajj season.

The enemies of Islam had been constantly outspoken about their future plans of using force to stop the spread of Islam among tribes. If Believers were successful in converting desert Arabs to the Ideology of Sovereignty of Allah, then the superior position held by Quraysh would end and they would lose all existing privileges. Quraysh, like most rulers of mankind, were advocates of Sovereignty of man and man-made laws. They had no desire to lose their freedom to indulge in worldly pleasure by accepting Sovereignty of Divine Laws which once accepted could not be transgressed without inviting censure and resulting in social imbalances. They realised all these aspects of Islam and were, therefore, determined to fight for perpetual continuity of a secular society.

The mention of force again and again, the stress on loyalty and the mention of certain possibility of fighting in order to defend Believers' right to proclaim the Sovereignty of Allah, leads us to believe that the atmosphere at Makkah, at that time, must have been very tense. The Oath of Allegiance was hardly completed when the news was conveyed to the Quraysh and some one was heard saying:-

> "O people of the station of Mina, do you want this reprobate and the apostates who are with him. They have come together to make war on you."

This also shows the prevailing trend of general conversation among Quraysh, at that time, and their psychological state of war-mania, which had captured their minds.

Men in power and desirous of retaining that power at all costs are all the time on the look-out to find every possible excuse for using physical force against those who in spite of being weak dare to challenge their authority. The news that the Prophet (PBUH) had succeeded in getting supporters among the people of Yathrib must have upset the elders of Quraysh a great deal. Discussions to counter this development and to use physical force must have commenced among the younger generation of Quraysh, even before a proper meeting of the elders could be called.

Believers from Yathrib are certain to have been aware of these developments as is clear from their question and the secrecy maintained by them in arriving at the rendezvous. When they were told to disperse and had returned to their camp, al-Abbas bin Ubada said, "By Allah, if you wish it, we will fall on the people of Mina, tomorrow with our swords." The Prophet (PBUH) did not like any harm to fall on the Believers from Yathrib. He had not yet received any Commandment from Allah to use force even when threatened. He replied, "We have not been Commanded to do that; go back to your caravan."

The Quraysh heard about the Bayah and sent some men to find out the exact position. The Mushrikeen from Yathrib, whom these people asked, knew nothing of the Bayah. They, therefore, denied that any such ceremony had taken place. Believers from Yathrib had kept the news limited to Believers only. The Makkan agents went back and the news remained a secret until after the departure of Yathribite caravan from Mina. It shows the extent to which Quraysh were prepared to go to stop the spread of Islam. If they had come to know of the details of the meeting at this second Bayah of Aqba, they would have taken extreme measures immediately even before the Prophet (PBUH) had made preparations for departure to Yathrib. As long as the Prophet (PBUH) could remain physically interned in Makkah, they could prevent the spread of Islam. Once he and his Companions of the stature of Abu Bakr, Omar and Hamza succeeded in establishing Islam any where outside Makkah, they felt that they would be handicapped and would have to resort to war against those who gave him protection. Makkan leaders were, therefore very keen to avoid the trouble of going to war by putting a ban on the emigration of any Believer from Makkah. This attitude of Makkans is not in conformity with the behavior of earlier people, who did not accept the teachings of prophets sent to them. In all cases they turned them out or desired that those prophets who insisted on preaching the true religion, should leave their tribal cities and go elsewhere. The attitude and behavior of Makkans, since the beginning, had been to contain Islam, by all possible means, to Makkah alone and then by bribery, cajoling, persecution and all other possible means to see that the movement died out. This difference in the behaviour of Makkans from the behaviour and conduct of earlier people needs further study. In the case of Prophet Lot, may Allah bless him, his people said:-

> "Expel the household of Lot from your township, for they (forsooth) are folk who would keep clean." 27: 56

It appears that the reason why the Makkans were bent upon compelling, by force, the Prophet (PBUH) and his Companions to remain as hostages in Makkah so that Islam does not reach a place where its socio-economic organization can be implemented. Later events, after the success of Hijrah confirm this view.

The opposition shown at the time of migration of a few Muslims to Habsha was the result of the same policy decision. Details of the news of Bayah of Believers from Yathrib must have leaked out, particularly because the Prophet (PBUH) gave permission to individuals to migrate as and when an opportunity arose. It was more than permission. As the historian says, "The Prophet (PBUH) commanded his Companions...to emigrate to Madina and to link up with their brethren, the Ansar." Allah will make for you, brethren and houses, in which you may be safe. "So they went out in companies, and the Prophet stayed in Makkah waiting for his Lord's permission to leave Makkah and migrate to Madina."

The first to migrate to Yathrib was Abu Salma bin Abdul Assad of Banu Makhzum, but he had gone before the Second Bay ah of Aqba. There were scenes at times when the head of the family wanted to migrate and efforts were made to retain the wife or the children. When houses were found empty the blame of dividing families was put on the Prophet (PBUH): "He has divided our community, disrupted our affairs, and driven a wedge between us." Some of those intending to migrate were caught by their relatives, bound by ropes and forced to apostatize. Most of those migrating to Yathrib did it secretly. Omar ibn al Khattab, went to Ka'aba, performed Tawwaf and left openly. He was neither molested nor any effort made to detain him. People were afraid of him even when he was a young man.

New Destination

The Prophet (PBUH) waited for permission from Allah to leave Makkah and move to Yathrib. The Quraysh, however, knew that he would leave Makkah, and they got together to chalk out a plan to decide on the best possible way of preventing his migration to Yathrib. They called a meeting of the elders in the conference hall known as *Nadwah*. "The discussion opened with the statement, that as Muhammad (PBUH) had gained adherents outside the tribe, they were no longer safe against a sudden attack and the meeting was to determine the best course to pursue. One advised that they should put him in irons behind bars and then wait until the fate overtook him as befell like the poets Zuhyr and Naabigha, and others. The Shaikh objected to this on the ground that the news would leak out that he was imprisoned and immediately his followers would attack and snatch him away; then their number will grow to the extent that they would destroy the authority of Quraysh altogether. They must think of another plan. The alternative suggested was that they should drive him out of the country and did not care where he went or what happened to him. Once he was out of sight, they would get rid of him. They could then restore their social life to its former state. Again the Shaikh objected to the plan saying that his fine speech and beautiful diction and the compelling force of his message were such that if he settled with some Beduin tribe he would win them over so that they would follow him and (he would) come back and attack them in their land and rob them of their position and authority and then could do whatever he liked with them. They must think of a better plan.

Thereupon Abu Jehl said that he had a plan which had not been suggested hitherto, namely that each clan should provide a young, powerful, well–born, aristocratic warrior; that each of these should be provided with a sharp sword; then that each of them should strike a blow at him and kill him. Thus they would be relieved of him and responsibility for his blood would lie upon all of the clans."

The Prophet (PBUH) came to know of this plot, but before they could decide on the day and time of attack he received permission from Allah to migrate to Yathrib. He informed Abu Bakr, who had already purchased two camels for the journey and supplies. He took with him all the cash which he possessed. Allah had informed the Prophet (PBUH) through Jibraeel of the plan of the Quraysh. He decided to leave on the very night, that had been fixed to kill him. It was an unwritten law in Arabia, which is still honoured in some parts that the privacy of the house of a person is inviolable. If a man is to be murdered he will be killed when getting out of the house. Ali was asked by the Prophet (PBUH) to lie on his bed and return all valuables placed with the Prophet (PBUH) by people as trust, and then migrate to Yathrib. The Prophet (PBUH) then left in the company of Abu Bakr and as arranged reached the cave of Thaur. Next day Ali got up in the morning, and when he emerged from the house the men waiting for the Prophet (PBUH) were surprised but nothing could be done.

They searched for him, in the neighbourhood, for three days, while he and his most intimate friend and Companion lay in the cave of Thaur. Abu Bakr's daughter, Asmaa supplied them with food during these three days. The Makkans had announced a reward of one hundred camels to anyone who would bring him back dead or alive. The stakes were extremely high. If he could not be killed the Makkans would lose their power, prestige, socio-economic superiority over Arabs and the affluence which resulted from their unique position as leaders of socio-religious and economic life simultaneously, which no other class in any nation has ever occupied.

There was a third man with them. He was the guide, Abdullah bin Arqat, who had joined them after they emerged from the cave of Thaur. He guided them along a route not normally used for going north to Syria or even to Yathrib. He reached outside Yathrib on Monday 12th of Rabiul Awwal at about noon. Some say that it was eighth of Rabiul Awwal,which would be 20th of September 622 A.C. After staying in Quba for three days and having constructed a mosque there, he moved to the central part of Yathrib and stayed at the house of Abu Ayub. There was great rejoicing on his arrival in Yathrib by the local Believers, their families, friends and acquaintances. A vacant plot of land was purchased and the construction of mosque taken in hand. Walls were made of stone, the pillars and beams were trunks of date trees and the rest of roof of branches and leaves of this very useful tree. The area then covered by the Mosque of the Prophet (PBUH), as it has been known ever since, is marked by large stone pillars with decorations of flower wreaths upto about two feet from the floor.

On the south and sides were constructed rooms for Ahle-Bait, the family of the Prophet (PBUH). Each room was a few feet in length and breadth and had the barest minimum of household items found even in humblest abodes. A mattress stuffed with leaves of date palm was the only item of luxury.

Until the end of his life he did not change his style of life. In later days, when his share of war booty was considerable and he often presented hundred of camels to visiting embassies he did not use any of it for making his life a little more comfortable even though he needed rest and comfort due to his advancing age. He used to spend a greater part of the night in prayers until the end. Advancement in age and tremendous increase in responsibilities did not make any difference. In Sura Al-Moemenoon, when in Makkah, he had been directed to ask for Allah's forgiveness.

> And, O (Muhammad) say: My Lord! Forgive and have mercy, for Thou art best of all who show mercy. 23: 118

Until the end this remained his favourite Recitation. He had been known in Makkah as a mild, gentle and kind young man. In Madina, when he wielded great power and had a great load of administrative and judicial duties to perform; and, for the first nine years, a great deal of defence responsibilities had fallen on him alone, he would stop in the street to shake hands with people and cheer up children. He was not known to have withdrawn his hand first when greeting people and shaking hands with them. He would utilise the first opportunity to go and visit the sick and never missed offering Janaza prayers for the dead.

The news of his safe arrival was bound to reach Makkah, and it reached without any loss of time. Traffic between the two cities flowed regularly. Now that he had reached Yathrib where there were already local Muslims in addition to his Companions who had slipped away ahead of him the situation had become grave from Makkan point of view. Though the Muhajirs were hardly forty odd in number, they had started playing an active role in the communal affairs of Believers and were exercising healthy influence over the civic life of the city. It was evident, from Makkan point of view, that the Muhajirs would soon be absorbed into the stream of social and cultural life of Yathrib which meant that when they felt home sick, after some time, they would succeed in persuading their protectors to join them in attacking Makkah. The refugees from Habsha would also join them and with new converts to Islam from neighbouring tribes the force would swell to proportions beyond the defence capacity of Makkah. This was the trend of reasoning in Makkah when news of daily developments started reaching them. The reception given to the Prophet (PBUH) on arrival in Yathrib was unprecedented. No guest in the history of tribal Arabia had ever received such rousing reception. They knew his talents. They had already admitted to themselves that he possessed persuasive powers.

Now that he had settled with, not exactly a Beduin tribe, but all the same a powerful adversary, who, as a result of war among themselves in the recent past had experience of fighting, the Prophet (PBUH) appeared to them a source of serious danger. This fear was not new. During the past few years they were afraid that such an eventuality would develop if they permitted him to leave Makkah. They had failed to keep him under their watchful eye but they decided to take some positive action which was to attack Yathrib, but Arab chivalry demanded that they must warn the Yathribites first. The fact of Yathrib being close to their caravan route to Syria, was to be seriously considered, but if they could win over the people of Yathrib, and persuade them to kill or turn out Muhammad (PBUH) and his Companions, the matter could be ended without any future danger to their trading activities to the North.

The Makkans called a meeting of elders in their usual meeting hall, the Nadwah, the house of Qusayy bin Kilab. It was decided to write a letter to Abdullah bin Ubbay, the head of Khazraj, the largest tribe of Yathrib. It so happened that a little earlier the two tribes of Yathrib, Aus and Khazraj, had come to terms and it was under consideration to declare Abdullah bin Ubbay as the king of Yathrib. A crown studded with jewels was being prepared for him. The conversion of a considerable number of his tribe to Islam and the arrival of a batch of disciplined Believers from Makkah had altered the situation. Attention, for the past many months, had been fixed on the expected arrival of the Prophet (PBUH). The news of change in the internal politics of Yathrib and the resulting disappointment of Abdullah bin Ubbay must have reached Makkan leaders as well. This may have prompted them to have addressed the letter to him and not to any one else. They wrote to him:-

> "You have given protection to our men. We swear by Allah that you should either kill them or turn them out of Yathrib. If you do not do that we will attack you and having destroyed you will capture your women folk."

This was, in a way, an ultimatum of war but in actual fact it amounted to the declaration of war. There was no period or date mentioned by which time the Believers from Makkah had to be tumed out of Yathrib. The Quraysh knew that this protection had been given as a result of Bayah, which meant in the presence of Almighty Allah and Bayah is not broken, just because, some unreasonable and illegal threat is received.

When the letter reached Yathrib and Abdullah bin Ubbay found an excuse of re-establishing himself as the leader of Yathrib, he gave out that he would use force against the refugees and if they did not leave Yathrib, he would kill them all. He said he was not strong enough to repulse an attack by an adversary as strong as the Quraysh. The news reached the Prophet (PBUH). He did not wish that trouble should arise between the Muhajirs and Yathribites, even though the majority of them were those who had not yet accepted Islam. He went to meet Abdullah bin Ubbay personally and told the Khazraj chief that when thinking of using force against the Believers he did not realise that Yathribite Believers will side with Muhajir Believers. The Prophet (PBUH) told him in the end that if he used force against Muhajreen he will find that "the blood of his people has been shed on both sides." This quietened him. The realisation that a Believer severs all old connections and every moment of his is offered on the Path of Allah. Believers cannot array themselves in opposite camps. Peace for one is peace for all or none. This philosophy was to be interpreted by him in the Charter under study. He must have explained to Abdullah bin Ubbay that Believers will all be in one camp. They only fight on the Path of Allah. When fighting is on the Path of Allah, all Believers take part in it, but, on the side of Allah and His Prophet (PBUH). Abdullah understood.

History is silent on the issue as to whether he asked the Prophet (PBUH) as to how will Yathrib be defended. We feel that he must have asked the question and the Prophet (PBUH) must have put him at rest by saying that the Believers were duty bound to fight the invaders. Allah had Commanded while he was still at Makkah:-

> " Sanction is given unto those who fight because they have been wronged; and Allah is indeed able to give them victory. 22: 39

This was only permission because the Muslims had not yet organized themselves into an Ummah and had not yet established a state. War demanded the organization of the Muslim Community and a piece of land to established the Law of the Quran. War can be fought only after proper preparation and organization. This was possible in Yathrib. When the Prophet (PBUH) had the conversation referred to above it is more than probable that the following two Verses had been Revealed. They are:-

> "Warfare is ordained for you." 2: 216

and

> "Fight on the way of Allah against those who fight against you, but being not hostilities. Lo! Allah loveth not the aggressors." 2: 190

As mentioned earlier the Philosophy of War, Ordained by Allah and demonstrated by the Prophet (PBUH) of Allah, can be summed up in one sentence. Believers cannot be aggressors but they have a duty (Faridha), to repulse any attack against them. If they do not fight back, then they are likely to be punished to the extent that the land occupied by them is given over to some one else.

> "If ye go not for the He will afflict you with a painful doom, and will choose instead of you a folk other than you. You cannot harm Him at all. Allah is able to do all things." 9: 39

We feel that when the Prophet (PBUH) answered Abdullah bin Ubbay's question by accepting the responsibility of defending Yathrib through the Believers and "others," who would be prepared to follow the leadership of Believers and fight alongside with, then Abdullah bin Ubbay could not object. He could always play the role of remaining neutral. If the Believers succeeded, he and those who followed him, would reap the fruits of the efforts of Believers. If, on the other hand, Believers were likely to be defeated he would not join in the battle. As a result he would not be punished by the Makkans. His conduct, throughout the period of war with Makkah supports this view. There must have been a certain amount of further discussion with him and the Prophet (PBUH) who had a very disciplined mind and who believed in straight dealings, must have told him that he would like to issue a Document giving details of the manner of defending Yathrib and legal basis of affairs of the people of Yathrib. If he was to defend Yathrib, he must have the last word in the Land, which was being defended. This meant that a state and a country had to be established in which Sovereignty would rest with Allah, because it was the Believers who had accepted the responsibility of creating the state, and running it, including the Internal Security and the Defence of the state. Abdullah bin Ubbay had no grounds to oppose this decision of the Prophet (PBUH).

This was the background and the basis of the Constitutional Charter of Yathrib, the town which had given him and his

Companions asylum and which had now no option but to accept to be defended by him and his Companions, as a result of the Command of Allah.

> "He is Allah, than whom there is no other God, the Sovereign Lord, The Holy One, Peace, The Keeper of Faith, The Guardian, The Majestic, The Compeller, The Superb. Glorified be Allah from all that they ascribe as partners (unto Him). He is Allah, The Creator, The Shaper out of naught. The Fashioner. His are the most beautiful names. All that is in the heavens and the earth glorifies Him, and He is Mighty, the Wise." 59: 23-24

> "Glorified be Allah, the Lord of the Throne." 21: 22

3

Last Phase in Mecca

The last years of Muhammad's stay in Mecca were very eventful. The tidal wave of Islam had been constantly growing stronger and the Prophet had won a sizeable following in spite of the hostilities of the Quraysh. It was during this period that two eminent personalities Muhammad's uncle Hamzah and ' Umar, the son of Khattab (who later became the Second Caliph), joined the new faith. The pledge of 'Aqabah' took place and the Prophet was asked to undertake his night journey which is known as Mi'raj (ascension).

It is recorded in Ibn Hisham that the Holy Prophet was one day seated on the hillock of Safa when Abu Jahl happened to pass by and accosted the religion preached by him. Muhammad (peace be upon him), however, kept quiet and did not utter a single word. He left the place and came to join a party of the Quraysh who were sitting near the Ka'bah. It so happened that, shortly after that, Hamzah, while returning from his hunting expedition, passed by the same way, his bow hanging by his shoulder. A slave-girl belonging to 'Abd Allah b. Jud'an, who had noted the impertinence of Abu Jahl, said to him: "O Abu 'Um-mardh! would that you witnessed the scene when your nephew was abused by Abul Hakam. He accosted him with reproaches and uttered such words as were most repugnant to Muhammad (peace be upon him), but he did not answer him back." On hearing these words Hamzah was deeply offended and hurried to the Ka'bah and there, in the courtyard of the holy sanctuary, found Abu Jahl sitting with a company of the Quraysh. Hamzah rushed upon him and struck bis bow upon his head violently and said: "Ah! you have been abusing Muhammad; I too follow his religion and profess what he preaches. Hit me back if you can." The men of Band Makhzum came to his help, but Abu Jahl sent them away saying: "Let Abu 'Ummarah alone, by God I did revile his nephew shamelessly." Therefrom, Hamzah proceeded direct to the house of lrqam and professed Islam at the hand of the Prophet. The conversion of Hamzah to Islam proved to be a source of great strength to the new faith and its followers.

Another significant addition to the strength of Islam was 'Umar, the son of al-Khattab, a man of dauntless courage and resolution, feared and respected in Mecca, and hitherto a bitter opponent of the new religion. The traditional account reveals that the Holy Prophet once raised his hands in prayer and said: "O Allah! give strength to Islam especially through 'Umar b. al-Khattab," The prayer was granted and he embraced Islam. The account of his conversion is very interesting.

One day 'Umar set out from his house sword in hand, with the intention of killing the Prophet. He was in a fit of anger and was fretting and fuming. Nu'aym b. 'Abd Allah, a friend of 'Umar, met him accidentally half way. What had caused so much excitement and on whom was the fury to burst, he inquired casually. 'Umar said furiously: "To destroy the man Muhammad (peace be upon him), this Sabean, who has shattered the unity of the Quraysh, picked holes in their religion, found folly with their wise men and blasphemed their gods." "By God, 'Umar, your soul has deceived you, do you think that Banu 'Abd Manaf would let you walk on earth if you slayed Muhammad. Why don't you take care of your own family first and set them right?" Which of the folk of my house?" asked ' Umar angrily. "Your brother-in-law and cousin, Sa'id b.Zayd, and your sister Fatimah, for by Allah they have embraced Islam and have chosen to become the followers of Muhammad, so look thou to them." 'Umar directed his footsteps to his sister's house. As he drew near he heard the voice of Khubbab b. Aratt, who was reading the Qur'anic chapter "Taha" to both of them. Khubbab, perceiving the noise of his footsteps retired to a closet. Fatimah took hold of the leaf and hid it under her knee. But 'Umar had already heard the voice. "What sound was that I heard just now" shouted the son of al-Khattab, entering angrily. Both his sister and her husband replied: "You heard nothing." "Nay," said he swearing fiercely, "I fear that you have become the followers of Muhammad in his religion." He plunged forward towards Sa'id b. Zayd but Fatimah rushed to the rescue of her husband. Thereupon, 'Umar fell upon his sister and struck upon her head. The husband and the wife could not contain themselves and cried aloud: "Yes, we are Muslims, we believe in Allah and His messenger Muhammad (peace be upon him) so do what thou will." When 'Umar saw the face of his dear sister besmeared with blood, he was softened and said: "Let me see what you were reading, so that I may see what Muhammad has brought." Fatimah hesitated and said: "I feel afraid to trust you with it." Umar swore by God that he would return it to her when he had read it. Fatimah was satisfied with the assurance but said: "O brother, you are unclean on account of your idolatry, none but pure may touch it. You must at least clean your hands." So 'Umar arose and washed his hands and took the page and read the opening verses of the chapter Taha.

> "We have not revealed unto thee (O Muhammad this Qur'an that thou shouldst be distressed, but as a reminder unto him who feareth; a revelation from Him

Who created the earth and the high heavens, the Beneficent One Who is established on the Throne. Unto Him belongeth whatsoever is in the heavens, and whatsoever is in the earth and whatsoever is beneath the soil." (xx: 2-6)

'Umar read it with great interest and was much entranced with its rhythm, fascinating charm and appeal so that when he came to the verse: Verily! even I am thy Lord. There is no god save Me. So serve Me and establish worship for My remembrance,"he remarked: "How excellent it is, and how graceful!" And when he heard that, Khubbab came out of concealment and said: "O 'Umar, I hope that Allah has answered the prayer of the Prophet (peace and blessings of Allah be upon him) for only yesterday I had heard him say: 'O Allah! strengthen Islam through 'Umar.' 'Umar said: "O Khubbab direct me to Muhammad that I may go and submit myself to him."

Khubbab led him to a house in Safa where Muhammad had been living along with his Companions. 'Umar reached that place with the sword swinging by his arm. He knocked at the door. Companions of the Holy Prophet turned to see who the intruder was? One of them peeped through a chink in the door and reeled back exclaiming: "It is 'Umar with his sword." Hamzah, the son of Abd al-Muttalib, dispelling the fears of his friends, said: Let him in. As a friend he is welcome. As a foe he will have his head cut of with his own sword." The Prophet asked his Companions to open the door. In came the son of Khattab. The Prophet, advanced to receive the dreaded visitor and asked him the reason of his visit. At this 'Umar replied: "O Messenger of Allah; I come to you in order to believe in Allah and His Apostle and that which he has brought from his Lord." Filled with delight Muhammad cried aloud: "Allah-u-Akbar" (Allah is the greatest).

The conversion of 'Umar, a simple incident, reflect admirably the powerful influence that the Holy Qur'an had on the hearts of those who listened to or recited it. It shows how the Word of Allah could conquer their souls. Couched in concise and exalted style, its short pregnant sentences, often rhymed, possessed an expressive force which could turn even the bitterest enemy into an ardent admirer. The transmutation of dust into gold seems trivial compared to the overnight transmutation of an avowed foe into a passionate believer. Moreover, this incident also gives us an idea of the deep love the Prophet had for mankind. His calm and dignified personality had a charm of its own. His heart was burning with the keen desire to summon people to the path of righteousness and he was always ready to show the greatest affection even to his most bitter enemy. His mind was absolutely free from all sorts of prejudices.

The conversion of Hamzah and 'Umar was a real triumph for the cause of Islam. So great an instant was the effect of their conversion on the situation that the believers who had hitherto worshipped God within their own four walls in secret now assembled and performed their rites of worship openly in that sanctuary itself. This raised their spirits, and dread and uneasiness began to seize the Quraysh.

The last days of the Meccan phase of the Prophet's life is noted for his miraculous journey from Mecca to the farther mosque at Jerusalem, and an ascent through the sphere of the heavens and then enjoying the company of adoring prophets and angels and getting into immediate presence of God Almighty, far beyond where none except Gabriel could ascend.

This important journey is known as Mi'raj which literally means ascent or ascension. In Islamic parlance, the ascension of the Prophet Muhammad (peace be upon him) to the heavens is called Isra' which signifies a night journey. This journey is described in chapters 17 and 53 of the Holy Qur'an:

> Glory be to Him, who carried His servant by night from the sacred Mosque to the distant Mosque—the precincts of which We have blessed—in order that We might show him some of Our signs. (xvii: 1)

This verse describes the initial stage of the journey from Mecca to Jerusalem, and explains its purpose to be the manifestation of the extraordinary signs of Providence. The noteworthy feature is that the journey took place within a part of the night in spite of the fact that the distance between Mecca and Jerusalem is several hundred miles. Another chapter of the Qur'an which gives an account of Mi'raj is liii and it reveals some details of the Prophet's experience in the heavens where he is described as having witnessed the Divine Glory and Manifestation at the closest possible propinquity.

In both these places, the events have been described as extraordinary and the Qur'anic version belies the conclusion that the whole event was merely a dream-experience.

There are many authentic traditions from the Prophet concerning the night journey contained in Bukhari and Muslim and other reliable collections of Hadith. Here we quote a few of them. The Prophet described that extraordinary experience in the following words:

> "I was one night sleeping at Mecca in the house of Umm Ham, daughter of Abu Talib and a sister of 'Ali, when Gabriel came to me. He rent the roof of the house and brought to Hatim near the Ka'bah. He opened my chest on the side of the heart, washed it with the water of Zamzam in a golden basin, filled it with wisdom and mercy and put it back in its place. Then he brought a horse (Burraq) to me, which resembled lightning in swiftness and lustre, was of clear white colour, medium in size, smaller than a mule and taller than an ass, quick

in movement that it put its feet on the farthest limit of the sight. He made me ride it and carried me to Jerusalem. He tethered the Burraq to the ring of that temple to which all the prophets in Jerusalem used to tether their beasts, and led two Rak'ahs of prayer with them. After that, Gabriel took me to the heavens on the same horse. When we reached the first heaven, the guarding angel said: "Blessed be thy arrival" and opened the door of the heaven. The angels congratulated me and opened the gate. I visited Jesus and John (peace be upon them) and saluted them. They returned my salutation and said: "Good brother, blessed be thy arrival!" Then they expressed their faith in my prophethood. Then I reached the third heaven and met Joseph (may peace of Allah be upon him) and saluted him. He welcomed me and returned my salutation and expressed his faith in my prophethood. Then I was carried to the fifth heaven. There I met prophet Ha'run (may peace of Allah be upon him), I saluted him and he returned my salutation and expressed his faith in my prophethood. Then I reached the sixth heaven, I met Moses there. I saluted him and he returned my salutation. Thence, I reached the seventh heaven and met Abraham and saluted him. He returned my salutation. Thence, I was carried to the Sidarat al-Muntaha. Then I was shown the Bait al-Ma'mur which is a Ka'bah encompassed daily by seventy thousand angels, so that the angels who once encompassed it would not have their turn again till the resurrection. I saw paradise and hell. Then Gabriel stopped there and I was presented to the Divine presence and experienced the thrill of witnessing the Divine Glory and Manifestation. Fifty daily prayers were ordained for my followers. On my return, I spoke to Moses that my followers had been enjoined to pray fifty times in a day. Moses said: "Your followers cannot perform so many prayers; I have already

> tried the children of Isra'il. Go back to God and ask for a remission in number." I went back to the presence of God and stated that my followers could not bear (the burden of) so many prayers. The Almighty God, glory be to Him, made a reduction of ten prayers. When I reported this to Moses, he urged me again to request for a further reduction. I again begged my Lord to reduce the number still further. I went again in the presence of Allah at the suggestion of Moses for reduction in the number of prayers till these were reduced to five only. Moses again asked me to implore for further reduction, but I said: "I feel ashamed now of repeatedly asking God the Holy and High, for the reduction. I accept five daily prayers. God commanded that these five prayers shall be rewarded as fifty prayers."

It is also recorded in Hadith that the Prophet led a congregational prayer of the prophets-in Bait al-Maqdis.

The account of the Mi'raj, as given in the Qur'an and Hadith, is clearly indicative of the fact that it was not a dream, but an astounding experience. The description in chapter xvii begins with the glorification of the Lord for the extraordinary favour that he had conferred on Muhammad. Had it been merely a dream, its special mention was absolutely uncalled for and the limited span of time i.e. a part of the night, would have been meaningless, because one can have a glimpse of both the worlds in a state of slumber even in the fraction of a minute.

Moreover, the Mir'aj has been expressed by the word Isra', which signifies a journey both of body and soul together in a part of a night as it has been pointed out in the Holy Qur'an:

> The angels said: O Verily we are messengers of the Lord; they shall not reach thee. So travel with thy people in a part of the night. (xi: 81)

Likewise in another chapter of the Qur'an, it has been clearly stated:

> And We inspired Moses saying: Take away my slaves by night, for ye will be pursued.

Here the word asra denotes travel by night, and it is obvious that it refers to bodily movement.

It is also recorded that as the story of the Mi'raj spread around, the unbelievers scoffed at it, Had it been only a dream, there would have been no occasion for such a reaction about it.

The Qur'an, however, tells us that this event raised a good deal of stir among the people and the sceptical audience plied Muhammad with all sorts of questions:

> And We appointed the vision (of thy ascent) which We showed thee as an ordeal for mankind. (xvii: 60)

This verse clearly indicates that this extraordinary event became an ordeal for the people. The ordinary mind could not imagine that a man could ascent through heavens with his body. A dream, however, could never have created such a widespread discussion as this event did. 'Abd Allah b. 'Abbas, who had a deep insight in the Holy Qur'an, says that the word 'ru'ya' as used in the above mentioned verse, signifies the observation with the help of an eye. He emphatically refutes those who claim that it was vision in the state of sleep.

It is, however, significant to note in this connection that the word 'ru'ya' is used in the Arabic language both for the vision in dream and seeing with the physical eyes, corresponding to the context of the use of that word. The well-known poet Mutanabbi while praising Badr b. Ammar, says:

The night is over, but your praise is not exhausted. Your seeing with the eyes is more enchanting than your vision in a state of slumber.

The Holy Qur'an testifies to the bodily ascension of Muhammad in Surah Najm as well:

> Then he drew nigh and came down. Till he was (distant) two bows' length or even nearer. And he revealed unto His slave that which He revealed. The heart lied not (in seeing) what it saw. Will ye then dispute with him concerning what it seeeth.
>
> And verily he saw him yet another time by the Lote-tree of the utmost boundary, nigh unto which is the Garden of Abode. When that which shroudeth did enshroud the lote-tree. The eye turned not aside, nor yet was over-bold. Certainly he (the Prophet) saw some of the greatest signs of his Lord. (vii: 6-8)

The famous scholar of Hadith, Nauwwi, in his well-known commentary of Muslim's Sahih succinctly remarks:

> The fact is that an overwhelming majority of the people including the early servants, jurists, muhaddithun and the scholars agree that the prophet ascended to the heavens with his body. Any person who would carefully reflect over the traditions and the accounts narrated by the Companions would be convinced of this truth.

This opinion of the illustrious commentator of Hadith clearly points to the fact that the Mi'raj was a unique experience of the Holy Prophet in which both the body and the soul participated. The view is accepted universally by the Muslim scholars and mystic philosophers of the various schools of thoughts. The difference, if there is any, is on the issue whether the Prophet saw the Lord with his naked eye or not. In this connection, the disagreement rests on the fact that the Companions gave different interpretations of the verse:

And verily he saw Him yet another time descending. 'Abd Allah b. Abbas says that "Him" stands for God whereas Abd b. Mas'ud and 'A'ishah claim that "Him" denotes the angel Gabriel.

This unique experience of the Holy Prophet led to different reactions. The unbelievers found it a suitable opportunity to jeer at the Muslims and their creed. They pestered the Prophet with questions as to the description of the temple at Jerusalem, where he had never gone before and, to the astonishment of many, the Prophet's replies furnished accurate information about that city, etc.

But for the true Muslims there was nothing unusual about it. The Almighty God, Who is powerful enough to have created the heavens and the earth by an act of His Will, is surely powerful enough to take His messenger beyond the heavens and show him those signs of His at first hand which are inaccessible to man otherwise. This deep belief of the Muslims in the Omnipotence of Allah and in the variety of the Prophet is expressed in the answer of Abu Bakr, when he was asked to make his comment about this extraordinary episode. It is recorded in the Hadith that the unbelievers came to Abu Bakr and inquired whether he believed in the truth of the story of his friend Muhammad, that he went to Jerusalem and then came back within a part of the night. Abu Bakr inquired if the Holy Prophet had actually said that. "Yes" they answered. Upon this he said: "Yes, I do verify it." The unbelievers then said: "Do you testify that Muhammad went to Jerusalem and then returned within the short span of a night?" He replied: "Yes, I am prepared to testify to events even more wonder-provoking than this one, i.e. the heavenly messages come to the Prophet day and night. This event (his ascension) is not more astounding than that."

To Abu Bakr, therefore, the acceptance of the Mi'raj was just like the acceptance of the prophethood of Muhammad. It was on this occasion that he earned the title of al-Siddiq (the verifier of the truth).

The apt reply given by Abu Bakr is very meaningful and beautifully epitomises the Islamic point of view about God and the universe and their mutual relationship and the significance of miracles in the scheme of revealed religions.

Great Miracle

There can be no doubt that one who believes in the prophetic doctrine about Allah, the Creator and the Sustainer of the universe, can find no a priori difficulty about verifying the miracles of the prophets. These are not unworthy of God, nor are they arbitrary acts. These are in fact occasional expressions of God's special purpose in the universe in connection with His messengers, expressions which are designed to serve as eyeopeners against the blindness of a world perverted by sin. These are not so much disturbance in the natural order of the universe as they are acts of the Lord meant to shake people out of their heedlessness and to wrench back a sinful world into its proper order. They are part of a redemptive process which seeks the restoration of the Divine Order in nature, not its overthrow. For the man who holds the mechanistic view of the universe, nature might be a system, closed and complete in itself, and therefore, the idea of any intrusion into it of anything "from beyond," or the idea of any interruption of its regular law or order is unthinkable. But for a Muslim, there is nothing irrational in miracles because he does not look upon the universe as the creation of blind forces, but of an ever-living Lord Who is always concerned with its affairs and Who moulds them according to His Will. There is, no doubt, a uniformity in nature, but this does not mean that the universe is a finished product which left the hand of its Maker at its completion and is now lying stretched in space as a dead mass of matter with which God has now no active relationship. Such a view is repugnant to the spirit of Islam. The uniformity in nature signifies the perfect orderliness of God. But the principle of the order of nature should not be taken in the sense of blind mechanism. It denotes perfectly free will of the Supreme God, the Creator.

The idea of moral freedom is not in itself antagonistic to the idea of a perfect law. If nature is to be animated by freedom, and not by a blind necessity, then there is nothing unreasonable in miracles because in the heart of this world of determinate and determined forces and laws there lies this mysterious and unique thing—the free Will of the Creator which the modern scientists have failed to comprehend.

There is no gainsaying the fact that a modern man who is exclusively absorbed in the scientific conception of nature as the scene of inevitable law cannot accept the possibility of miracles. But we should bear in mind that science is not the only legitimate avenue to Reality. There is also a moral avenue to Reality which justifies the existence of miracles. It is not contrary to reason to expect from the Almighty God that under exceptional circumstances. He should show some special signs which might attract the attention of the people quite effectively.

It is true that the testing of faith lies in enduring and seeing Him Who is invisible in the ordinary course of natural life, but when the hearts of men almost fail to perceive the real worth of the teaching of the Prophets, it is quite logical if they are revived with the force of some extraordinary event. It would be sheer arrogance on the part of human reason to hold this to be necessarily impossible.

We find no basis in the Qur'an for encouraging any childish love for the supernatural. But does it not amount to denying reason and power of God, if we were to assert that the Lord is tied to the rigid laws of nature? When a miracle is performed what happens is that God innovates upon the moral physical order solely in the interest of the deeper moral order and the purpose of human life.

"Miracles, it must be remembered, are very rare. That is of their essence. These are occurrence in the process of nature of something which nature, that is the experienced order, cannot account for, and which constrains men to recognize a special or extraordinary action of God calling attention to a special purpose."

This definition of miracles is very exhaustive. It tells us that these are not common occurrences, but are quite rare. Secondly , it tells us that they are astounding events. Lastly, that although these are shown at the hands of some prophet, they are actually performed at the behest of God. Ghazali in the well-known book Ihya' 'Ulum al-Din observes:

The mu'jizah (miracle) testifies to the truth of the prophets, because human beings fail to perform it. It is a work of the Lord.

Similarly, Shaykh 'Abd al-Haqq Muhaddith Dihlavi remarks:

Miracle is not the act of the Prophet, but that of the Lord only which is exhibited at the hand of His Messenger.

Imam Ghazali has further elucidated this point in another work known as Tahafat al-falasifah. He believes that miracles are the works of Allah only, but adds that the time qualified for the occurrence of a miracle comes only when the prophetic resolution is directed to it, and then as a means of strengthening the system of the sacred Law, its appearance becomes a specific condition for the establishment of the system of God. The Holy Qur'an is the greatest miracle of the Holy Prophet, his character, morals and manners are the resplendent proofs of his truthfulness. "The mu'jizah (i.e. a departure from the usual course of nature which the human intellect fails to comprehend as a matter of cause and effect)," says Ibn Rushd, is not a purpose in itself but it lends support and strength to man's belief in Allah and His Apostle.'

Preaching Hard

The working of miracles was not thus the main pre-occupation of the Prophet. His energies were concentrated on preaching the Word of God and he lost no opportunity in calling people to the path of righteousness. He visited all those tribes who were often drawn to Mecca or to fairs in the neighbouring towns. He addressed assemblies at 'Ukaz and other places and preached to the pilgrim encampments at Mecca and Mina. On these occasions, he made fervent appeals to the people to give up idolatry and accept the sovereignty of Allah, the sole Creator and Sustainer of the universe, and assured them that the worship and service of the true Lord would not only open for them the gates of heaven in the next life, but would secure for them prosperity and dominion here on the earth as well. Abu Lahab, the sworn enemy of Islam and that of the Holy Prophet would shadow Muhammad's steps crying aloud, "O men, this man exhorts you to cast off the yoke of Lat and 'Uzza from your necks. Do not listen to him."

The Prophet was not dismayed at all. He persisted in his mission for the fulfilment of which he had been commissioned to strive despite all odds. He moved amongst the tribes, he came across, awakened them to the consciousness of the great destiny that beckoned them and hurled defiance at the forces of doubt and darkness that stood in his way.

It was during this period that he got the opportunity of inviting the tribes of Medina (then known as Yathrib) to Islam. It is narrated that he once met a group of six or seven men whom he recognised as visitors from Medina. "Of what tribe are you?" asked the Holy Prophet. "Of the tribe of Khazraj," they replied. "Then, why not sit down for a little and I will speak to you." The offer was readily accepted for the fame of Muhammad (peace and blessings of Allah be upon him) had spread to Medina and the strangers were curious to know more of the man who had created a stir in the whole area. The Prophet presented to them an expose of his faith, explained its implications and the responsibilities that fell upon the men who accepted it.

Hadith further records that both the Jews and the polytheists of Medina were eagerly waiting for the advent of a new prophet. The Jews, however, excelled others both in wealth and knowledge. So, whenever there was any fight amongst them, the Jews always threatened their opponents by telling them that a prophet was about to rise for the time for a new dispensation had arrived. Him they would follow and then smite their enemies as the children of 'Ad and Iram had been smitten.

So when Muhammad addressed a group of pilgrims from Medina they testified him and said:

> Know, surely, that this is the prophet with whom the Jews are ever threatening us; wherefore let us make haste and be the first to join him.

Call from Yathrib

They, therefore, embraced Islam, and said to the Prophet: "We have left our community for no tribe is so divided by hatred and rancour as they. God may cement our ties through you. So let us go to them and invite them to this religion of yours; and if God unites them in it, no man will be mightier than you.It is doubtless the Ansar had some awareness of the truth when they accepted the doctrines of Islam, but the majority of them presumably became Muslims primarily because they believed that God had sent Muhammad with a message to the Arabs.

The handful of Medinese converts remained steady to the cause and they preached the new faith with full zeal and devotion with the result that they succeeded in winning adherents for Islam from amongst their fellow-citizens. So the following year, on the occasion of the pilgrimage there came a group of twelve faithful disciples ready to acknowledge Muhammad as their prophet. Ten were of the Khazrhaj, and two of the Aws tribe. They avowed their faith in Muhammad as a prophet and swore:

> We will not worship any but One God: we will not steal; neither will we commit adultery, nor kill our children, we will obey the Prophet of God (Muhammad) in all that is good.

When they had taken the oath or pledge, Muhammad (peace and blessings of Allah be upon him) said: He who carries it out has Paradise for his reward and he who neglects anything and is afflicted in this world, it may prove redemption for him in the hereafter and if the sin remains hidden from the eyes of men and no grief comes to him, his affair is with Allah. He may forgive him or He may not."

This oath is known as the First Pledge of 'Aqabah, named after a little terraced mound where it was taken.

When the twelve men returned to Medina, the Holy Prophet sent Mus'ab b. 'Umayr b. Hashim so that he might teach them the doctrines of Islam and give them practical guidance as he had learnt in his company. He lived in Medina with 'Asad son of Zurara. "So prepared was the ground, and so zealous the propagation that the new faith spread rapidly from house to house and from tribe to tribe. The Jews looked on in amazement. The people whom for generations they had vainly endeavoured to convince of the errors of heathenism were of their own accord casting their idols to the moles and the bats and professing belief in the One True God."

The next year during the pilgrimage season, the converts of Medina met the Holy Prophet once more at the same place where they had met a year ago. This time, however, unlike the previous year, their number was eighty-eight as against twelve previously, they pledged their faith to him in the presence of his uncle 'Abbas b. Abd al-Muttalib who (though himself still not a Muslim), abjured them not to draw his nephew away from the protection of his own kindred unless they were fully prepared to defend him even at the risk of their lives. He was the first to speak:

> O ye people of the Khazraj! you all know the position that Muhammad (peace and blessings of Allah be upon him) holds among us. We have protected him from our people as much as we could. He is honoured and respected among his people. He refuses to join anyone except you If you think you can carry out what you promise while inviting him to your town, and if you can defend him against the enemies, then assume the burden that you have taken. But if you are going to surrender him and betray him after having taken him away with you, you better leave him now because he is respected and well defended in his own place.

The Medinese assured 'Abbas and his companions of their whole-hearted support to the Holy Prophet and the noble cause for which he stood then addressing him said: "O Messenger of Allah! It is now for you to speak and take from us any pledge that you want to take regarding Allah and His Messenger."

The Prophet once again preached the faith and said: "I call you in the name of Allah, to worship none but one God and to give me a pledge that you will give me whole-hearted co-operation in the cause of Allah."

Bara' b. Ma'rur stretched out his hand and said: "We pledge, O Prophet of God! that we accept all these conditions."

Then Abul-Haytham b. Tayyihan said: "O Prophet of God between us and the Jews there are agreements which we would then sever. If Allah grants you power and victory, should we expect that you would not leave us". The Prophet replied:

> Nay, it would never be: your blood will be my blood. In life and death I will be with you and you with me. I will fight whom you fight and I will make peace with those with whom you make peace.

The audience were ready to take the pledge but Abbas b 'Ubadah son of Nadia Ansari remarked:

> O ye people of the Khazraj! do you know the significance of the pact that you are entering into with this man? You are in fact avowing that you will fight against all and sundry. If you fear that your property will be at stake or the lives of your nobles will be endangered, then leave him now, because if you do this after the pledge it will be degrading for you both in this world and the world to come. But if you think that you can carry out what you are called upon to do in spite of the loss of precious lives and property, then undertake this heavy responsibility, and I swear by God, that herein lies the good of this world and that of the next."

Good Days Ahead

The people said with one voice: "We accept this even at the cost of our lives and property. But, O Prophet of Allah! if we remain unshaken in our resolution, what will be in store for us? "Paradise," was the reply. Then they all stretched out their hands and took the pledge which was as follows:

> We all will obey you, O Prophet of Allah! in all sets of circumstances: in plenty as well as in scarcity, in joy as

> well as in sorrow, that we would not wrong anyone. We will speak the truth at all times; and that in God's service we would fear the censure of none.

The Prophet of God appointed twelve deputies to preach Islam to the people at Medina and to guide the respective men of their own tribes in matters relating to the propagation of Islam.

Somehow or the other, the news of these secret desert meetings with the Medinese leaked out and, in order to know the facts with certainty, the Quraysh interrogated some of the pagans of Medina, who answered in good faith that there was no truth in the report.

As time rolled by, the Quraysh learned more about the pledge and in a fit of rage they pursued the pilgrims from Medina but did not succeed in catching hold of anyone except Sa'd b. 'Ubadah. They subjected him to unspeakable tortures, but he was later rescued by Jubayr b. Mut'in and Harith b. Harb with whom he had trade relations and whom he had given shelter before.

After the pledge of "Aqabah, Muhammad (peace be upon him) began encouraging his followers to migrate to Medina. Abu Salamah is said to have gone there even before the pledge. This movement aroused the hostility of the Quraysh still further. They were unhappy with emigration because it would remove the Muslims to a place entirely beyond their reach, and plant them in a safe place whence they might securely work out their plans. The Quraysh, therefore, renewed their persecution, and, wherever they had power, they sought either to force the believers to recant, or to prevent their escape by confining them. It was in pursuance of this unwise policy that Umm Salamah (who, after the death of Abu Salamah was married to the Holy Prophet) was forcibly detained in Mecca and her child was also snatched from her. She succeeded in joining her husband along with her child at the end of the following year. After this 'Amir b. Rabi'a and his wife Layla, the daughter of Abu Hathma migrated to Medina. Then came Abu Ahmad bin Jahsh, and his brother 'Abd Allah. This is how a speedy movement of the Muslims to Medina went on till the entire quarters of the city became deserted; and 'Utbah, the son of Rabi'ah at the sight of these vacant abodes, once so full of life, sighed heavily and recited the old verse: "Every dwelling place, even if it has been blessed ever so long, will one day become a prey to desolation and bitter wind." "And", he sorrowfully added, "all this is the work of the son of our brother, who has scattered our assemblies, ruined our affairs, and created dissension amongst us".

Within two months nearly all the followers of Muhammad, except Abu Bakar, 'Ali, the Prophet himself and those helpless noble souls who had been detained in confinement or were unable to escape from slavery, had migrated to their new abode. "They were welcomed with cordial and even eager hospitality by their brethren at Medina, who vied with one another for the honour of receiving them into their homes, and supplying their domestic wants." In the words of Muir:

> Qureish were paralysed by a movement so carefully planned, and put into such speedy execution. They looked on in amazement, as families silently disappeared, and house after house was abandoned. There was here a determination and self-sacrifice on which Qureish had hardly calculated.

This situation alarmed the Quraysh and at last they convened a meeting to take some effective measures with a view to stopping this tidal wave. Imprisonment for life, expulsion from the city, each was debated in turn. Assassination was then proposed, but assassination by one man would have exposed him and his family to the vengeance of blood. The difficulty was at last solved by Abu Jahl who suggested that a band of young men, one from each tribe should strike Muhummad simultaneously with their swords so that the blood-wit was spread over them all and therefore could not be exacted.

This proposal was accepted and a number of young men were selected for the sanguinary deed. Muhammad was informed of all that had been conspired against him and the angel Gabriel revealed this verse to the Holy Prophet:

> They are devising a plan against thee and I will devise a plan for thee. Wherefore, bear with the infidels and let them alone for a while. (xxxv: 1517)

How splendidly did it come true! Eleven of the conspirators were killed shortly after in the Battle of Badr, and the remaining three, namely Abu Sufyan, Jabir and Hakim were converted to Islam, and the Prophet escaped safely from their hands. Referring to their deliberations the Holy Qur'an says;

> And call to mind when the unbelievers devised their plans against thee, that they might imprison thee or slay thee or expel thee from the city. Yes, they devised plans, but God also devised plans. (viii: 3)

The situation was no doubt critical but Muhammad was not at all perturbed. Abu Bakr was, however, urging the Prophet to depart from Mecca. He was also eagerly waiting for an opportunity to accompany Muhammad on this eventful journey. But the Prophet told him that the time had not yet come: the Lord had not given him the command to migrate.

This delay in the command might have been caused by the overpowering desire of Muhammad (peace be upon him) to see all his followers safely go away from Mecca before he himself left for Medina. Moreover, by deferring his departure God perhaps purposely wanted to show to the people that Muhammad was the

Messenger of God and he had been deputed by Him to call people to the path of righteousness and that the Prophet had, therefore, no cause for fear. The events also made it plain that the safety and security of the Prophet's life depended upon God alone and that the Prophet, therefore, need not bank upon the support of any other individual or agency; that the Almighty Who had the power to create man and the universe also had the power to save Muhammad from the danger that beset him.

In anticipation of the command of Allah, Abu Bakr had made preparations for the journey. He had purchased two swift camels and had fed them properly so that they could successfully stand the ordeal of the long desert journey.

Four months rolled by. One day the Holy Prophet came to the house of Abu Bakr and informed him that God had commanded him to leave for Medina. The faithful admirer of Muhammad (peace and blessing of Allah be upon him) shed tears of joy. The hour for emigration had at last arrived and he was to be the companion of the Prophet's journey. Abu Bakr offered him one of the camels which he had already bought for the occasion. The Prophet accepted this offer on condition that he would pay its price.

Abu Bakr's daughter Asma' prepared a bag containing meals for the trip. On the other hand, the Meccans were on the alert. As night advanced, they posted assassins around the Prophet's house. Thus, they kept vigil all night long, waiting to kill him the moment he left his house early in the morning, peeping now and then through a hole in the door to make sure that he still lay on his bed. Muhammad had with him people's trusts, which he entrusted to his cousin to return All them safely to their respective owners and assured him full surety under God's protection and told him that no harm would come to him. 'Ali (may Allah be pleased with him) lay in Muhammad's bed covered with his green mantle. The Prophet came out of the room and cast a handful of dust at the assassins and reciting verses of the Holy Qur'an, passed unperceived through them.

The assassins remained on the watch until the day dawned when they rushed in and to their utter surprise, found that the person lying in the Prophet's bed was 'Ali rather than Muhammad (peace be upon him). This created a stir in the whole town.

Muhammad proceeded direct to the house of Abu Bakr who immediately accompanied him and both set out southward, clambered up the lofty peak of Mountain Thawr, and decided to take refuge in a cave. Abu Bakr first entered the cave, closed all the holes with pieces torn off from his clothes, cleaned it and then asked the Prophet to step in.

The Prophet and his companion stayed in this cave for three nights. 'Abd Allah, the son of Abu Bakr, would go to see them daily after dusk and apprise them of the situation in the city. Amir b. Fuhayrah, while in the company of other shepherds of Mecca tending his master Abu Bakr's flock, stole away unobserved every evening with a few goats to the cave and furnished its inmates with a plentiful supply of milk.

The Quraysh, on the other hand, were quite baffled and exasperated. A price was set upon Muhammad's head. The news that the would–be assassins had returned unsuccessful, and that Muhammad (peace be upon him) had escaped made them gnash their teeth in anger and frustration. Horsemen scoured the country. Once they even reached the mouth of the cave where the Prophet was hiding along with Abu Bakr. When he saw the enemy at a very close distance Abu Bakr whispered to the Prophet: "What, if they were to look through the crevice and detect us? We are two and unarmed and at the bottom of the cave."

God's Gift

The Prophet in his God-inspired calm replied:

> O Abu Bakr! What do you think of those two with whom the Third is Allah.

Alluding to this important scene of the cave the Holy Qur'an says:

> If ye will not assist the Prophet, verily God assisted him aforetime when the unbelievers cast him forth, in the company of the second only; when the two were in the cave alone; when the Prophet said unto his companion: "Be not cast down, for verily Allah is with us! And Allah cause to descend tranquillity upon him and strengthened him with hosts which ye saw not, and made the word of unbelievers to be abased; and the word of the Lord, that is exalted, for God is Mighty and Wise." (xi; 40)

For three days, Muhammad (may peace of Allah be upon him) and Abu Bakr lived in the cave and the Qur'aysh continued their frantic efforts to get hold of them.

"Abd Allah b. Arqat, who belonged to the family of ad-di'l b. Bakr, and had as yet not embraced Islam, but was trusted by Abu Bakr, and had been hired by him as a guide, reached the cave after three nights according to a plan. His report satisfied the noble fugitives that the search had slackened. The opportunity to depart bad come. They could move unobserved, the sooner the better.

They rode the camels, Muhammad (peace be upon him) with the guide and Abu Bakr with his servant Ibn Fuhayra behind him, and resumed their journey. Having come down from mount Thawr and having left the lower quarter of Mecca a little to the right, they struck off by a track considerably to the left of the common road and, hurrying westward, soon gained the vicinity of the seashore near by 'Usfan.

The little caravan travelled during the night and rested in the noon when the heat grew scorching. One day, they could find no shelter. Abu Bakr cast a glance and found a little shade beside a rock. He cleaned the ground, spread his mantle for the Prophet to lie upon and himself went off in search of food. Coming across a bedouin boy who was tending his goats, Abu Bakr asked him to supply milk, which he did.

The Quraysh, as we have mentioned above, had declared that whoever would seize Muhammad (peace be upon him) would receive a hundred camels as reward. This had spurred many persons to try their luck. Among those who were on the lookout for the Prophet and his companion in order to win the reward was Suraqah, the son of Malik. He, on receiving information that a party of four had been observed on a certain route, decided to pursue it secretly so that he alone should be the winner of the reward. He mounted a swift horse and went in pursuit of them. On the way, the horse stumbled and he fell on the ground. On drawing a lot so as to divine whether he should continue the chase or not, as the Arabs used to do in such circumstances, he found the omens unpropitious. But the lust for material wealth blinded him altogether and he resumed the chase. Once more he met with the same fate but paid no heed to it. Again he jumped into the saddle and galloped on at a break-neck speed till he came quite close to the Prophet. Abu Bakr's heart agitated and he said to the Prophet: "O Messenger of Allah! we are lost." But the Prophet remarked in his calm and confident tone: "Be not cast down, for verily Allah is with us."

This marvellous steadfastness of the Prophet in the midst of overwhelming perils was due to Divine revelation that strengthened him and comforted him at every step of his life.

The repeated stumbling of Suraqah's horse and his falling from it awakened him to the situation and he realised that it was a constant warning of Allah for his evil design which he contemplated against the Holy Prophet. His heart was immediately changed and the sworn enemy was converted into an honest believer. He approached the Prophet with a penitent heart and begged of him forgiveness in all humility. The Prophet forgave him and confirmed it with a token written by Abu Bakr on a piece of parchment. Suraqah showed this writing to Muhammad (peace be upon him) on the day when be entered Mecca in triumph. The Prophet rewarded him and said: "It is the day of favour and fidelity." Suraqah hurried back to Mecca and tried to foil the attempts of those who were running in pursuit of Muhammad (peace be upon him) and his noble companions.

The party continued its journey till it reached the encampment of Umm Ma'bad al-Khuza'iyah. She was a gracious lady who sat at her tent-door with a carpet spread out for any chance traveller that might pass that way. Fatigued and thirsty, the Prophet and companions wanted to refresh themselves with food and a few draughts of milk. The lady told them that the flock was out in the pasture and the goat standing nearby was almost dry. The Prophet with her permission touched its udders, reciting over them the name of Allah, and to his great joy, there flowed plenty of milk out of them. The Prophet first offered that to the lady of the house and what was left by her was shared by the members of the party.

After having refreshed themselves the emigrants moved further. In the evening when Abu Ma'bad, the husband of Umm Ma'bad, came to his house, the lady narrated to him this strange incident. Upon this he remarked: "By God, he is the same man whom the people of al-Quraysh are searching for. Can you give me his description?" Umm Ma'bad said:

"His was an innocently bright and broad countenance. His manners were fine. Neither was his belly bulging out nor was his head deprived of hair. He had black attractive eyes finely arched by continuous eyebrows. His hair, glossy and black, inclined to curl, he wore long. His voice was extremely commanding. His head was large and well formed and set on a slender neck. His expression was pensive and contemplative, serene and sublime. The stranger was fascinated from the distance, but no sooner he became intimate with him, this fascination was changed into attachment and respect. His expression was very sweet and distinct. His speech was well set and free from the use of superfluous words, as if it were a rosary of beads. His stature was neither too high nor too small so as to look repulsive.

He was a twig amongst the two, singularly bright and fresh. He was always surrounded by his companions. Whenever he uttered something the listeners would hear him with rapt attention and whenever he issued any command, they vied with each other in carrying it out. He was a master and a commander. His utterances were marked by truth and sincerity, free from all kinds of falsehoods and lies."

On hearing these words, Abu Ma'bad said, "By God, he is the man who is zealously debated about amongst the Quraysh now-a-days. I have determined cheerfully to accept his yoke."

Leaving the encampment of Umm Ma'bad, Muhammad (peace be upon him) and his companions lost no time and resumed their journey, going through unfrequented paths and suffering great hardships on account of scarcity of water and severity of heat. It was during this time that they met Zubayr at the head of a caravan returning from Syria. Warm greetings were exchanged, Zubayr gave them the tidings that Medina was eagerly waiting for their arrival. He also presented to them two white garments which they thankfully accepted.

As soon as rumours of Muhammad's arrival began to spread, crowds came flocking out of Medina. They would come every morning and wait eagerly for his appearance until forced by the unbearable heat of the midday sun to return. One day, they had gone as usual and after a long trying watch had retired to the city when a Jew, catching a glimpse of three travellers winding their way to Medina, shouted from the top of a hillock: "O ye people of Arabia! He has come! He has come! He, whom ye have been eagerly waiting for, has come!"

The joyful news soon spread throughout the city and people marched forward to greet their noble guest. The shouts of "Allaho Akbar" (God is the Greatest) resounded in Banu 'Amr Muhammad's elation (may peace of Allah be upon him) correspondingly increased, but with rare sense of timing and propriety, he called a halt. It was Monday, the eighth day of Rabi'al Awwal, thirteen years after the inauguration of the prophetic career of Muhammad (peace be upon him) i.e. on 20th September 622.

Muhammad (peace be upon him) stayed in Quba, with Kulthum b. Hadam a hospitable chief of the tribe of 'Amr b. 'Awf, who had already received many of the emigrants on their first arrival. It was here that the party was joined by 'Ali. He brought the news that the rest of the family would soon be arriving. Zayd was leading one party which included his own wife Zaynab, the Prophet's wife Sawdah, and his daughters Fatimah and Umm Kulthum. 'Abd Allah b. Abu Bakr was bringing his sisters 'Aishah and Asma', as well as his mother Umm Ruman.

During his period of stay at Quba which, according to Bukhari, extended to a fortnight, was laid the foundation of a mosque which has been glorified in the Qur'an in the following words:

> The mosque which was founded upon piety from the first day is more worthy that thou shouldst stand (to pray) therein. (ix: 108)

Exemplary Cooperation

The Prophet worked side by side with his other companions for the construction of the mosque. He even carried stones on his back and helped in setting them in proper place.

On the morning of Friday, Muhammad (peace be upon him) rode towards Medina amidst the cordial greetings of his Medinese followers who had lined his path. He halted at a place in the vale of Banu Salim and there performed his first Friday prayer. The address which he delivered is marked by matchless eloquence, exhortation and eulogy of the Faith and succinctly sums up the spirit of Islam:

> Praise be to Allah, I seek His help, guidance and Kufr. I declare that Allah is One and Muhammad is His Messenger whom his Lord has blessed with guidance, light and wisdom and has sent him to the people at the time when the Apostles had ceased to come and the people had forgotten the teachings of the previous apostles and were led astray. The Day of Resurrection was at hand. Who ever obeys Allah and His Prophet finds righteousness and whoever disobeys goes astray beyond doubt, and is in error manifest. I admonish you to fear Allah. The best advice that a Muslim can give to his brother is to exhort him to observe piety. Avoid that which Allah has commanded you to avoid. There is no better precept than that of piety and fear of God. These are the sources of strength and help in the next life. Your relation with Allah, whether in the seen or unseen sphere of your life, should be based on truth and fidelity and this objective can be best achieved when you have no other end to pursue except that of seeking the pleasure of Allah. Such a course of life will enable you to get honour and fame in this world and it will prove to be a boon in the

Hereafter, when man stands badly in need of good actions and wishes that there had been a great distance between him and misdeeds. Allah admonishes you with His power and Authority and this He does because He is very compassionate and Merciful towards His men. Allah is Truthful and fulfils His promise as He says in the Qur'an: My words cannot be changed nor am I indeed unjust to the slaves" (L: 29). Therefore, fear Him in this world and the world to come in the seen and in the unseen since who fears Him, God grants him redemption for his sins and favours him with great reward. This person alone is, in fact, highly successful. Fear of Allah saves man from His wrath, His punishment and anger. This will brighten the faces of people and elevate them on the Day of Judgment. Fear Allah, walk on the path of virtue and piety. Do not show any slackness in obedience to forgiveness and declare my implicit faith in Him and abhor God. Allah has revealed the Book for your teaching and, has made the right path clear for your guidance so that truth can be distinguished from falsehood. Just as Allah has shown you His favour, likewise you should obey Him in right earnest. Look upon His enemy as yours and exert your best for winning His favour. Allah has chosen you for Himself and has given you the name of Muslims, God has ordained that those who are to be destroyed will be swept away and those who are to survive, after the clear signs have come to them, would live, with insight and on the strength of evidence (from the Lord). No power is of any avail to any one except that of the Power of Allah. Therefore, remember God as much as you can and live for the Hereafter. The man whose relation with God is based on sincerity, Allah will help him against evil. None will be able to harm him. Allah's command is supreme over the people. But people cannot command God. Allah alone is the Master of all men and men have no share in His lordship. Therefore, keep your relation with Allah on the right footing. Do not bother about others. Allah is the Greatest Protector. Allah is the Greatest and there is no Power but that of His."

The address is so eloquent that it needs no comment. A man suffers for thirteen years all kinds of insults at the hands of the Quraysh; stones and filth are thrown at him; he is beaten by the young and the old, and is excommunicated. Then a plot is hatched to put an end to his life and he is forced to leave his hearth and home. He is put to all kinds of torture physical and mental, for no fault of his. He only says: Surrender yourself to Allah. After having been driven from his native place and having suffered hardships and perils of long journey, when he finds an opportunity to address people, not a single word of bitterness is uttered by him. He has nothing to say of his personal sorrows and griefs, of the atrocities perpetrated on him by the people of Mecca, of the privation that he has constantly suffered. The noble heart is free from all stains of personal anguish. The audience is repeatedly exhorted to develop God-consciousness and adopt the path of righteousness.

After leading the Friday prayer, the Prophet resumed his journey towards Medina. The tribes and families of Medina came streaming forth, and vied with one other in inviting the noble visitor to their homes. It was indeed a triumphal procession. Around the camel of Muhammad (may peace and blessings of Allah be upon him) and his immediate followers, rode the chief men of the city in their best raiment and in glittering armour. Everyone was anxious to receive him and said: "Alight here, O Messenger of God I Abide by you." Muhammad (peace be upon him) answered everyone courteously and kindly: "This camel is commanded by God, wherever it stops, that will be my abode."

The camel moved onward with slackened rein and entered the quarter of the city inhabited by Banu Najjar, a tribe who was related to the Holy Prophet from the maternal side. There it stopped before the house owned by Abu Ayyub. The fortunate host stepped forward with unbounded joy for the Divine blessing appropriated to him, welcomed the holy guests and solicited them to enter his house. Abu Ayyub, out of the profound respect that he had for the Prophet, offered to vacate the upper storey, but the Prophet preferred the lower one, being more accessible to his visitors. The Prophet stayed in this house for seven months until the building of the mosque and his own apartments was completed.

Grand Success

Islam no doubt achieved tremendous success in Medina, but the achievements at Mecca too were not insignificant. It was in Mecca that the new religion was founded and a phenomenal transformation was brought about in the life and thought of the Muslims. In the words of Muir:

> Never since the days when primitive Christianity startled the world from its sleep and waged mortal combat with heathenism, had men seen the like arousing of spiritual life, and faith that suffered sacrifice and took joyfully the spoiling of goods for conscience sake...
>
> ...What a change had those thirteen years produced! A band of several hundred persons had rejected idolatry, adopted the worship of One God, and surrendered themselves implicitly to the guidance of what they believed a Revelation from Him; praying to the Almighty with frequency and fervour, for looking for pardon through His mercy and striving to follow after good works, almsgiving, purity, and justice. They now lived under a constant sense of the omnipotent power of God, and of His providential care over the minutest of their concerns. In all the gifts of nature, in every relation of life, at each turn of their affairs individual or public, they saw His

hand... Muhammed was the minister of life to them the source under God of their newborn hopes; and to him they yielded an implicit submisson.

...The Believers bore persecution with a patient and tolerant spirit. And though it was their wisdom to do so, the credit of a magnanimous forbearance may be freely accorded. One hundred men and women, rather than abjure their precious faith, had abandoned home and sought refuge, till the storm should be overpast, in Abyssinian exile. And now again a still larger number, with the Prophet himself, were emigrating from their fondly loved city with its sacred Temple, to them the holiest spot on earth, and fleeting to Medina. There, the same marvellous charm had within two or three years been preparing for them a brotherhood ready to defend the Prophet and his followers with their blood."

4

Shift of Seat

Only few Muslims were left in Mecca and among the high ranking companions only Abu Bakr (R) and 'Ali (R). And so the Quraysh deemed it a golden chance to kill the Prophet (PBUH).

A meeting of the elite of Quraysh was held in Camera at Dar al-Nadwah. It was a representative gathering of the chiefs of all the well-known tribes and classes, including a seasoned old devil from Najd. The satanic suggestions that came from these enemies of Allah and His Prophet Muhammad (PBUH) were: 1. "Yoke and chain him" suggested one and putting him in a room permanently closed with brick work, so that he too, like, Zuhair and Nabigha, may taste of agony before death."

The old man from Najd disagreeing said: "No this is not right. The news of Muhammad's incarceration is sure to find its way to his followers and these Muslims will as surely take him cut and when in power are most likely to annihilate you as well.

Another suggestion was that he should be put on a camel's back and this driverless animal be left alone. Let him go anywhere, settle where he likes, he may live or die should be none of our concern:

The old fellow from Najd: "This suggestion too is unsound. Have you forgotten the charming words of Muhammad (PBUH) Do you not observe that he charms every one he talks to? How easily he wins the hearts of men? Wherever he goes the residents thereof shall get attracted to him and follow him. And they are sure to avenge their Prophet (PBUH) at your cast.

The Approved Plan of Prophet's Murder and Selection of Murderers

Finally Abu Jahl put up a plan that was unanimously upheld.

1. A brave strong man should be selected from every well-known tribe of Arabia.

2. And all of them should surround the house of Muhammad (PBUH) on all sides.

3. When Muhammad (PBUH) comes out for the early morning prayer, all these murderers should follow him with their swords.

The advantage of this ingenious plan was pointed out that since all the tribes of Arabia shall be involved in the murder, neither his own tribe nor yet his followers can create any trouble.

Almighty's Order

Utter shameful failure of the best human plans where Divine Decree starts working can be witnessed when we find that on Muhammad's (PBUH) house being surrounded by the murderers, he said to his cousin 'Ali (R): Occupy my bed and covering yourself with my sheet and need have no worry, for nobody can do you any harm. And while 'Ali (R) slept soundly surrounded by so many murderers and the apostle of Allah (PBUH) came out, under Allah's protection and before the very eyes of the intending murderers who failed to see him, reciting Surah Yasin ("And we have put up a bar in front of them and a bar behind them. And further, we have covered them up so that they cannot see.

(Q. XXXVI: 9) he went his way unseen and unharmed. It happened on 27th of Safar, the 13th year of the Prophet's raising. Thursday, 12th September 621 C.E.

The apostle of Allah (PBUH) went to the house of his closest friend among men, Abu Bakr (R). They hastily made necessary arrangements for the impending journey. Asma (R) the daughters of Abu Bakr (R) closed the open end of the bag of parched and ground barley with a part of the string binding her drivers out off for this emergency need. In the darkness of the night both of them started on their journey. About four or five miles from Mecca, there is mount Thaur which makes journey toilsome due to ascent on a rocky path. Pointed rough stones were wounding the feet of the Prophet (PBUH) and stumbling also was causing him trouble and pain. Abu Bakr (R) lifted him on his shoulders and finally approached a mountain cave (where they decided to stay during the day light, considering pursuit by the enemy. Abu Bakr (R) asked him to rest outside and himself went into the cave, dusted and cleaned it and with pieces torn from the clothes on his body, he plugged the holes in the cave. And then he requested the Prophet (PBUH) to enter.

When the day dawned, 'Ali (R) got up from his bed and the Quraysh recognized him at close quarters and enquired about Mohammad (PBUH). 'Ali (R) replied: "What do I know about him. I had not been keeping watch over him. You yourself let him get out and he left. Their repentance for their negligence infuriated them and they fell upon 'Ali and beating him they brought him to Ka'bah, kept him in custody and freed after some time.

Then they came to Abu Bakr's (R) house, knocked at his door. Asma (R), his daughter, responded and came out. Abu Jahl asked her about her father to which she showed her total ignorance. Evil natured as he was, he slapped her so violently that her ear ring fell on the ground.

A small incident is worth mentioning here. Asma (R) says that her father, departing, had taken all the money he found in the house for the use of the Prophet (PBUH). At her grandfather's remark that Abu Bakr had left, leaving them penniless, she managed to put something where money was kept and leading her blind old grandfather to make sure through touch that the money was there, she had reassured him since he was worried about Abu Bakr's family and its livelihood. Abu Bakr's daughter was no ordinary girl. She had both, a strong faith and unusual wisdom for her age.

These two, the moon and the sun (Abu Bakr (R) and Mohammad (PBUH)) remained in the cave for three days. During the dark nights Asma (R) used to bring food for the duo and Abdullah, Abu Bakr's (R) son, used to bring to them the talk of town of the day and 'Amir (R) bin Fahirah (R) a slave of Abu Bakr's family entrusted with Abu Bakr's (R) flock of goats, used to come to the mouth of the cave and milked some goats for them. On the return journey the first foot prints were wiped out by the flock itself.

Abu Bakr (R) was rewarded for his loving care and devotion by Allah in his (Abu Bakr's) mention in the Quran, "Allah is surely with us." where the word "us" includes the Prophet's most devoted companion Abu Bakr (R).

On the fourth night, two she-camels came to the cave from Abu Bakr's house that had been carefully pampered for this long journey. The Prophet and Abu Bakr mounted one and the other was used by 'Amir bin Fahirah and Abdullah bin Ariqat, hired for guidance of route. They started on this journey on Rabi I, Monday which accords with September 16, 622 C.E.

Migration for the sake of Allah alone and the unhampered propagation of His Faith was the sunnah (way) of the earlier prophets like Ibrahim, Moses and Da'ud (P.B.U.T.) as borne out by both the Quran and the Bible and Allah's aid came to his and their rescue (earlier) after migration.

Their guide had now taken to a change in the route, by the sea now (as a measure of safety against pursuit). However Suraqah bin Jaysham, helmeted and fully armed on horse back was in hot pursuit, tempted by the reward announced by the Quraysh for the Prophet (alive or dead), and on seeing him was glad at heart for his success. But the divine plan of rescue came to the aid of the Prophet and Suraqah's mount was on its knees. In another attempt by him the mare under him sank in the sand of the desert and falling down he became alive to the divine protection and his failure. The Prophet who had all the time in communion with Allah, entreating Him for His Allah was informed about the pursuer and Suraqah also very humbly requested to be spared. He was given assurance of safety of life and the pursuer sincerely promised to guard them against other pursuer if any. Then at his own request and the Prophet's bidding, 'Amir bin Fahirah gave him a letter of immunity for future use.

As a prophesy by the Prophet on this occasion Suraqah had received from him the glad tidings of the jewel studded golden bracelets of Kisra (the ruler of Iran) which he actually received from Caliph 'Umar when Persia was conquered and rich booty came to Medina, and the prophesy had come true.

The first day after coming out of the Thaur cave, this blessed caravan came upon the camp of Umme-Ma'bad. She came from Khuza'ah and well-known for the care and feeding of the travellers. She offered water to the passers by and those who need rest were offered that facility too for a while.

When the Prophet (PBUH) and his companions (R) came to her camp they enquired if she had something to eat. She expressed her regrets saying that if she had any she would have offered before their asking for it. On entering the tent, the Prophet saw a goat in a corner and enquired why was standing there. Umme-Mabad told him that it was too weak to go out for grazing with the flock. At this, he sought her permission to milk the goat and the old woman permitted adding that if you expect milk from it do as you please.

The Prophet touched the teat of the goat invoking Allah's name and taking a milk pot started milking. Soon the pot was brimming over with milk. This was taken by him and his companions. Repeating the operation they took it together. A third operation too gave as much milk and this was handed over to Umme-Ma'bad, the owner of the goat, and started once again on their journey.

After sometime Umm-e-Ma'bad's husband came home and seeing the milk enquired about it. Umme-Ma'bad explained to him how a blessed person came here and it is the miracle that he performed. He said, this person you mention appears to be the same Qurayshite I have been looking for. Let me hear from you something about his appearance. Umm-e-Ma'bad described the features of the Prophet thus:

"Attractive face, open countenance, good natured, neither with a pot belly nor a bald head, handsome to look at, big bright black eyes, and black long thick hair, commanding tone, high neck, fine and joint eye brows. Curly hair sparing in speech and speaking with dignity and confidence, so as to touch the heart, looked from a distance fascinating in appearance, and at close quarters sweet and perfect in charms, sweat and perfect in charm, sweet of speech, clear words in a clear tone, neither sparing in words nor verbose, neither short statured nor unusually talk, companions always at his service command, who like to hear his words attentively and rush to obey and do his bidding. And he the master neither very brief (sparing in words) nor a prolix (long winded speaker)."

On hearing so much about him from his wife he said that he is certainly that 'Sahib-e-Quraysh' (the Qurash supremo). I must go and see him.

Years Passed

We have given a brief account of the thirteen years activity of the Prophet in Mecca. Although the number of Muslims did not exceed a couple of hundred but it was a unique success since it had won over men.

1. Like 'Ali, Abu Bakr, 'Uthman and 'Umar (R) to him as companions, whole excellence of knowledge, practical charm, power, mental vision and traits of the best capabilities which made them the leaders and guides of the-then known world.

2. Or they were men of such talents and competency as Mus'ab bin 'Umair, Ja'far Tayyar and Abu 'Ubaidah bin-al-Jarah (R). They converted the entire populations of Yathrib, Abyssinia and Najran through their magical sermons.

3. Or there were people of the high grade like Abd-Allah bin Mas'ood and Abd-al-Rahman whose traditions of learning and knowledge are the store house of innumerable fine points of religious instruction.

4. Or those of the rank of Zubair, Talhah and 'Ammar Yasin (R) whose devotion and love of Truth are unparalleled in the world history.

5. Or the type of Bilal, Sumayyah, Yasir and Ka'b, Khabbab (R) who had, with their patient perseverance and firmness of stand, tired the Pharaohs (tyrants) of the times in the exercise of tyranny and future.

6. Or yet those with courage and resolution of Sakran. Shamoos, Umm-e-Habibah and Khanees who had, for the sake of the Faith of Truth, left their country of birth, near and dear ones, to go to a strange country, Abyssinia, and settled there.

7. Or eloquent, learned and fluent in speech like Labeed and Swaid bin Samil, called Kamil (the Prophet) and Anees brother of Abu Zarr (R) who got the better of several tribes with one speech or another and were unique in the world of their own times, at least to themselves.

And it was during this period that Islam had spread outside Mecca also. A few examples from that lot of Muslim:

1. Tufail bin 'Amr Dausi who ruled over a territory, close to Yemen had embraced Islam in Mecca and due to the efforts of Tufail Islam had found ascendancy in his country.

2. Abu Zarr Ghifari (R) his brother Anees (R) and his mother and half his tribe Banu Ghifar had become Muslims.

3. Twenty persons from the Christians of Najran.

4. Damad-al-Azdi, the famous sooth sayers of Yemen.

5. The bani Abd-al-Ashhal tribe.

6. Tamim and Na'im and a few citizens of Syria.

7. Many people in Abyssinia and so on.

The Historic Journey

On his way to Yathrib, the Prophet came across Baridah Aslami, the chief of his tribe. The Quraysh had announced a reward of hundred camels for the arrest of Muhammad (PBUH) and Baridah had come out looking for him to win this reward. But when he came face to face with the Prophet and had an occasion to speak to him, Baridah (R) along with seventy companions of his embraced Islam. Taking off his turban he tied to his lance and thus unfurling the white flag of peace and amity he went forward, conveying the glad tidings to all those who could hear, that the king of peace, supporter of concord and friendship and to make justice and equity rein supreme in the world is coming.

On his way, the Prophet (PBUH) met Zubair (R) bin-al-'Awam, coming from Syria with the Muslim traders of Mecca. He presented white cloth to the Prophet (PBUH) and Abu Bakr (R).

Majestic Reception

On 8th Rab I, 13th year of the Prophet's (PBUH) raising, Monday the 23rd of September 622 C.E., the apostle of Allah reached Quba (the entrance to yathrib). The Yathribites having heard of the Prophets leaving Mecca had made it their daily programme of waiting at the entry to Yathrib from morning to midday. One of these days they had hardly left their places of waiting (only a few minutes earlier) that the Prophet approached and at somebody's loud call they one and all turned back, came together and with the cries of Allah-u-Akbar (Allah is the greatest) as their slogan of reception they greeted him from all sides around him. There were among them those who had not seen the Prophet before that were often in doubt about the identities of the Apostle of Allah and his companion Abu Bakr (R). The latter had the perception of the need of identification and stood up protecting the Prophet from the heat of the sun.

The apostle of Allah (PBUH) stayed here until Thursday. And during the three days of his stay here, the first thing that he took in hand was to lay the foundation of a mosque here for the worship of Allah the One and Only, without any partners. And it was here that Ali (R) having travelled all the way from Mecca to Yathrib, (a distance of 300 miles) on foot, joined the Prophet (PBUH). He had stayed back in Mecca, under orders from the apostle of Allah, to return the Trusts (articles entrusted to the care of the Prophet in Mecca) to their rightful owners.

On 12th Rabi I of the finest year of the Prophet's migration to Medina (12.3.1 A.H) it was Friday. The Prophet (PBUH) mounted his camel and reached the habitations of Bani Salim when it was time for Friday congregation, and he got down and led the prayer with a hundred persons following him. This was the first Friday congregational prayer in Islam fifteen hundred years back, (during the prophethood of the Final Prophet of Islam, though it had continued earlier under all other prophets also).

Holy Sermon

All praise is due to Allah. I praise Him and seek help, forgiveness and guidance from Him. I repose my faith in Him, I do not transgress against Him and have feelings of hostility towards those who are transgressors. I bear witness that there is no one worthy of worship save Allah. He is Unique (unparalleled). He has no partners. Muhammad (PBUH) his servant and Apostle. He sent Muhammad (PBUH) with guidance, light and exhortation, at a time when for centuries no apostle came to humanity for guidance. (True knowledge had become deficient and ignorance had pervaded (mankind). He was sent very close to the Doomsday and death. Whoever obeys Allah and His Apostle is on the right path and whoever disobeyed then went on the wrong track, and degraded himself and is entangled in serious misguidance. O ye Muslims! I command you to fear (displeasure of) Allah. The best induction from a Muslim to another Muslim is this that he should induce him to get prepared for the Last Day, and advise him to hear Allah's (displeasure). O ye people! keep away from those things Allah has forbidden. There is no better advice nor a better 'zikr' (remembrance of Allah). Keep in mind that relating to things pertaining to the Hereafter, for a person who is working in constant fear of Allah for a person who is working in constant fear of Allah taqwa (piety) is the best help. And when a person will set right the relationship between him and Allah, both overtly and covertly and so doing his intent is pure (sincere), in that case so doing will be remembrance of Allah in this world and after death (when man will factually realize and stand badly in need of good deeds) it will become a (most profitable source to save him (from damnation in the sight of Allah).

But if somebody does not act in that manner, he has come for mention in the verse: "It will wish there were a great distance between it and its evil, but Allah cautious you (to fear) Him and Allah is full of kindness to those that serve Him. (Q.III: 30) And whoever took Allah's command as true and fulfilled its conditions, he has been commented upon in the following words of Allah:

"The word changes not with Me and I do not the least injustice to My servants." (Q.L: 29)

O ye believers! Keep in view in your present and future and overt and covert deeds, fear of Allah since the evil deeds of the God-fearing are passed over cursorily (or overlooked). The pious are those who will attain great felicity. It is taqwa (piety) that takes away Allah's displeasure. His chastisement and His wrath. It is piety that turns darkness into luminosity, invites Allah's pleasure and elevates the position.

O ye Muslim! Do derive pleasure but do not neglect the divine rights. Allah has taught you His Book and shown you His Way, the righteous and those given to falsehood may be kept distinctly apart. Allah has treated you kindly so you too be kindly and generously disposed towards His servants (the people). And take the enemies of Allah as your enemies. And strive in the way of Allah as you ought to strive (with sincerity and under discipline)..... and has named you Muslim." (Q. XXII: 78). That those who died might die under a clear Sign (had been given), and all those who lived might live under a clear sign (had been given), (Q. VIII: 42). And all good deeds come into existence with Allah's Help. O ye people! Remember Allah and work for the life Hereafter. For, whoever sets right his relationship with Allah, Allah sets right his relationship with other people. And Allah exercises His Authority and rule and governs men's affairs. And nobody can have any say in His Affairs. Allah is the Lord and Master of His servants and they have no authority where Allah comes in. Allah is the Greatest and we derive our will and power for good deeds solely from that Lord of all Greatness.

Grand Arrival

Having done with Friday congregation the Prophet (PBUH) entered Yathrib proper from the southern side and it was from that day that Yathrib came to be called Medina-al-Nabi (the town of the Prophet) or Medina in short.

His entry was grand indeed the streets of the town were resounding with the slogans of praise and sanctification, and men, women and children were all eyes for a glance at the luminary from Allah. Watching this grandeur and sanctity of his reception, it was disclosed to the learned men of the people of the Books what the following statement in Habakkuk Prophet's Book chapter III. V. 3:

God came from Teman, and the Holy One from Paran. Selah, His glory covered the heavens, and the earth was full of his praise.

Faran or Mecca, since Faran bin 'Aufbin Himyar had once occupied it.

The innocent little girls of Ansar were singing the following couplets in an enchanting tone and unsullied tongues:

The full moon has risen upon us from the southern mountains.

We owe thanks to Allah for the Superb Faith and its teachings,

We are duty-bound to obey thy commands for thou hast been sent by Allah the Patron Lord the Obeyed One.

These girls belonged to the fresh converts to Islam knowing pledged allegiance to Islam at the hands of the Prophet (PBUH) in Mecca or those whom Mus'ab bin 'Umair and Ibn Maktoom had converted in Yathrib.

The Ansar of Medina were not in an enviable position where material wealth was concerned but so large-hearted, great lovers of Islam that they kept nothing back from sharing with their migrant brothers with whom they had been formally fraternized by the Prophet, prepared to divorce an extra wife for a muhajir brother. They fed the hungry mouths often on a hungry stomach themselves as evidenced by the Quran also:

> "And those who before them, had homes (in Medina) and had adopted the Faith, show their affection to such as come to them for refuge, and entertain no desire in their hearts for things given to the (latter), but give them preference over themselves, even though poverty was their (own lot)."
>
> —Al Quran LIX: 9

A New Phase

Mecca was populated by Quraysh alone who were dominant and ruled over it. They had also a common creed iconolatory. Medina was a mixture of various communities and religions, including idolaters and Judaic race and religion, a sprinkling of Christians. The Jewish tribes Banu Nadeer, Banu Qaningra', and banu Quraiza, lived in separate fortresses and due to their trade and usury were rich and had sway over other communities.

According to the prediction of Moses, the Jews had been expecting the promised messiah (that prophet) to be born among Banu Isma'il of Arabia, who would restore the demigrated Jewish community to its former glory and had staged so long in Medina, particularly after expulsion from Syria.

Now the news of the arrival of the prophet of Banu Isma'il had gladened their hearts. But once they learnt that he supports Jesus Christ as a true apostle of Allah and believing in him is an inseparable part of his faith, Islam, and thus acknowledging his true exalted position brings the Judaic people to the dock for their grave injustice in rejecting, insulting and handing him over to the pagan roman governor, they one and all became deadly enemies of their "one time expected redeemer."

Noblest Hosts

The Christian citizens of Medina too were longing for the promised messiah the comforter, whose arrival had been foretold by 'Isa in his last sermon, he had ordered his followers, Muslims, who, latter in their misguidance, came to call their faith Christianity (as if it was a faith founded by Christ, and themselves Christians) to follow him. From that time (for six centuries) they had waited for him, who would avenge them against the Jews, raise the Christians to a higher position in the world, bring out the true position of Christ lowered by the Jews. But when they found him rejecting their self-invented (innovative) elements of Faith like making 'Isa ibn Maryam, "Isa ibn-Allah (the son of God), trinity, atonement, asceticism and the almost divine right of Pope, they too became sworn enemies of 'that prophet.'

It would be worth while casting a glance at Abd-Allah bin Ubai bin Salool to grasp the true position of Medina of this period. Besides the sway of the Jews, he too enjoyed a position of great influence over Madinites and he had been nursing hopes of becoming the crowned king of Medina with the support of these tribes who held him in great esteem and it is said preparations were already afoot for his formal coronation before the arrival of the Prophet (PBUH) and other Muslim migrants from Mecca. Under drastically changed conditions, he also accepted Islam hypocritically. But finding the Jews opposing the Prophet he strategically tried to maintain friendly relations with them (the Jews), and the tribes converted to Islam may also remain under his influence as of late. So this hypocrite resorted to double-dealing. And since he had the mistaken notion that the advent of Islam had put cold water on his ambitious plans, he never hesitated in harming the Muslims and their cause. So Medina too had many difficulties in store for Islam and Muslims. But Islam got over their difficulties due to its true nature. The Quran had predicted it. "And the later period is better for you than the former."

Q. XCIII: 4

5

The First Statute

A modern writer defines constitution as "codes which aspire to regulate the allocations of functions, powers and duties among the various agencies and offices of the government...." When we apply it, to a document which was signed within a few months of the Hijrah of the Prophet (PBUH), fourteen hundred years ago, we do not get the exact sense and meaning given to it by either the Prophet (PBUH) himself or those to whom the document was being given. He had called, the Document under study, as:-

"A Writing from Muhammad, the Prophet of Allah."

It could also mean a letter and a document, the last being the most appropriate. This settles one thing. It was neither a 'treaty' nor an agreement, because it was "From Muhammad, the Prophet of Allah," and not an agreement between him and others. They had no objection in receiving it as a Charter laying down the Code of Life for Yathrib. They also accepted his position as "The Prophet of Allah," even though some of them desired to retain their attachment to the religion they already professed. They had, as a matter of fact, no option but to accept it or else live in Yathrib as aliens.

A few points need to be borne in mind while studying this Document. First, that the Document must be placed chronologically before any of the other objects is studied. This is necessary, because of two reasons. The first reason is that unless its period is determined it will not be possible to determine the object for which it was promulgated.

We have referred to the immediate object of this Document as the Defence of Yathrib in the last Chapter. The Document is of a permanent nature. There must, therefore, have been other reasons which are of a lasting nature. The Constitution, if we consider it as such, of the first Islamic State, brought into existence by the Prophet (PBUH) himself has to remain, in most respects, if not all, a model Constitution for all states established by Muslims. We, therefore, feel that it needs studying from a number of angles.

It is important to bear in mind that the Document was dictated by the Prophet of Allah (PBUH). He had been receiving Sublime Guidance, for thirteen years, from Allah. A person of his calibre would not issue a document of this nature without an adequate and a set purpose. Furthermore a person of his knowledge, experience and capabilities would not issue a self–contained document piece meal. If a document is issued by instalments it loses consistency and results in being misunderstood. His actions subsequent to the issue of this Document have also great relevancy. They show, if he was in the habit of tackling problems in a consistent or a disjointed manner. It must be kept in mind that he is The Law Giver and laws given by him have stood the test of time. Persons who create and promulgate laws have to consider problems from all angles, otherwise their laws fail to receive such reception as desired. There has to be logic and consistency in the words and actions of men placed in the position he occupied. Written documents become out of date if they are void of consistency. Lastly, it has to be borne in mind that this Document was issued under certain conditions. Therefore, to gauge its proper importance we must bear in mind all the time, the circumstances which necessitated its issue. These have been discussed briefly.

We have referred to the Document as a Constitutional Charter.

"The form and nature of a constitution are dictated by the relationship prevailing among the various sections or classes of people." There was no organized group with whom the Prophet (PBUH) could have executed a treaty or an agreement. Hence we find that it was neither a treaty nor an agreement. It is important to bear in mind its heading, which also forms the very first Clause.

The heading needs to be given in full.

> "This Document (writing) is from Muhammad The Prophet of Allah (PBUH) to Quraysh and Yathribite Believers and those who will follow them and fight alongside with them. They will form ONE UMMAH to the exclusion of others."

Primarily the Document has been issued to administer the affairs of Muhajir and Ansar Believers. Its jurisdiction is then extended to those who live and fight Jehad under the leadership of these Muhajir and Ansar Believers. Leadership has been given to the entire Muslim community. The Prophet (PBUH) has not spoken of his leadership. This point has great significance for future generations of Believers.

Historic Charter

The manner of promulgation of the Charter may also have a bearing on the circumstances at the time of its issue and the keenness of the recipients to be favoured by inclusion in the Ummah. From the wording and placing of concessions to various tribes, it creates the impression that the dictation of the Charter took place in an open Darbar, and as the Arab custom was and still is, those to whom a clause did not apply they spoke up to be included and at once another clause was dictated for inclusion.

The Document was issued within a few months of the Hijrah of the Prophet (PBUH) which took place in July or August 622 A.C. This is the period when, "a few years earlier, the reign of the grandson of Nousherwan was extended to the Hellespont and the Nile, the ancient limits of the Persian monarchy; the Christians of East were scandalized by the worship of fire and the impious doctrine of the two principles; the Magi were no less intolerant than the bishops, and the martyrdom of some native Persians, who had deserted the religion of Zoroaster was conceived to be the prelude of a fierce and general persecution. The oppressive laws of Justinian, the adversaries of the Church were made the enemies of the state; the alliance of the Jews, Nestorians and Jacobites, had contributed to the success of Chosroes, and his partial favour to the sectaries, provoked the hatred and fears of Catholic clergy."

The Persian monarch was so full of arrogance that, as his predecessors used to carry away the gods of the defeated, back to Persia, he carried away to his capital the Holy Cross from Jerusalem. The situation, however, altered, within a few years as predicted in the Quran. Byzantium, "rallied under Heraclius, who had led his troops in 624 A.C., into the heart of Iran. Chosroes was deposed and executed by his own subjects, and Heraclius recovered the Cross".

It meant a great deal for the prestige of the Emperor. To have brought back Holy Cross, the symbol of true Christianity, to Jerusalem, where the Jews were supposed to have been instrumental in having Jesus Christ crucified, was a great achievement. Syria, at that time was a truly Christian land. "In fact this is the only period in which Syria has been a fully Christian country..... Not only was the country Christian, but the age was an ecclesiastical age".

It was in this age of persecution, religious prejudices, taboos, ethnical differences, and acute hatred resulting in mass killings, when this Document was dictated to an assembly of Believers,

Mushrikeen and Jews, not far from a totally Christian land, where at about the same time controversies raged, which ended in a, "sentence of excommunication on the tomb of St. Peter; the ink was mingled with the sacramental wine, the blood of Christ; and no ceremony was omitted that could fill the superstitious mind with horror and affright".

It was the same period, when in India, Harsha ruled and according to a Chinese pilgrim, "The penalty of imprisonment, inflicted after the cruel Tibetan fashion, which left the prisoner to live or die was freely awarded and mutilation was often adjudged".

In spite of it all we are told that in every one of these lands their particular civilization was at its peak and yet man was in bondage and writhed with pain at the feet of other men. Man had forgotten that he and other men were all descended from Adam and Adam had been created from clay:-

"He it is Who hath created you from clay". 6: 2

How unnatural that men should be regarded as unequal and yet inhabit the same planet. Many prophets had come and tried to teach men and women that they were equal as human beings, but it was left to the Last Prophet of Allah to establish complete equality in those who believed in Allah and him as His Messenger and Servant.

While he was dictating this Document of great consequence he was observing the principle of equality. It would take centuries for mankind to realise the effect and importance of this principle.

Real Authority

The ultimate destination of mankind, while on this planet is the mastery of elements of nature. He has to achieve vast knowledge of nature of things and elements to an extent that very few can imagine. Acquisition of knowledge at the level of entire humanity demands peace, justice and equality among mankind. This will come about when mankind rises above the level of present ignorance and becomes one Ummah. This is the most important lesson taught by the Last Prophet of Allah, while dictating this unique Document. Universal peace will be achieved when the principle of equality of man is universally accepted. The Prophet (PBUH) when dictating this Document brought the level of all men on an equal pedestal. Jews who, at the time, were looked down upon, except may be in Iran were given equality with Arabs of Quraysh and Ansar origin. Equality of man appears to be one of the main features of his Mission, and, "It is difficult to portray the events of the life of the Prophet (PBUH) unless we first understand the nature of the Mission entrusted to him"."

This Mission, according to the Quran is complete guidance of mankind in all walks of life. Man has to enter Islam completely.

> "O ye who believe! Come, all of you, into submission".
> 2: 208

And the Prophet has to bring mankind into Islam-submission to the Will of Allah.

> "(This is) a Scripture which We have revealed unto thee (Muhammad) that thereby, thou mayst bring forth mankind from darkness unto light, by the permission of their Lord, unto the Path of the Mighty, the Owner of Praise". 14: 1

The Eternal Message of Allah happens to be placed in a world which, in certain respects, alters with changes in time and geography. And yet this Eternal Message guides men to the straight path. "The glory of Islam is that it distinguishes the universal from the changing particulars".

If we study the Quran and try to locate Eternal Commandments we will find that these happen to be all in respect of those aspects of human life and nature, which remain constant and are not subject to any great changes as a result of time and place. Those aspects of life whether at the level of an individual or at the collective level of society, which are subject to changes due to change in surroundings, have been left to the individual or the society, as the case may be, to find the best solution as long as no other Commandment is violated in the process. This means that no restrictions have been placed on "the changing particulars."

It is the same with the Sunnah of the Prophet (PBUH). He has set precedents in all walks of life but restrictions are placed only in the field of universals and particulars are left to be decided by the individual and the society, as the case may be. He was the Messenger of the Code of Life Revealed by Allah. He was not sent as a military commander and yet he demonstrated the "why, when and how" of war, because the Ummah needed guidance in it. He was not a statesman and yet he demonstrated how justice tempered with mercy was to be administered in a society of equals. He led his army to many a battlefield, keeping in view the principles of war and compulsions of strategy and tactics dictated by geography and other factors and demonstrated all the qualities of a great commander.

His critics fail to keep his Mission in view when commenting on his activities as a soldier or as a statesman because their view of a Way of Life is limited to acts of prayers only. To say that, "Muhammad (PBUH) himself was not a warrior and had few military gifts. In battle he invariably followed behind the front line, never, if avoidable, himself engaged in hand to hand fighting", amounts to disregarding his role as a guide of commanders. The writer forgets that commanders do not engage, normally, in hand to hand fighting. They have to direct, control and deploy troops as the situation may demand. This vague statement of a British general does not mention those qualities of martial nature which in his opinion were absent in the Prophet (PBUH). He would have probably liked to see in him qualities displayed by British generals like Kitchner, who, "sword in hand and Bible in pocket he enjoyed a career of spectacular warfare in Russia, China, India, and Africa...." Kitchner's enjoyment of war amounted to perversity, when he had defeated Mehdi's Army he arranged a victory parade, on 10th of April 1898, in which, he treated the captured enemy commander Amir Mahmud in the most cruel manner. "Dragging chains which were riveted round his ankles, and wearing a halter round his neck the defeated army commander was made to walk, and sometimes run, behind the cavalry. His hands were bound behind his back, and he was driven forward by Sudanese guards who lashed him with whips when he stumbled. Kitchner rode on a white horse in triumph". What a spectacle of British chivalry and martial excellence during the closing years of nineteenth century when European civilization was at its height.

This British general of whom many generations spoke with admiration, gave orders, that the tomb of Mehdi be razed to the ground and his bones to be cast into the Nile. Mehdi's skull which was unusually large was kept aside to be used as inkstand. One suggestion was to use it as a drinking cup. He had ordered Wingate, another famous British soldier, to "loot like blazes. I want any quantity of marble stairs, marble payings, iron railings, looking glasses and fittings, doors, windows, furniture of all sorts". A victorious general who pardoned his life-long enemies must have appeared to General Glubb, to lack martial qualities common among European generals and conquerors. The objective of the Prophet (PBUH) was to establish peace as a precedent for Believers until the end of Time. He had to demonstrate what was an ideal life. This included both war and peace. It included the life of a labourer and also that of a ruler. He demonstrated the life of a man of all walks of life, when he was being persecuted and we find no change in the way he lived, when he was the ruler of entire Arabia and his army had a successful round of exchange of arms with the Byzantian Imperial Army, at the battlefield of Mowta. As a general his strategy was not only to win the war but to succeed in the days after the war as well, and his war stands alone in the annals of military history, which brought happier days both for the winner and the vanquished although a winner in earlier battles he had accepted armistice on the enemy's terms.

It has been recorded by his biographer "When there was peace and war was abolished and men met in safety and consulted together none talked intelligently about Islam without entering it. In these two years double as many or more than double as many entered Islam as before".

Throughout his life he was keen to use all his resources to bring about peaceful atmosphere in which his Message could be understood and accepted. Today, fourteen centuries after him, the world has accepted the point of view that peace alone can solve mankind's problems. A modern writer has said, "In an age of Total War we will need Total Peace". War, however, has to be catered for." Wars do not break out of themselves, but they may change the course of history and the fate of mankind.... War has, therefore, become the greatest of social problems". For him and for Islam war had become the greatest of not only social but also political problem. He gave to the world, Islam—The Message of Peace-when war had been brought to his doorstep. This Document is of great consequence as it gives an answer to a multi-national Ummah, as to how they should face an aggressor and survive. One of the outstanding features of this Document, which cemented the citizens of Yathrib was justice with Equality for all. Peace within communities and, at international level, cannot be established without equality and equal status to men and groups of men—the nations. This equality was not acceptable either within Arabia or at the international level at that time. The Arabs of Makkah, steeped in the idea of racial superiority, their minds clouded with racial prejudices, and having a class ridden society, were in no mood to accept equality between Abu Jehl, the high born Qurayshi chief and Bilal the Negro slave.

Equality for All

It was the principle of equality of man which evoked the animosity of the two neighbouring mighty empires of Iran and Byzantine, towards Islam and Muslims. The ruling classes of both these empires were securely entrenched as the high born elites, who held the birth right of princely and regal positions. The birth of an Ideology of "Equality before the Eyes of Allah," both in this and the next world, was a revolutionary reality which had to be nipped in the bud. The rest of the world was to array itself on the side of these to Empires, one after the other. The prophesy of Abbas bin Ubada was fulfilled soon enough but it was to continue being fulfilled for ever.

It was during the Second Bayah at al-Aqaba that Abbas bin Ubada al-Ansari, said to the Ansars who were swearing allegiance to the Prophet (PBUH), "O men of Khazraj, do you realise to what you are committing yourselves in pledging your support to this man? It is to war against all and sundry. If you think that if you lose your property and your nobles are killed you will give him up, then do so now, for it would bring you shame in this world and the next. But if you think that you will be loyal to your undertaking even if you lose your property and your nobles are killed, then take him for by God. It will profit you in this world and the next".

The men from Khazraj and many others who followed their footsteps are still being challenged by the enemies of Justice and equality for all. It is, outwardly, that people oppose Islam, while their real opposition is against the principle of equality of man, by those whose vested interest are in danger or being jeopardised. It was a question of life and death in that age. Religion during that age made men of religion oblivious of cruelties perpetuated in the name of religion. Minor differences or even suspicion of minor differences led men to throw others into flames. As has been remarked, "It remained for the Medieval Church, however, to put cruelty and burning and gruesome public executions on the firm popular basis of exalting religious spectacles".

There can be no peace in the world unless the world led by Muslims observes laws relating to Jehad on the Path of Allah and in conducting their foreign affairs as ordained in the Quran. This Document was the first writing, directing towards the principles and the policy according to which human societies should conduct their affairs. It has been universally accepted that in the world of today there is no international law, relating to the conduct of states in matters of conflict or mutual interest, obligations and the making and breaking of treaties. There have been usages in various parts of the world, which have been overlooked more often than not and in all conflicts national interests have prevailed. "International Law, so called, is in reality national law regulating international relations of those states".

Prefect Document

Islam has a complete Code of International Law. It, however, operates at the level of the Millah of Islam, on the principle that Believers are an Ummah when considered with respect to the rest of humanity. If Muslim States observe in their inter-state relations, the Commandments of the Quran, the super powers will find it difficult to drive humanity in World Wars, as they have done twice during twentieth century. These Quranic Injunctions dictate relations between Muslim states and also between Muslim states and others. Islamic Law is the only Law which forbids states to undertake aggression of any kind; not even for the spread of religion.

This Document, apart from being the Constitutional Charter of the state of Yathrib was at the same time the document on the authority of which this state had come into existence. The person proclaiming the coming into being of this new state was Prophet Muhammad (PBUH), the last of the line of prophets, who had received Revealed Word of Allah. As a result of the contents of this Document, the state of Yathrib received all those elements which add up to the formation of a state. "A state exists as soon as the four formal elements (a people, a territory, a government and the characteristics of sovereignty) can be found in it and that recognition by other states merely recognizes the social fact", and non-recognition does not alter its status. The newly created state of Yathrib was, however, recognized soon after its establishment. The Prophet (PBUH), immediately after the promulgation of this Document went out of Yathrib, stayed with various tribes, each of which held sovereign status within its tribal territory, and executed friendly treaties with them. Apart from establishing treaty relations with neighbouring tribes, these journeys of the Prophet (PBUH) fixed approximate limits of the territory of Yathrib. The boundaries of an Islamic State, cannot be a permanent feature. Islam cannot have and does not have fixed boundaries. Islam attracts people because of principles of justice and equality. It spreads and with its spreading are extended its boundaries. Islam has not remained static even during its days of political eclipse. The spread of Islam in Africa has been when a greater part of Africa had been occupied by European Colonial powers.

In Malay Archipellago Islam was spread by Muslim merchants at a time, when Spain held sway over the area. "They did not come as conquerors, like the Spanish in the sixteenth century, or used the sword as an instrument of conversion; nor did they arrogate to themselves the privileges of a superior and dominant race so as to degrade and oppress the original inhabitants".

It is said of Al-Mamun that when a certain Yazdanbakht a leader of the Manichaean sect came on a visit to Baghdad and held a disputation with the Muslim theologians, in which he was utterly silenced, the caliph tried to induce him to embrace Islam. But Yazdanbakht refused saying, "commander of the faithful, your advice is heard and your words have been listened to: but you are one of those who do not force people to abandon their religion".

It was the same in Eastern Europe where, "The Calvinists of Hungary and Transylvania, and the Unitarians of the latter country, long preferred to submit to the Turks rather than fall into the hands of the fanatical house of Hapsburg; and the Protestants of Silesia looked with longing eyes towards Turkey...." The writer speaks in the same vein of other countries and other lands. "Even in Italy there were men who turned longing eyes towards the Turks in the hope that as their subjects they might enjoy the freedom and the toleration they despaired of enjoying under a Christian government".

As said earlier, this toleration of Muslims, in all the then known lands of the Globe, was the result of magnanimity shown by the Prophet of Islam (PBUH) when dictating this Document in Yathrib, at the time, when the first state of Yathrib was coming into existence. The Muslims have honoured the spirit of this Document throughout these fourteen centuries, which is not a mean achievement. In spite of it, and may be because of it and the resulting popularity of Islam, it "inspires perfidy of the Balkans, the hate of the Jews, the apprehension of the Hindus and the animosity of the Russians".[1] The remarks of Abbas bin Ubada Ansari have been referred to above. His prediction continues to come true and may continue much longer. The basic reason for this opposition is the fear of loss of vested interests of the ruling classes and the religious hierarchy, of many faiths which upholds these classes and are a hindrance towards universal equality of man and the resultant justice and fairplay for the masses.

The tenacity with which Muslims have held on to the principle of equality is due to the fact that, they believe staunchly in the Sovereignty of Allah, which is the core and basis of all Islamic teachings. Islam stands for the Sovereignty of Allah alone and of none else. This, in practice, means that the Eternal Laws enjoined by Allah cannot be altered. If this principle was accepted by the ruling classes they would, after that, not be able to frame laws as and when it suited their vested interests. They desire to keep the framing of laws in their own hands and thus they and their institutions set aside for framing and promulgating laws retain Sovereignty in their own hands.

People's Power

The law assures that Parliament is omnipotent and paramount. It can make or unmake laws on any matter whatsoever.... The power and jurisdiction of parliaments, says Sir Edward Coke, is so transcendent and absolute, that it cannot be confined, either for causes or persons, within any bounds.... It hath sovereign and uncontrollable authority in making, confirming, enlarging, restraining, abrogating, repealing, reviving and expounding of laws, concerning matters of all possible denominations, ecclesiastical or temporal, civil or military, maritime or criminal. This fact is contained in their Constitutions, whether written or based on practice, precedence and legal judgements. Speaking of the Constitution of England (which included English possessions in Scotland, Ireland and Wales) Dicey, an eminent lawyer, has mentioned "three leading characteristics in the existing Constitution of England; they are now generally designated as the Sovereignty of Parliament, the rule of law and the convention of the constitution"." If a similar analysis was to be made of the Constitutional Charter of Madina, its leading characteristics, that would emerge would be firstly, the "Sovereignty of Allah and His Prophet" (PBUH), secondly, "The Rule of Law" and thirdly, "The Equality of Man." As composed to the Sovereignty of Parliament which means sovereignty of man made laws, and Convention of the Constitution, these characteristics certainly carry more weight.

Mankind has, time and again, failed to convince itself that it can successfully conduct its affairs, without Guidance from Allah. Mankind, in nearly every land, "has been the victim of disastrous illusion—the illusion of our ability to emancipate ourselves from natural laws". Whether we call them as Natural Laws, (Revealed to prophets of earlier eras) or openly admit that they are Laws given by Allah who alone is our Creator and Sustainer and Knows our needs far better than us, makes no difference. These are laws which are based on Truth from Him, who has set a destination for mankind which cannot be arrived at except by conducting ourselves in accordance with these Laws. Man has been given knowledge and intelligence, but both these qualities are limited as compared to the knowledge and Power of Allah. "It is evident that human intelligence has not increased simultaneously with the complexity of the problems involved." To-day, as much as in the past, civilized humanity has shown itself incapable of directing either its individual or collective affairs. The modern world, like the Quraysh of Makkah, needs to be bold and pay homage, to the basic principle of the acceptance of the Sovereignty of Allah.

This Document, The Constitutional Charter of Madina, laid down, in no uncertain terms, that Allah alone wielded Supreme Power and that the method of invoking that power is Allah Himself and His Prophet (PBUH) is the interpreter of His Laws. This Document also lays down priorities to be adopted for the security and defence of states established by Muslims. The test of Constitutions whether they are capable of meeting the needs of their respective states has been suggested by a modern American writer as follows:-

> "How effective is the constitution in enabling us to come to grips with periodic crises? What are the principal objectives of our national institutions? What service do they render? What are the rights and obligations of American citizenship"?

The Constitutional Charter of Madina, as a Document, is fourteen hundred years old. If modern constitutions are examined in the light of the above mentioned questionnaire it would clearly come out that human mind has not made any perceivable advance in this respect. The history of events in Madina, subsequent to the issue of this Constitutional Charter, has been recorded in greatest possible detail. We can, as a result of its perusal, say that the periodic crises that occured, in Madina, after the promulgation of this Document, were conveniently solved through actions based on it.

There is no doubt about the fact that at the time of its promulgation, the entire population of Yathrib had rejoiced about it and had unanimously accepted to live under its protection and abide by its laws.

This Document, "brought into existence a voluntary association of all sections of Madinites-Muslims and non-Muslims, emigrants and locals, principals and clients,..." Aus and Khazraj, the two Arab tribes, were the only people who could claim that Yathrib belonged to them. They had been at war with one another but had settled their differences, lately. An agreement had been reached tentatively that in order to give the place semblance of an organized community they should choose a king. Abdullah bin Ubbay the leader of Khazraj was being talked of as the future king of Yathrib when Bayate Aqba Thani took place. Soon after this, Muhajirs started arriving in Yathrib. They and the Ansars were a far more organized group, than any tribe could be, and Abdullah bin Ubbay's crowning ceremony was soon forgotten.

There were Jews also in Yathrib. They were all engaged in trade and commerce and being rich had built themselves strong forts outside the main city of Yathrib. The Jews, however, did not either own or belong to the place. A number of theories have been advanced, but the most plausible theory is that they were immigrants from Syria as a result of one of purges that used to be carried out from time to time, to rid the Holy Land, of them. They were living under the protection of various sub-tribes of Aus and Khazraj. They did not possess any right other than what the Haleef-protecting tribe-cared to allow them.

This Document had completely altered their social and political status. They were being raised to the status of citizens of Yathrib like any other person from amongst the tribes of Aus and Khazraj. This was a great elevation in their status. They were no more aliens or emancipated slaves. They would, henceforth be able to speak up to the Arabs as equals and the word Jew would soon loose the sense of inferiority which it had, hitherto, carried all the world over. The Prophet (PBUH) was allowing them a further concession, which would soon make them a political force to be reckoned with. He was, on certain conditions, inviting them to become a part of the Ummah of Believers. This invitation happened to be under Divine Guidance and was, therefore, all the more attractive. Although this invitation was also given to the Christians but they were so few in Arabia that the Jews would have been certain to overshadow them always. This invitation, however, had one point which in the end was likely to be unacceptable to them. It was that they had first to accept the Sovereignty of Allah. The invitation being the result of an Ayah of Quran must have made them hesitate but they do not seem to have shown any such hesitation in the beginning. The Words of this Ayah of Quran, are:-

> "Say, O People of the Scripture! Come to an agreement between us and you: that we shall worship none but Allah, and we shall ascribe no partner unto Him, and that none of us shall take others for lords besides Allah. And if they turn away, then say, Bear witness that we are those who have surrendered (unto Him)".
>
> 3: 64

The Prophet (PBUH) was trying to create a multi-national Ummah which was to form a coalition of all those who believed in Allah and thus were being asked to form a united front against the godless. He had advocated an idea, which the West have taken up lately but not with the intention of finding a united platform for all religions, but, to find out means of accelerating Christian Missionary activities in Africa and South East Asia. What would have been the shape of a society, in which, all those who believed in Allah, were to form one Ummah, and yet continue calling themselves by their old denominations, would be difficult to imagine.

Hijrah of the Prophet (PBUH) had brought about a fundamental change in the society of Yathrib. There were, in Yathrib, Mushrekueen, who were pagan Arabs and did not follow any set rules, which could fall under the heading of Laws of a Religion. There were, as mentioned earlier, Jews, who, at least in principle, followed the law of Moses (May Allah's Blessings be on him). Because of being the followers of a Revealed religion, they considered themselves as superior to the pagan Arabs, although they lived under their protection. There were some Arabs who had adopted the law of Moses but their position was strangely unidentifiable. They lived among their own families and observed Arab customary law but considered themselves as possessing a higher intellectual creed. If they were asked to choose one of the two camps, in case of a quarrel, they would have joined their particular tribe and not gone to the Jewish camp.

The arrival of the Prophet (PBUH) altered the social structure of Yathrib completely. In fact, it had started undergoing a change since the Bayate Aqba Thani. The Prophet (PBUH) had appointed twelve leaders from among the Madinites who had come to Makkah to embrace Islam. The Prophet (PBUH) had told the gathering, "Bring out to me twelve leaders that they may take charge of their people's affairs.' They produced nine from al-Khazraj and three from al-Aus".This was the beginning of Muslims bringing into existence an organized Islamic Society. "With the appointment of these twelve leaders an organized Islamic Society came into being". On their return to Yathrib, these twelve leaders conducted the affairs of Madinite Muslims, until the arrival of the Prophet (PBUH).

Supremacy of God

The Jews had not been able to set up any communal life with the few Arabs who had accepted the Shariah of Prophet Moses. The Prophet of Islam was inviting not only Arabs but Jews, Christians and all others to share with the Believers higher values of the activities of a community organized on the basis of Sovereignty of Allah and equality of man, His most Balanced creation. The result was that, even when the Believers were in a small minority, the social life of Yathrib, due to their presence, had started taking its direction from the Muslims and adopted Islamic values in an imperceptible way. The Prophet (PBUH) and the small band of his Companions set the pace and texture of social life and thus became the centre of all communal activities. Whenever any issue demanded Allah's commandment for its settlement or the Prophet's own verdict in the matter, the Muslims did make all possible efforts to arrive at the authentic views of Islam on the basis of these two sources. The earlier Revelations of the Quran of Madina period are all relating to laws regarding various aspects of life. Many of them resulted from questions asked at these gatherings where the Prophet (PBUH) invited people to embrace Islam. He is known to have gone to a Jewish school to preach Islam to them. If there passed a group of people, by the road, he would stop and join them to invite them to Islam, even though they disliked it.

A new social structure based on the Sovereignty of Allah and equality of man was taking shape. A new culture was emerging out of this social structure. Man was being given, for the first time in his cultural life, the proper place in the scheme of things, and man's mind was awakening to his place in this universe. One can find no better key to the internal logic of a society than its conception of man and his place in nature. This high position had been bestowed upon man by Allah Himself, in His Eternal Code of Life. The result was that the social and cultural trends of life in Yathrib, at a time when the Believers were in a small minority, took a turn towards adoption of Islamic values, and life became centralised around the personality of the Prophet (PBUH) and his Companions.

The Significance

As mentioned earlier the Constitutional Charter of Madina has importance for more than one reason. It is the earliest written document of the Government and State of Madina. Later documents like the Peace Treaty of Hudaybiya, the Victory Proclamation of Khayber, and the Overlordship Gazette Notification of Aila granted to the Christian population of that place,-were all of the nature of proclamation of cessation of hostilities due to one or the other reason. This Document stands in a different position. It established a state and a government in order to meet aggression. Invasion by Quraysh of Makkah had to be stopped. Defence of a society cannot be assured without first organizing that society. When a society is organized it takes the shape of a state. The state must have law and it must also lay down as to what was the source of law and who in future would be entitled to amend or add to this law. All these steps were being finalised through the Constitutional Charter of Madina. This process has been explained in modern terminology in the following words. "Peace among men and a civilized society, which are one and the same thing, are imaginable only within a legal order equipped with institutions to give effect to principles and norms in the form of law..." The Prophet (PBUH) was laying down that the final authority in Islam would be Allah, through revelations to him. Arabian society was losely governed by custom.

There was no written law. Absence of law was a great hindrance to the establishment of a progressive and stable society. The Charter was removing this imbalance. "Whenever men group together and approve of a given standard morality, they must speak finally in terms of a law. Law permits morality to grow and as it grows the standard of law is elevated and morality is further advanced, for the two have reciprocal influence".

In this case, although hostilities had not started, war had been declared and arrangements had to be made to face the enemy. Allah had also Commanded.

> "O ye who believe! Take your precautions, then advance the proven ones, or advance or altogether". 4: 71

It is beyond doubt that the Document was promulgated to bring into existence the State of Madina so that it could be defended against the impending attack by the Quraysh of Makkah. Discussion leading to the declaration of its contents, if any, are conspicuously absent from both the Seerah and Hadith literature.

No Flaws

Its authenticity is, however, above doubt of any kind. It cannot be a spurious document. Once Islam and the Muslims had emerged as victorious, not only within Arabia, but had also liquidated the two strongest empires of the then civilized world, there was no need for them to concoct a document of the early period when Muslims were very few and not very strong. In actual fact once they stepped out of Arabia, they paid no particular attention to it. It is genuine both from external evidence and from the inner evidence of its contents. The idea that it is the sum total of a number of agreements arrived at on a number of occasions is so illogical that it should be ignored completely. As is well known, the events which took place after the promulgation of the Charter, developed with such after, and in such an unforseen manner that a situation had arisen where there was no need of fresh terms being issued, or new agreements gone into with any party. The idea that the document in its present shape is the result of numerous agreements is the result of the basic misconception, that it was an agreement. One may ask "agreement between whom, because the Document was being issued with the heading "From Muhammad, The Prophet of Allah." Its contents were Legal Orders and not paragraphs of an agreement. A charter from some one in power can be amended or additions made to it by the authority issuing the original charter. From Badr onwards the Prophet (PBUH) did not have to issue new instructions to any one in Yathrib. The Jews were getting weaker every day and signs of rebellion on their part had developed immediately after Badr. They had not "followed the Believers and not fought along with them." They had not, therefore, qualified for any of the concessions granted to them through the Charter. If anything, any fresh document, would have curtailed concessions granted to them from the incidence of rebellious behaviour of the Jewish tribe, Banu Qainuqua, immediately after Badr, the Jews were not in a position to request for a reappraisal of their relations with the ruling party.

The arrival of ultimatum from the Quraysh of Makkah was a serious affair. They were a powerful tribe and had the influence which leaders of thought possess in a society. They exercised the sole authority of laying down the religious ceremonies and the Arab way of life. They held the monopoly of carrier trade between southern Arabia and the flourishing market of Middle East, and were very rich as compared to the rest of Arabia. An attack by them, against Yathrib, would wipe out this small agricultural town of Najd. War in any case "is not a pass time. It is a serious means for a serious object". The Makkan object was very serious. Muhammad (PBUH) had "mocked their Way of Life," and taken refuge in Yathrib to save their Way of Life they had to destroy him completely. They had awoken to the danger from the time of the second Bayah of Aqba. As already mentioned when some of the Companions started migrating to Yathrib they "assembled in their council chamber, the house of Qusayy bin Kilab, where all their important business was conducted, to take counsel what they should do in regard to the Prophet (PBUH), for they were now in fear of him." It was suggested that "they should put him in irons behind bars." This was objected "on the ground that news would leak out that he was imprisoned, and immediately his followers would attack and snatch him away then their numbers would so grow that they would destroy the authority of the Quraysh altogther".

After some further discussion Abu Jehl came out with a new plan. This was "that each clan should provide a young, powerful, well born, aristocratic warrior; that each of these should be provided with a sharp sword; then that each of them should strike at him and kill him. The Banu Abde Manaf could not fight them all and would have to accept blood money which they would all contribute". Having failed to kill him they were not able to liquidate Islam in Makkah. They could not, however, let it prosper in Yathrib. They were afraid, as they said that "Their numbers would so grow that they would destroy the authority of Quraysh altogether". They decided not to permit their numbers to grow and decided to act quickly. They knew of the disappointment of Abdullah bin Ubbay. His people had made a sort of jewelled diadem to crown him and make him their king, when Allah sent His Prophet (PBUH) to them; so when his people forsook him in favour of Islam he was filled with enmity realizing that the Prophet (PBUH) had deprived him of his kingship. However, when he realised, that his people were determined to go over to Islam, he went too, but unwillingly, retaining his enmity and dissimulating.

The Quraysh sent a letter to the people of Yathrib, but addressing it to Abdullah bin Ubbay. The letter was, in fact, a declaration of war. It said, "you have given protection with you, to our men. You should kill these people or turn them out of Yathrib. We swear by Allah that if you do not do that, we will all attack you and having destroyed you, will capture your womenfolk".

This was a very good excuse for him to use force and turn the Prophet (PBUH) and his Muhajir Companions from Yathrib. He was the head of a very powerful tribe, which appears to have been numerically stronger than others. Its members were alive to the needs of religious revival. Out of twelve leaders chosen to look after the affairs of Muslims of Yathrib, nine belonged to his tribe. He decided to use force if the occasion demanded to kill the Prophet (PBUH) and the few Muhajir Companions.

The Prophet (PBUH) heard of his decision and went to him. Very little of the conversation between them is recorded. Abdullah bin Ubbay was confronted with a new reality. Islam, although a religion of peace, denoted complete submission to the Will of Allah. It meant the acceptance of the Sovereignty of Allah which in practical life was demonstrated by obeying the Laws of Allah. This is what is meant by:-

> "I created the Jinn and humankind only that they might worship me". 51: 56

And one of the Commands of Allah is that He has Ordained fighting for the Believers.

> "Warfare is ordained for you". 2: 216

The occasion for which this Commandment has been primarily Ordained is when some other group fights against you. It says:-

> "Fight in the Way of Allah against those who fight against you, but begin not hostilities". 2: 190

It has to be remembered that this Ummah is One:-

> "Verily this Ummah of yours is One Ummah". 23: 52

The Prophet (PBUH) brought home to Abdullah bin Ubbay in these words:-

> Do you realise that if you use force the Muslims from Yathrib will fight alongside the Muhajir Muslims and you will be shedding blood of your tribe on both sides.

He realised the mistake he was making and decided not to use force against the Prophet (PBUH) and his Companions. His change of attitude was the result of his fear of being defeated at the hands of determined fighters. History is replete with instances, where people have had recourse to peace for fear of being hurt, in the end. The philosophy of Ahimsa—non-violence—is also the product of such logic, because the same people believe in Kali Devi, the goddess, who quenches her thurst from blood of gory murders. Peace accepted by him was of this kind. When we could not use force he resorted to mischief and remained a hypocrite and a tool of the Jews until his death.

History books are silent on further details of the conversations, that took place between the Prophet (PBUH) and Abdullah bin Ubbay, it would be correct to assume that the latter must have asked the Prophet (PBUH) the way Yathrib was to be defended against the Makkans. The details of the Charter lead us to the conclusion that the Prophet (PBUH) must have replied that the Muslims would defend Yathrib and if the others would like to share that responsibility the Believers would permit them to join in this great honour. It could also be said that, as a result of the urgent need to defend Yathrib, the Prophet (PBUH) formulated the plan of establishing the state of Yathrib, giving it a Constitution, and laying down the responsibility of defence on Believers. Abdullah bin Ubbay could not help accepting this plan. The next event mentioned in history books is the Constitutional Charter itself.

The Charter was dictated under the shadow of an impending war of extreme intensity. Its defence paragraphs must belong to the same period. The concessions granted to the Jews are linked with defence paragraphs and must belong to the same period. The paragraphs covering general administration were also the demand of the time. There are no further events in the history of Yathrib, which could have resulted in the issue of further the documents. The division of the Document of Professor Sergeant in 'A, B, X, Y, etc, amounting to eight different documents can certainly be called a futile effort, made merely to create doubts and with no fruitful object. The war that was visualised when dictating this Document lasted for nine years and had, before ending, embroiled the largest Empire of that period in it, thus initiaing the longest war of history— The war between the Crescent and Cross—which is raging even today, fourteen centuries after the Charter came into force, and is no-where near its end as yet. Islam until then had laid greater stress on the building of character of individuals. The Charter ushered in the collective life of the Ummah. The principle that Muslims formed a nation by themselves, even when they lived in surroundings, which were not purely Islamic and it was given prominence by the Charter. The contents of the Charter make it clear that even when living as a numerical minority. Believers take over the administration of the society on condition that the principle of the Sovereignty of Allah is being acted upon. As mentioned earlier, as far as details are concerned, when dictating the Charter, greater emphasis has been paid to matters relating to the defence of the state, than to other matters. The Prophet (PBUH) as a result of the wisdom and insight granted to him by Allah, kept his mind centered on the period after the war when need would arise for rehabilitation of people. In the words of a modern military thinker, "The true national objective in war lies in the 'after war'. If the civilized world is to be saved from collapse, there is urgent need to produce true grand strategists to replace the blind exponents of mass destruction". He argues that "If you concentrate exclusively on victory, with no thought for the after effect, you may be too exhausted to be profited by the peace, while it is about certain that the peace will be a bad one, containing the germs of another war". The author is speaking from experience of two World Wars. Britain won both of them but lost the peace that followed.

The experience of modern world over the last two centuries has shown that the war to end war has yet to be fought, unless laws of war laid down by Allah are observed in total. The war that was initiated by the Quraysh of Makkah and won by the Prophet (PBUH) ended, as far Arabia was concerned, because the Prophet (PBUH) keeping the after-war period in view had done nothing, during and at the end of war, which could keep alive the hatred generated by war. Modern wars have tended to increase hatred to a point, when, a rapprochement becomes impossible. We need, therefore, to study his life, his teachings, his foreign policy and the manner in which he fought his war and then magnanimously pardoned his enemies. It will show a pattern of human behaviour unparalleled in the annals of human history.

The Prophet (PBUH) had accepted the responsibility of defending Yathrib against the threatened attack, when Yathrib had yet no state, no government and no army. He and his Companions were the total force available for this onerous task. There were no armaments, no provisions, no transport animals and no finances to provide all these instruments of war. He had, however, men, who were prepared to lay down their lives on the Path of Allah. He had trained them to such unchartered heights of Belief in Allah, that no weapon could force them to abandon their positions.

He also knew his enemies. They were resourceful. They were rich merchants and could furnish their army with the most sophisticated weapons. They also had the means to last them during a long drawn war. They had friends among Arab tribes.

They could, as a result widen the zone of war and have him surrounded and they had the means and facilities to make the blockade permanent, but his Belief in Allah outweighed those considerations. It is true that "once war begins, no one can tell how it will go. There are some who urge that we should abolish all armaments, and refuse to fight on any pretext. If this view is put forward on religious grounds, I will not deal with it beyond saying that it does not seem to me in accordance with the Bible... If on the other hand, its advocates believe that it would make for peace, it is inconsistent with recent events. China offered little or no resistance to Japan, yet that did not save her from the loss of territories as large as Europe, and the slaughter of some thousands other citizens".

The position of Believers, at the time of declaration of war by Makkah, was far more precarious than any community of peaceful and peace-loving people, who are threatened by a neighbour, who does not approve of their Ideology and their Way of Life. The enemy was the same, who had persecuted them in Makkah, ignoring relation of blood and friendship. A small number, a little over seventy had migrated to Habsha, and now less than fifty males had reached Yathrib and found a place, where they hoped to live according to Allah's given Way of Life, and they were being threatened with war and possible extermination. They had no alternative but to accept war. If they decided to avoid war, where could they go. They would have become stateless. The result would have been that the Islamic Society, which was visualised by the Prophet (PBUH) as a result of Revelations to him, from Allah, would not have been possible to be established. Allah's Promise was that they would be uppermost if they were Believers, was enough for them:-

> "It is a promise from Allah in truth; and who can be more truthful than Allah in utterance"? 4: 122

And:-

> "(It is) a Promise of Allah. Allah faileth not His Promise". 39: 20

And Allah has promised that:-

> "Faint not nor grieve, for ye will overcome them if ye are (indeed) believers". 3: 139

> "And verily Our word went forth of old unto Our bondmen sent (to warn) that they verily would be helped. And that Our host, they verily would be the victors".
> 37: 171-173

They were indeed Believers in its fullest meaning. No group of any Ummah of days gone by had reached heights of Belief in Allah which they had proved to have reached, and were yet to prove on many an occasion.

Most Required

Documents of this nature are not issued in a vacuum. There is always a background and a pressing need for them. In fact, pressing necessity, for the execution and enforcement of such documents alone made them acceptable to people. Such documents, whether they are named as agreements, treaties, charters or constitutions, are promulgated because the very existence of those societies depends on bringing into existence means of laying down the pattern of communal life, and such documents provide and guarantee a disciplined life of the community. Apart from rights and duties of individuals and groups such documents lay down restrictions and penalties for the breach of rules of conduct, expected of those for whose guidance they are issued. Preparations to meet the threat of war are taken in hand, when the danger is real and the entire society recognises it. War cannot be taken lightly because it "is a social phenomenon too complex to be governed by any simple formula". Except the Prophet (PBUH) himself no one was either qualified nor was there anybody who had the moral strength to accept the responsibility of making the decision to defend

Yathrib or when the decision had been taken to take defensive preparations in hand and then conduct the war.

To accept the duty of defending a state and its people is a decision of great moral character. An ill prepared nation is in serious danger of losing its war. To lose a war means to surrender the "right of freedom of thought" and to lose freedom of thought means to lose the right to live according to one's chosen Way of Life, which includes one's mode of worship. The Muslims could not afford to lose the war. They had chosen the Islamic Way of Life of their free will. It was being challenged by the people, who had persecuted them for nearly thirteen years. They were determined that if they could not win the war they would fight to the last man. The battles fought by the Believers for the defence of Yathrib were all fought with the determination that they would fight until each one of them had achieved Shahadah. The Prophet (PBUH) had trained his Companions to wish for Shahadah and he was certain that they will come up to his expectations. His historic words, just before the attack of Makkan Army started at the battlefield of Badr are a testimony of the Believers having absorbed this philosophy. He had said:-

> O Lord!
> If this little band of Believers
> Is wiped out to-day
> There shall be none left
> To obey your Commandments
> Until the Day of Judgement.

There had been wars before and there were to be wars in future as well, but this war was different both in conception and the manner in which it was expected to terminate. Both sides were fighting to defend their respective Way of Life. It could end in not only the defeat of one army or the nation it belonged to but it was to end with the end of the Way of Life to which the loser belonged.

It was a war aimed at the extermination of the Muslim's Ideology and Way of Life. The idea, that all wars are fought for differences, which can be solved peacefully, does not appear to be applicable to this war. Normally it can be said that, "Just how senseless and futile an expedient it really is, can usually best be judged by those who lose rather than by those who have won". In this case it was not applicable because the losers were to forego the freedom of living in accordance with their chosen Way of Life.

This Document had been dictated keeping in mind this Philosophy of War that to remain a Believer in Allah was only possible when Sovereignty of Allah could be proclaimed and life was led in accordance with His Commandments. To achieve that it was essential, that land occupied by Believers had to be defended to the last. It was, therefore, necessary, that Yathrib had its Basic Law—its Constitution—promulgated in a manner that its defence preparations could be taken in hand legally and constitutionally. Hence the correct heading of the Document can be "The Constitutional Charter of Yathrib... Madina".

It was not an agreement with the Jews as Allama Shibli Noamani calls it. He says "The Prophet (PBUH) sent for Ansars and Jews and dictated an agreement....which was accepted by both parties". Another eminent writer Jalal-ud-Din Jaffery writes, "When the Prophet (PBUH) arrived in Madina, he had an agreement written between the Ansars and the Jews".Naeem Siddiqui, the only one out of all Urdu writers has shown a different approach to the problem. He writes, "The Prophet (PBUH) created an organization for the arming of the State of Madina, through which he integrated the Muslims, the Jews and the un-believers, into a new society. He had a written document of the nature of an agreement, prepared. The nature of this document was of a proper constitution and it can be correctly called as the first written constitution".

Nearly all writers of Seerah in Urdu have called the "Charter" as an "Agreement," between either the Prophet (PBUH) and the

Jews, or between the Believers and the Jews. An eminent learned man like Syed Abul Hassan Ali Nadvi has termed it as an agreement of peace with the Jews. Having correctly said that, "The Prophet (PBUH) on this occasion gave a writing to the Muhajirs and Ansars, "he adds "which contained an agreement of peace with the Jews". Another eminent historian writes, "On arrival at Madina, the Prophet (PBUH) during the very first year of Hijrah considered it appropriate to execute an agreement with all nationalities on the principle of internationalism so that a national solidarity should continue in spite of the ethnic and religious differences". Khalid Alvi, referring to the Jews writes, "He (the Prophet PBUH) made an agreement with them".

It could be that the word agreement has crept in because of absence of a proper equivalent of the term "Charter," in Urdu. The mistake dates back to Ibne Hisham, due to absence of a technical term for "Charter" in that age. He has used the word Aahadahum which has been translated as "covenant." The sentence as a result reads " the covenant between the Muslims and the Madinans and with the Jews".

Muslim and non-Muslim writers of Seerah in English, who belong to the present age, have also relied on Ibne-Ishaq, in more or less the same manner as Urdu writers. Abu Bakr Sirajuddin (Martin Ling) who has written with great devotion says, "and the Prophet (PBUH) now made a covenant of mutual obligations between his followers and the Jews of the Oasis".

A non-Muslim writer of Pakistan origin says that before the signing of the agreement a thorough exchange of views had taken place. This may be correct but no work of early period seems to mention a thorough exchange of views. He writes, "After a thorough exchange of views, an agreement was reached and was reduced to writing".

Muir while translating the Document uses the words "Charter of Muhammad the Prophet" instead of "Charter from Muhammad," but in introducing it he writes, "It was natural that Muhammad, holding these sentiments should desire to enter into a close and binding union with the Jews, and this he did in a formal manner shortly after reaching Madina. He associated them with himself by a treaty of mutual obligation drawn up in writing".

The difference between an agreement and a Charter is very vast. An agreement is between two equals and a Charter is given from one to others. An agreement can be rescinded by either party. A Charter can be altered, amended or cancelled only by the authority which promulgated it. Apart from the heading given to the document its contents alone can guide later researchers to give their verdict on it, whether it was a treaty, an agreement or a Charter.

Treaties are between states and usually the heading says so For instance, "Security Treaty between Australia, New Zealand and United States of America". Similarly Pacts are between independent sovereign states. For instance, "Pact of Mutual Co-operation (CENTO)" was signed between a number of states including Pakistan, Turkey and Iran. Recently a new name for mutual treaties has appeared. This is called a "Convention." For instance, "Convention regarding the Regime of the Straits"

Let us, once again, look at Meethaq-e-Madina in a little greater detail, particularly its heading. It says:-

> "This Document (writing) is from Muhammad, The Prophet of Allah (PBUH.)"

It is clear that it is neither an agreement nor a treaty because it is not between Muhammad (PBUH) and some others. It is from him and he is the Prophet (PBUH) of Allah. Those receiving the

Document are being told that the person issuing this Document is doing so in his capacity as the Prophet of Allah. Then it goes on to say that it is being given

"To"

"Quraysh and Yathribite Believers".

Believers whether from Makkah or from Yathrib were all his followers known as his Companions. No group of people in the history of mankind have shown their devotion to their leader as was shown by his Companions to Muhammad (PBUH) the Prophet of Allah. When marching out to the battlefield of Badr, the leader of Ansars of Yathrib, Saad bin Muadh said, "We believe in you, we declare your truth, and we witness, that what you have brought is truth, and we have given you our word and agreement to hear and to obey; so go forth where you wish, we are with you, and by Allah, if you were to ask us to cross the sea and you plunged into it, we would plunge into it with you, not a man would stay behind. We do not dislike the idea of meeting your enemy tomorrow. We are experienced in war, trustworthy in combat...."

Whatever else description or name may be given to this Document it cannot be called an agreement between the Prophet (PBUH) and his followers. It was being given by him to them and they were all included in it, both the Muhajirs from Makkah and the Ansars of Yathrib.

There were others as well. They were:-

"those who will follow them and fight alongside them."

It would be applicable to others as well, provided these others followed the lead of his followers, the Believers, from Makkah and Yathrib. Apart from following the Believers they had to take part in fighting alongside the Believers to qualify themselves as recipients of this august Document.

This heading ends with a brief last remark, "They will form ONE UMMAH to the exclusion of others." It means that if the others qualified as recipients of the Document, then they and the Believers, the Companions of the Last Prophet of Allah, will form an Ummah apart from the rest of humanity. It was a great honour, that was being bestowed on them but the price was also very high. They had to accept the Believers as their leaders and continue to follow them by joining in war with them against their enemies.

Thus the Document was primarily issued as the Basic or Fundamental Law The Constitution of Yathrib, so that defence arrangements could be taken in hand, on behalf of the entire population. The Believers, being the group which had sworn allegiance to him as a result of the Bayah formed the manpower of his army. The march to the battlefield of Badr proved this fact. None others were prepared to sacrifice themselves for a cause, in which they did not believe.

Revolutionary Character

History has recorded one more Charter given by the head of a state. This was King John of England. This Charter, however, was taken by force by the barons of the realm, because, "King John was very unwilling to grant it. This was on the 15th of June 1215 A.C., that the Great Charter was sealed with the king's great seal. He agreed that 24 barons shall be appointed to see that he kept the promises which it contained. He agreed only because he was compelled.... He never meant to keep the promises that it contained, and he did not keep them. He sent to France for soldiers and when they came he made war on his own people. He asked his friend the Pope for help and the Pope helped him by ex-communicating all barons, by London under Interdict, and by telling John that he had no need to keep his promises". The surprising part of the whole story is, that, there was not much in the Charter, which an honest ruler of an average society need to have objected to.

It may seem strange that the Pope of all the people, should have advised a Christian ruler to go back on his promises. It was, however, not the first time, nor the last time, that the head of Church had advised a prince to go back on his promises. In one case, "the Pope, who seeing his plans being nullified, by this (peace treaty) initiated the Magyars to break the peace; oaths sworn to infidels not being binding".

The Charter given at Yathrib was in the spirit of Islam, the New Way of Life. It had to be in accordance with all ethical, moral and legal principles laid down by Allah, for Believers in Him and His Prophet (PBUH). The time of its issue was the most critical period in the history of Islam—a time when the threat against Islam and Muslims was the greatest. This fact must be kept in mind while studying the Clauses of the Charter.

The position in which the Muslims were placed at this time has been misrepresented by some Western writers. Preparations for defence of Yathrib have been interpreted as aggressive designs against the Makkans. A well known British historian writes that "Muhammad had now, as it were, thrown down the gauntlet, which the Makkans could not but pick it up. He had effectively challenged them to a full scale trial of strength". It appears that after writing a few more sentences he remembered that it was the Makkans who had declared war. He adds; "The Makkan belief thought Muhammad would avoid them rested on a misappraisal of the relative strength and fighting qualities of the two parties". He has avoided to give the source on which he has based the superior strength of the Muslim Army.

6

Head of State

Let us now turn to the story of the Prophet's achievements in Medina. Muhammad's mission is spiritual first and spiritual last, his programmes, which to a superficial observer, appear to be "temporal", were fully inspired by spiritual motives. He was the Messenger of God and it was in this capacity as the last of the Messengers that he had transmuted into reality the word of his Creator. All his energies and efforts were directed to his single end. Whatever he thought or planned, whatever he uttered or did was the outcome of the desire that humanity should recognise its Master, i.e. should recognize the perfect guidance vouchsafed by Him and carry out His Will and Commands with full devotion.

New Centre of Power

The first task to which the Holy Prophet attended on his arrival at Medina was the construction of a mosque. A suitable site was selected for it and the land which belonged to two orphans was purchased for ten gold coins and then donated to the mosque. The ground was cleared of weeds and shrubs, palm trees and rubbish, and the construction of the mosque commenced. The Prophet joined in the work which encouraged the Muslims. Both the Muhajirun and the Ansar laboured hard to complete it as soon as possible. One of the Muslims chanted:

If we sat down while the Prophet worked

This action of ours would be the worst.

As they constructed the mosque the Muslims sang a rajaz

There is no life but the life of the next world,

O God I have mercy on Ansar and Muhajirun.

The Apostle of God, (peace and blessings of Allah be upon him) however, changed its rhythm or order and said:

There is no life but the life of the next world,

O God! have mercy on Muhajirun and Ansar.

This mosque was square in form, each side measuring approximately 50 yards, facing towards the north and having three gates on each of the remaining three sides. The southern door was for public entrance and the western gate was called Bab al-Rahaman and the eastern gate, reserved for the Prophet's household, was called Bab al-Nisa'.

To the north of the mosque, a place was reserved for those companions of Muhammad (peace be upon him) who had neither family nor home. They were known as Ashab al-Suffah (the people of the Suffah). This was a kind of seminary attached to the mosque for those who devoted full time to the study of religion. Adjoining the mosque were erected two apartments for the household of the Prophet. The mosque was a monument of simplicity—the walls were made of mud bricks and the roof supported by trunks of palm trees. Being covered with palm leaves and twigs it could not keep out rain, which sametimes made the unpaved floor muddy. This simple mosque was the venue of glorious scenes. It was here that the Holy Prophet imparted his teachings to the Muslims. It was here that embassies from different tribes were received. It was here that edicts were issued to kings and emperors. The residence of the Holy Prophet was, however, even simpler than the mosque. Some of the rooms were built of raw bricks whereas the others were mere cells made with the twigs of the palm trees. Worn out blankets were used with a view to providing privacy and seclusion to the inmates of the house. "During the time of the caliphate of 'Uthman," observes Hasan b. 'Ali, "when we visited the residential quarters of the wives of the Holy Prophet, we found their ceilings so low that we could easily touch them." Similarly another observer Dawud b. Qays, describing the house of Muhammad (peace be upon him) says, "I have had the good fortune to see with my own eyes the quarters where the wives of the Holy Prophet lived. These were apartments made out to the branches of palm-trees, and blankets of camel-hair hung at their doors. The courtyard was hardly six to seven paces in length and breadth and rooms did not extend beyond ten paces." After the death of the Prophet's wives all these quarters were annexed to the mosque and the land thus acquired was used for its extension. "Were these rooms kept intact, the world would have seen the austere and simple living of the last of the prophets in whose hand had been placed the keys of the worldly treasures", to which the Prophet showed no inclination.

We have noted earlier the persecution of Muslims in Mecca. They could not even perform their prayers openly. Up to that period, these prayers had to be conducted in secret. Every precaution had to be taken not to let it be known that the prayer service was taking place. In the peaceful conditions of Medina, where Muslims enjoyed full religious freedom, the problem which figured prominently was how to summon the Muslims to the mosque. The Jews summoned their congregations to the temple by blowing trumpets, the Christians by striking gongs. Muhammad (peace be upon him) did not feel drawn at all towards these customs and he considered them inappropriate for such sacred purposes. He felt that the human voice could better communicate the inspiration and emotion which should be dedicated to the solemnity of the occasion. It is narrated that when this problem was discussed, one day 'Abd Allah b. Zayd came to the Holy Prophet and told him: I saw last night a visitant in a dream who had a clapper in his hand and I asked him to sell that to me.

When he questioned what I wanted to do with that, I replied that it was to summon people for prayer, whereupon he said: Should I not show you a better way than this? I replied in the affirmative. Upon this he said, say:

Allahu Akbar, Allahu Akbar

Allahu Akbar, Allahu Akbar

Ashhadu an la ilaha illa Allah

Ashhadu an la ilaha illa Allah

Ashhadu anna Muhammad ar Rasul Allah

Ashhadu anna Muhammad ar Rasul Allah

Hayya ala al-Salah

Hayya ala al-Salah

Hayya ala al-Falah

Hayya ala al-Falah

Allahu Akbar, Allahu Akbar

La ilaha illa Allah

(Allah is the Greatest. Allah is the Greatest. Allah is the Greatest. Allah is the Greatest. I bear witness that there is no god but Allah. I bear witness that there is no god but Allah. I bear witness that Muhammad is the Messenger of Allah. I bear witness that Muhammad is the Messenger of Allah. Hearken to prayer. Hearken to prayer. Hearken to salvation. Hearken to salvation. Allah is the Greatest. There is no god but Allah).

The Holy Prophet said: "Your vision, by the grace of God, is true. Go to Bilal and communicate it to him so that he should call to prayer accordingly." When ' Umar heard this in his house, he came there dragging his cloak on the ground and said: "By Him who has sent you with the truth, I have seen precisely the same vision which has been shown to 'Abd Allah b. Zayd." The Holy Prophet said: 'God be praised for that.' For the morning prayer, the following reminder was added:

As-Salatu khayrum min al-nawm,

(Prayer is better than sleep)

Every day, at the five appointed times, this familiar call summoned the people to their devotions. For over thirteen centuries, the same call has continually sounded from myriad minarates.

It is not only a summons to prayer, but also sums up very concisely the teachings of Islam. There is no god but Allah, the Sole Creator, the Master and the Law-Giver. Muhammad (peace be upon him) is His Apostle and it is through him alone that we can find out the will of God which should be followed. Prayer is the basis of religious life and it is through prayer alone that one can find the path of salvation.

The Fraternity

Prayers being thus regulated, the Prophet next turned his attention to cementing the ties of brotherhood amongst the Muslims of Medina, who were called Ansar and the Muhajirin, i.e. emigrants from Mecca. It was a necessary step since the refugees who had left their hearths and homes and had said goodbye to friends and relatives were feeling lonely. To raise the spirits of his homesick and suffering followers, to cast off their feeling of loneliness, and to attune them to the changed circumstances, a new fraternity was established amongst the Muslims of Mecca and those of Medina.

This brotherhood was indeed unique in the history of the world. The fellow-feeling and love on which this new relationship was established found a wonderful expression. For example Sa'd b. Sabi', a Helper said to his fellow brother 'Abd al-Rahman b. 'Awf, "I am the richest man amongst the Helpers. I am glad to share my property half and half with you. I have two wives, I am ready to divorce one, and after the expiry of 'iddah, you may marry her." But 'Abd al-Rahman b. 'Awf was not prepared to accept anything: neither property nor home. So he blessed his brother and said: Kindly direct me to the market so that I may make my fortune with my own hands. The Helpers were extremely generous to their brethren-in-faith. They once approached the Holy Prophet with the request that their orchards should be distributed equally between the Muslims of Medina and their brethren from Mecca. But the Prophet was reluctant to put this heavy burden upon them. It was, however, decided that the refugees would work in the orchards along with the Helpers and the yield would be divided equally amongst them.

These are not solitary expressions of the spirit of selflessness which the Holy Prophet had infused in his followers. It was a common trait of their character which they had developed under the influence of Muhammad (peace be upon him). So strong and cordial was this relation that it surpassed even the relationship of blood. When either of the two persons who had been paired as brothers, passed away, his property was inherited by his brother-in-faith. This practice continued till the following verse was revealed and the regular rule of inheritance was allowed to take its usual course:

> And those who believed afterwards and emigrated and strove hard along with you, these also are of you, and the kindred by blood are nearer unto one another in Allah's decree. Verily Allah is of everything the Knower.

The atmosphere of brotherhood and fellow-feeling created by the Holy Prophet produced very healthy results. Age-long enmities amongst the different tribes, especially those that had existed between the Aws and the Khazraj were almost forgotten amongst the converts from those tribes. "Acceptance of the faith required that as Muslims they should acknowledge not only the spiritual but temporal authority of Muhammad and, holding subordinate every distinction of race and kindred, regard each other as brethren." The Holy Qur'an refers to this brotherhood as a great boon:

> And hold ye fast, all of you, to the cord of Allah, and be not disunited, and remember Allah's favour unto you, in that ye were enemies, and He joined your hearts together, and so ye became by His favour brethren, and ye were on the brink of an abyss of the fire, and He rescued you therefrom. (iii: 103)

The pages of history bear testimony to the fact that it was a marevellous and spectacular reform. Before the advent of the Prophet, the Arabs were an uncompromising people, a nation torn into mutually hostile clans and tribes, who were always ready to unsheath their blood-thirsty sword for petty reasons. It was due to the teachings of Islam and the untiring efforts of Muhammad (peace be upon him) that the spirit of brotherhood began to surge across Arabia. The entire past of tribal animosities was obliterated and a new society was summoned into existence which had a deep-rooted sentiment for the brotherhood of man, a consciousness of mutual rights and duties and love, and a humane and noble outlook on life. The prophet had in fact eminently succeeded in creating a social pattern "which had none of the features of the ancient cults, no priesthood and no ceremonial, which was based on no forms, but upon a spiritual relationship to an Unseen God. It was not designed to give prestige to a social group but to create a universal brotherhood composed of all men of every race who would accept this God and promise loyalty to His Holy Prophet."

The Pact

Another important task which attracted the attention of the Holy Prophet was to establish friendly relations between the Muslims and non-Muslim tribes of Arabia, particularly those of Banu Nadir, Banu Qurayzah and Banu Qaynuqa. As this was the first political agreement between Muslims and non-Muslims, we mention only a few of its provisions which would clearly give an idea of the rights of non-Muslims in an Islamic state.

In the name of Allah, the Compassionate, the Merciful. This is a document from Muhammad, the Messenger of Allah, concerning emigrants and helpers in which he made a friendly agreement with the Jews and established them in their religion and property and stated the reciprocal obligations as follows:

They form one group to the exclusion of other people. The emigrants of Quraysh unite together and shall pay bloodwit among themselves, and shall ransom honourably their prisoners. The Banu 'Awf unite together, as they were at first, and every section among them pays a ransom for acquitting its relative prisoners. (This clause is repeated with the same phraseology concerning Banu Sa'ida, Banu al-Harith, Banu Jusham, Banu al-Najjar, Banu 'Amr b. 'Awf, Banu al-Nabit, and Banu Aws). Believers shall not leave any one destitute among them by not paying his redemption money or bloodwit in kind.

Whosoever is rebellious or whosoever seeks to spread enmity and sedition, the hand of every God-fearing Muslim shall be against him, even if he be his son.

A believer shall not kill another believer, nor shall support an unbeliever against a believer. The protection of Allah is one (and is equally) extended to the humblest of the believers.

The believers are supported by each other. Whosoever of the Jews follows us shall have aid and succour; they shall not be injured, nor any enemy be aided against them.

The peace of the believers is indivisible. No separate peace shall be made when believers are fighting in the way of God. Conditions must be fair and equitable to all.

It shall not be lawful for a believer, who holds by what is in this document and believes in God and the Day of Judgment, to help a criminal nor give him refuge. Those who give him refuge and render him help shall have the curse and anger of Allah on the Day of Resurrection. His indemnity is not accepted. Whenever you differ about a matter it must be referred to God and to Muhammad (peace be upon him).

> The Jews shall contribute to the cost of war so long as they are fighting alongside the believers. The Jews of the B. 'Awf are one community with the believers. The Jews will profess their religion; the Muslims, theirs. No one shall go forth to war except with the permission of Muhammad; but this shall not hinder any one from seeking lawful revenge. The Jews shall be responsible for their expenditure, the Muslims for theirs, but if attacked, each shall come to the assistance of the other. Medina shall be sacred and inviolable for all that join this treaty.

These are some of the clauses of the famous treaty. "It appears as a tripartite agreement between the Muhajirin or emigrants of

Mecca, the Ansar or adherents of Medina, and the Jews. A careful examination of the text shows, however, that it was more than a treaty of alliance. The first part indeed reflects to us more than an attempt at reconciliation between the tribes; it is in fact a convention for fusing all the rival attempts of the Arab tribes in Medina to constitute one nation in distinction from the rest of the people. It is, in other words, a constitution for the Islamic state in its embryonic stage rather than a loose alliance of tribes. In this Muhammad (peace be upon him) had attempted to dissolve the narrow tribal loyalties within a superstructure, by shifting their focus of attention to a new religion and state."

Secondly, this treaty sheds a good deal of light on the position of the Prophet as the controller of the affairs in Medina. The constitution states that wherever there is any dispute, it is to be referred to God and to Muhammad (peace be upon him). "It seems likely that it was contemplated in the original agreement between Muhammad and the Medinites that he would be able to act as an arbitrator between rival factions and thus help to maintain peace in the oasis."

The latter part of the treaty, which refers to an alliance between the Arabian tribes constituting one party and the Jews as the other, clearly lays down the broad principles on which cordial relations could be established between Muslims and non Muslims.

This treaty, which owed itself of the efforts of the Holy Prophet for establishing peace, is a landmark in human history. "It guaranteed mankind thirteen hundred and fifty years ago, free doom of thought and freedom of worship. Protection of life and that of the property was recognized and the crime in all its forms was legally banned. These are fact fresh laurels which Muhammad (peace be upon him) eminently won in the realm of civics and politics of that time, for it guaranteed peace and freedom to the people who had been woefully groaning under the heel of tyranny and opression let loose by despotism and autocracy and anarchy of that age."

After having united all the discordant elements of society, Muhammad (peace be upon him) turned his attention towards his household affairs. He had been living at that time with his wife Sawdah and his daughters Fatimah and Umm Kulthum.

'A'ishah, his new bride, was just attaining her puberty and was still in the house of her father. She was a precocious girl and was developing both in mind and body with rapidity peculiar to such rare personalities. At the suggestion of Abu Bakr and his wife, Muhammad (peace be upon him) decided to consummate the marriage.

Like everything else in Muhammad's life (peace be upon him), the ceremony was simple. 'A'ishah was washed and dressed in clean clothes, Umm Ruman, her mother, then took her to a room where some women of the Ansar had been anxiously waiting for the arrival of the bride. The moment 'A'ishah stepped in, they prayed: "May you be blessed, your fortune is enviable."

This marriage is significant in the history of Islam. It further cemented the ties between Muhammad (peace be upon him) and his devoted friend who always stood by him in hours of distress and who sacrificed his all for the cause of Islam. Secondly, by this marriage, a lady of rare qualities, both of mind and heart, was allowed to enter the haram of the Prophet at an impressionable age, and thus got an opportunity to penetrate into the innermost recesses of the life of Muhammad (peace be upon him). She shared his sacred company and was thus able to develop her potentialities and refine her taste. Even a glance at the life of this eminent lady clearly bears out the fact that her marriage with the prophet was a source of immense good to herself and to the world of Islam at large. She came into direct contact with the Prophet when her sensibilities were just developing. It was the august personality of the last of the Prophets- (peace be upon him) which nurtured them properly and directed their growth to the right channels. This young age was opportune for marriage, as it has been clearly shown in the researches of the psychoanalysts that much of the emotional life of a mature person and most of those seemingly unaccountable leanings, tastes and tendencies comprised in the term idiosyncrasies can be traced back to the experiences of his highly formative age, either later childhood, or early adolescence.

Moreover, even from the psycho-sexual stand-point, it was a happy union as it is evident from the records of Hadith. "When the difference (in ages)" says T.H. Von De Velde, Director of the Gynaecological Clinic at Harlem, "is great e.g. exceeds fifteen or twenty years, the results may be happier. The marriage of an elderly (senescent)—not, of course an old (senile)—man to a quite young girl, is often very successful and harmonious. The bride is immediately introduced and accustomed to moderate sexual intercourse."

Those Western critics of Islam who have criticized this marriage lose sight of the fact that this marriage did not involve sexual consideration alone. There was so many other reasons behind it. Firstly, there was the consideration of Abu Bakr's honour and status and an expression of due recognition of his glorious service. Then there was the problem of training a young girl who was gifted with penetrating intellect and zest for knowledge so that she might be able to guide young women in different spheres of their lives.

The wives of Muhammad (peace be upon him) with the exception of 'A'ishah, were all of advanced age, and thus could neither share the feelings of the younger generation nor could they properly appreciate their point of view. The difference of age always stood as a barrier between them and the ladies of younger ages. The only lady with whom young women could frankly enter into conversation and discuss their problems without any reserve could be none else but young 'A'ishah. Thus, the marriage of the Prophet with 'A'ishah at an age when she was at the threshold of puberty was a great necessity, as it was through her that instructions could successfully be imparted to the young ladies who had newly entered the fold of Islam. 'A'ishah performed this function most eminently and fully justified the choice of the Messenger of God (peace be upon him).

Moreover, this marriage struck at the root of a wrong notion which had taken a firm hold on the minds of the people, that it was contrary to religious ethics to marry the daughter of a man whom one declared to be one's brother. The Prophet, with the help of his personal example, showed to the people that there was great difference between a brother-in-faith and a brother by blood. The marriage which is forbidden in Islam is not that with the daughter of a man who is tied to oneself in the bond of faith, but with one who is one's niece in blood.

The main concern of the Prophet, however, was the spiritual and moral training of his followers. In a relatively free atmosphere though not totally free from the threat of Mecca vengeance and aggression the Prophet began to propound the principles of righteous conduct, including rituals of worship.

Other Developments

At the end of eighteen months after the Hijra, fasting was established as an obligatory ritual for the month of Ramadan. The word *'saum'* which literally means abstinence, is a worship of a very great significance. It serves as an effective means, in the religious system of Islam, for bringing about purification of the souls of Muslim. A Muslim, according to its implication, is strictly forbidden to take food or drink (and even to smoke) or to indulge in sexual intercourse from the moment when the first streak of light on the eastern horizon announces the coming of dawn, until sunset. And this continued for one full month every year. In the words of Muhammad Asad:

"Twofold, I learned, is the purpose of this month of fasting. One has to abstain from food and drink in order to feel in one's body what the poor and hungry feel: thus, social responsibility is being hammered into human consciousness as a religious postulate. The other purpose of fasting during Ramadan is self-discipline, an aspect of individual morality strongly accentuated in all Islamic teachings (as, for instance, in the total prohibition of all intoxicants which Islam regards as too easy an avenue of escape from consciousness and responsibility). In these two elements—brotherhood of man and individual self-discipline —I began to discern the outlines of Islam's ethical outlook."

Moreover, fasting is the means whereby our sense of gratitude towards Allah is awakened. We can rightly measure and truly appreciate the countless favours of the Lord when we are deprived of them, even though for a short span of time. Thus, we can thank our Creator for His infinite bounties that He has so benevolently showered upon us. The following verse of the Qur'an makes a pointed reference to this aspect:

> Ye should complete the number and that you should exalt the Greatness of Allah for His having guided you and that you may give thanks. (ii: 185)

It was at this stage that the payment of zakat was made obligatory by Allah upon all Muslims. Islam does not leave the orphans, the infirm and the old to subsist on what is called "charity." By making the payment of zakat obligatory for the rich, Allah has given the poor a right to share in the wealth of the community. The Qur'an explicitly lays down:

> And in their wealth, is the right of the needy and of those who are deprived of the means of subsistence. (ii; 19)

This verse clearly establishes that the portion of the wealth which the Muslims contribute annually in the form of zakat is a matter of duty for them and, on the other hand, whatever the poor receive is not an act of undue favour for which they should hang down their heads in humiliation. The wealth of the rich that they receive is a matter of right for which they have no reason to feel small. Then the Qur'an has also laid down the purposes for which zakat is to be used. It should be paid, according to the Holy Qur'an, inter alia to those who cannot make an independent living (e.g. the orphans, helpless widows, the infirm, the decrepit, the travellers in distress, and people who have been deprived of the means of sustenance or of opportunities of work through natural calamities over which they have no control), the slaves seeking freedom and the debtors who cannot afford to pay off their debts:

> The compulsory alms are only for the poor and the needy and the agents employed therein, and those whose hearts are to be conciliated, and those in bondage and debtors and for expenditure in the way of Allah and for the wayfarer, an ordinance from Allah. And Allah is Knowing, Wise.
> (ix: 60)

The Qur'an thus makes it obligatory on those who earn or produce wealth to pass on to the state a specific portion of their savings as God's share to be distributed among the above categories of the members of society. "So great is the stress laid on the levy called zakat, that the compulsory injunction of prayer is always clubbed together with the insistence on the payment of this levy; so much so that when in the time of the first Caliph Abu Bakr, some of the Muslim Arab tribes refused to pay zakat to the State Exchequer, he had to wage a jihad against them till they yielded" and resumed the payment of zakat.

It was during this period that a change in the qiblah, was also ordered by Allah. It is significant that while at Mecca and living among the idolaters of Mecca, the Holy Prophet (may peace and blessings of Allah be upon him) used to pray with his face turned to the holy temple at Jerusalem, but when he came to Medina, where the Jewish element was strong and powerful, he was directed by Divine revelation to turn his face to the Ka'bah as his qiblah. This was a change of far-reaching importance, and it had different reactions in different circles. It strengthened the loyalty of the Muslims to Islam and the Holy prophet. They expressed their implicit faith in Muhammad (peace be upon him) as the recipient of Divine revelation and accepted this change most willingly. The pagans of Mecca said: "The way Muhammad has changed his direction for prayer towards our qibla, gives us reason to hope that he will eventually come back to our faith also." The Jews were very indignant and said tauntingly: "Muhammad has, in this change of direction for prayer, opposed all the earlier prophets. If he were a genuine prophet, he would have never done like that." The hypocrites (i.e. those who falsely pretended to be Muslims) availed themselves of this opportunity to undermine the increasing influence of Islam. They were sarcastic in their remarks and said: "We are not sure in which direction the Prophet wants to turn for prayer. If the previous position was correct he has abandoned that; and if this new position is right, it means that he had erred before."

The Holy Qur'an refers, in its eloquent style, to these different objections raised from the different quarters, and observe:

> And We appointed not the qiblah, which you have had, but that We might distinguish him who follows the Apostle from him who turns back upon his heels, and this was surely hard except for those whom Allah has guided aright. (ii: 143)

"The change of direction", says Arnold, "has a deeper significance than might at first sight appear. It was really the beginning of the national life of Islam; it established the Ka'bah at Mecca as a religious centre for all the Muslim people, just as from time immemorial it had been a place of pilgrimage for all the tribes of Arabia."

A few words may now be added as a prelude to the coming events which are connected with the unsheathing of the sword by the Muslims in the path of Allah. Jihad is a matter of great importance in the history of Islam, but it is sad to note that so many doubts and misgivings are centred around it. The true nature and significance of Jihad can be well understood, when it is viewed in the context of the teachings of Islam as a whole as well as the objectives which it seeks to realize. Moreover, we also have to consider the role of war, in other words, that of power, as a means for the establishment of a sound social order.

It should be clearly borne in mind that Islam does not subscribe to the materialistic world-view which is in vogue among the Western nation. "It is an intense God-consciousness that expresses itself in a rational acceptance of all God-created nature: a harmonious side-by-side of intellect and sensual urge, spiritual need and social demand." It is thus clear that Islam, besides, laying a good deal of stress on the problems of belief, ritual and personal morality and as a consequence of that nursing a moral attitude in the individual—the bedrock upon which is raised the superstructure of Islamic society "also aims at translating the moral attitude into a definite social scheme which would ensure to every member of the community the greatest possible measure of physical and material well-being, and thus, the greatest opportunity for spiritual growth."

This important aspect of Islam, i.e. its social aspect, is woefully neglected by Western thinkers, while estimating the role of power in a comprehensive view of life. They lose sight of the fact that Christianity in its early history did not aim at setting up a state, whereas Islam, from the very beginning, was a politico-religious institution. In order to translate into reality, Islam had to contend with those evil forces which knew no reasoning and persuasion.

It should be made clear, however, that war in Islam is not a casual phenomenon of violence; it is one of the phases of man's striving (jihad) against all that is evil, whether in thought or feeling or action. The raising of the sword is only one aspect of the all-round struggle to establish Islam in the world, and it represents in Muslim Law what is known as an 'honest struggle.'

The word (jihad) is derived from the word jahada, which means "he exerted himself." Thus literally jihad means exertion, striving; but in juridico-religious sense, it signifies the exertion of one's power to the utmost of one's capacity in the path of Allah. This is why, the word jihad has been used as an antonym to the word qu'ud in Islam.

> Not equal are the holders-back among the believers save those who are disabled, and the strivers in the way of Allah with their riches and their lives. Allah hath preferred in rank the strivers with their riches and their lives above the holders-back and unto all, Allah hath promised good. And Allah hath preferred the strivers above holders-back with a mighty reward. (iv: 95)

The above-quoted verse speaks eloquently of the fact that Jihad (striving) is just the opposite of idleness.

It is necessary to winnow out one mistaken notion which has taken hold of the minds of so many people. The word jihad is often confused with the word qital (fighting) and these are used in one and the same sense, whereas the Qur'an has made a clear distinction between them. Jihad fi Sabil Allah (fighting in the way of Allah) refers to an all-round struggle, while the other signifies only one aspect of that struggle i.e. fighting. The verse iv: 9.3 mentioned above bears ample testimony to this fact. The Holy Qur'an has clearly pointed out that jihad denotes two kinds of striving; striving with the help of God-given faculties, both mental and physical, and striving with the help of resources which he has at his command.

Ibn Rushd maintains that jihad is an all-round struggle and makes it obligatory for a Muslim to exercise all his powers, maybe in the form of intellectual or physical capacities, or his gift of speech or his moral strength, courage and steadfastness in the face of hardship and his worldly riches.

The Holy Qur'an has elucidated this point, i.e. jihad as an all-round struggle in various surahs. We reproduce below a few of them in order to explain the true nature and significance of jihad in Islam:

> The believers are only those who believed in Allah and His Apostle and thereafter doubted not, and struggled hard with their riches and their persons in the cause of Allah. Those, they are the truthful.
>
> And strive hard for Allah, as is due unto Him. He has chosen you, and has imposed no hardship on you in matter of the religion, the faith of your father Ibrahim.
>
> (xxii: 78)

This verse of the Holy Qur'an sums up the spirit of jihad in Islam. It is a striving in the way of Allah, and has far wider scope than mere fighting. The Holy Prophet once explaining the true qualities of mujahid (the one who strives in the path of Allah) significantly remarked:

> The mujahid is one who tries to struggle against his self, i.e. evil self.

Ibn al-Qayyim in his explanation of this aspect of jihad has observed:

> The jihad against the enemies of Allah with one's life in only a part of the struggle which a true servant of Allah carries on against his own evil self for the sake of his Lord. This striving against the evil tendencies which have dominated his mind and heart is more important than fighting against the enemies in the outside world. It is in fact the basis on which the struggle in the path of Allah can be successfully launched.

Since jihad is an all-round struggle, a struggle directed to so many channels, it necessitates the employment of different methods to acquit oneself creditably of its wide and varied responsibilities. According to Imam Raghib, a Muslim is required to fight against three foes:

(1) against the visible enemy;

(2) against the devil;

(3) against his self (nafs).

Ibn Rushd maintains that the believer may fulfil this struggle in four ways; by his heart, by his tongue, his hands, and by the sword. The first of these implies that a Muslim should develop his sensitivities to the point of excellence, so much so that nothing evil should find its way either in his heart or in his mind. He should have a deep-rooted aversion to everything ignoble and a strong desire to fight it tooth and nail, whether it is found in his own self or in the world outside.

Then comes the function of the power of expression which has a vital role to play in the establishment of a sound and just social order, free from all kinds of exploitation. This power has a double responsibility in the sense that it has to clothe in noble words the noble ideals and sentiments which upsurge the mind and heart of man and then by dint of his eloquence, imprint their superiority in the minds of other people. Moreover, this gift of expression is to be used for protesting against evils in human life. The Holy Qur'an shows the way how the powers of expression is to be used for inviting the people to the path of Allah:

> Invite (all) to the way of their Lord with wisdom and goodly exhortation and argue with them with that which is the best. (xvi: 125)

In his characteristic style, the Holy Prophet has explained that jihad consists not only of using the sword, but that even when Muslim uses his tongue for protesting against the atrocities of tyrants, he is waging jihad. He once said:

> Whoever amongst you sees something abominable, he should endeavour to change it with his hand, in case he has the power to do it: but if he lacks the requisite power, he should then use his tongue, and if he is powerless in this also, he must then hate it from the heart, and this in fact is the weakest (state) of faith.

Then in other tradition which is narrated on the authority of Abu Sa'id al-Khudri, the Prophet is reported to have significantly remarked:

> The best of jihad is the uttering of the word of truth in the face of a tyrant ruler.

This would make it abundantly clear that jihad in Islam is not an act of violence. It is, in fact, an all-round struggle in the path of Allah.

In this all-round struggle, however, which covers all aspects of life, Islam has assigned a special place to qital (fighting) as well. There do arise such occasions in which the use of arms becomes a dire necessity and even a slight show of weakness under these circumstances leads to disastrous results. Islam has stressed the need of rising to such occasions and has exhorted its followers to face the dangers that might thus beset them bravely and manfully. Thus, the use of force is not only permitted in Islam, but its need has been duly stressed in the Holy Qur'an and the Sunnah. But it should be made clear that even qital in Islam is not an act of mad brutality. "It represents in Muslim law what is known among western jurists as just war."

In order to understand the true nature of qital in Islam, we must first analyse the different motives which incite people to fight:

(1) The desire for material benefits is the principal impulse to warlike aggression: "Territory, with the attendant booty of various kinds, has been the usual stake in war, coveted alike by peoples and by dynasties."

(2) "The fear of injury as well as the resentment due to actual injury has unfailingly prompted to defensive war when resistance was possible and often when it might well be deemed hopeless. The interests which nations have usually prepared to defend at all costs are, in addition to their territory, their jurisdiction and their honour."

(3) The desire for power and glory has been, in the main, dominant motive of the great conquerors and their armies. It is a fact that ambitious men have again and again resorted to the use of force as a means for appropriating territory and increasing their own wealth and of the people whom they represent, but there is no denying the fact that nations as well as individuals find satisfaction in the exercise of power as an end in itself. "This desire manifests itself positively in the attempt of a nation or class to acquire dominion over others. The love of power for its own sake has been an important factor in the movements which established the great empires of

history, and it has been not less conspicuous in struggle for a supremacy among allied states as illustrated in the ancient rivalry of Athens and Sparta, and in the modern contest of the German principalities which issued in the hegemony of Prussia."

(4) "The passions of hatred and revenge have also furnished a relatively independent motive. A nation can take up an attitude that is on a still lower plane than brutal selfishness; it can become inspired by a hatred of the diabolic kind which makes it disregard even the counsels of self-interest for the satisfaction of inflicting deadly injury on a loathed enemy. The spirit of hatred has sometimes even been engendered by centuries of conflict or oppression. Sometime, it has its spring in deepseated difference of racial character and culture."

Qital in Islam has not evil design behind it. Islam has the greatest respect not only for the lives of human beings but even for those of animals and plants, and it is only for the achievement of some nobler ends and those too, through noble means, that a Muslim has been exhorted to lay hands upon them. There are so many verses in the Holy Qur'an which speak eloquently of the sanctity of life:

> And there is not an animal on the earth, not a bird that flieth with its two wings, but are communities like unto you. Nothing have we omitted from the Book. Then they (all) shall be gathered to their Lord in the end. (vi: 38)

The Prophet repeatedly emphasised the fact that not to speak of the life of man, even the life of a small bird is extremely precious and cannot be taken without sufficient reason: Whoever kills the swallow, or even a more insignificant bird than that, without any reason, shall be answerable to God for this slaughter.

On another occasion he issued a warning to people about the high-handedness that they showed towards animals:

> If Allah in His infinite mercy pardons the maltreatment which is meted out to your animals, at your hands, it means that you have been relieved of the heavy burden of sins.

Such is the value and consideration which Islam shows to birds and other animals. It is due to the result of Islamic teachings that animals have been treated with utmost kindness and love throughout the Muslim world. "Nowhere in Christendom", says Bosworth Smith, for instance, "with the one exception perhaps of Norway, are beasts of burden and domestic animals treated with such unvarying kindness and consideration as they are in Turkey."

Human life is given still greater security and no one is permitted to lay hand upon it without sufficient reason:

> Those who invoke not, with God, any other god, nor slay such life as God has made sacred except for just cause. (xxv: 68)

> On that account; we ordained for the children of Israel that if any one slew a person unless it be for murder or for spreading mischief in the land—it would be as if he slew all human beings. And if any one saved a life, it would be as if he saved the life of all human beings. (v: 35)

The above-quoted verses show in unequivocal terms the value of human life. The life of every person is sacred and thus its safety is one of the primary duties of society. A well-known scholar of Islam has made the following observations with regard to the above mentioned verses:

> On close analysis of these verses of the Holy Qur'an, we find that human life has been made sacred by God and its security is, therefore, the foremost duty of mankind; but this clause is also appended with a certain condition, i.e. "except for just cause". Similarly, along with the words: "If any one slew a person it would be as if he slew all human beings," there occcurs this conditional phrase: "unless it be for spreading mischief in the land." It means that the safety of human life is guaranteed no doubt but with certain conditions. Justice demands that tyranny and oppression should not be allowed to work havoc in the world; that wickedness ought to be restrained and punished in human society in the interests of the peace and prosperity of the human race. Human life is sacred so far as its activities are confined to the reasonable limits, but when these transgress them and become a source of terror and aggression and constant peril to the lives of other persons, then it loses its sanctity and its termination becomes indispensable and therein lies the welfare of humanity. That is why, the Holy Qur'an says: "Mischief is more grievous than homicide."

The Holy Qur'an clearly brings out the that fact that qital is not an end in itself in Islam, but a means to a higher and nobler end—the welfare of humanity. That is why, Islam has exhorted its followers to raise arms not in a spirit of brutality but in a spirit of love for humanity—a spirit in which the surgeon applies the knife to the blistering sores of the human body. An individual or a community is no benefactor of humanity if it becomes a silent spectator to the atrocities which are perpetrated on innocent people by those who have no feeling for humanity and no consideration for moral principles. A person does not fulfil his responsibilities towards mankind if he does nothing to support the moral order which forms the bedrock of justice in the human race. A man, or a nation, who tries to exterminate evil in all its forms is the benefactor of humanity in the true sense of the term, for it is even a greater evil to commit injustice with impunity than to be punished for it. The Holy Prophet has beautifully summed up the responsibility of man towards his fellowmen in the following tradition:

> It is narrated on the authority of Anas (may Allah be pleased with him) that the Messenger of God once said: 'Help your brother whether he is the wrong-doer or the oppressed one.' Thereupon people said to him, "O Messenger of Allah, we can help the man when he is wronged, but we fail to know how a wrong-doer can be helped.' Upon this the Prophet (may peace and blessings of Allah be upon him) replied, 'You can do this by holding his hand from an act of oppression.'

> None having a grain of common sense can favour the granting of licence to the wicked people for committing crimes and then letting them go scot free. It is not love for humanity but act of enmity towards it that the weaker elements of society should be subjected to wrongs and injustices and no check should be imposed upon the wrong-doers. "It is absurd to maintain," says W. P. Paterson, "that the rulers of a nation are under obligation, not merely to sacrifice themselves, but to take the responsibility of sacrificing others who instinctively look at them for protection, and of abandoning old men, women and children, to privation, sufferings, and moral perils. The Christian spirit was surely better interpreted in the mediaeval code of chivalry."

Herbert Spencer declares:

> The doctrine of non-resistance is anti-social, as it involves the non-assertion, not only of one's own rights, but of those of others, while it holds out no prospect of leading to the desirable end of international peace.

Grotius argues that recourse to war is permitted and approved by the law of nature, by the consent of the manly and of the wise and by the law of nations, as well as by the divine law which was promulgated and attested by the scriptures.

> The law of nature has two branches, the course dictated by natural instincts, and the principles approved by reason. This law intimates its permission of war through the universal instinct of self-preservation, accompanied as it is by nature's disclosure of purpose in the provision of means of defence to all creatures and also by the voice of reason which makes it clear that the well-being of society is incompatible with the unchecked reign of violence.

These observations make it abundantly clear that the use of force is essential in certain conditions in order to maintain the sanctity of human life and to preserve the moral order in the world. The very first passage which gave the sanction of qital to the Muslims makes a pointed reference to all these noble ideals:

> Permitted are those who are fought against, because they have been oppressed, and verily to succour them, Allah is Potent. Those who have been unjustly driven forth from their abodes merely because they say: "Our Lord is Allah." And were it not for Allah's repelling or some by means of others, cloisters and churches, synagogues and mosques, wherein the name of Allah is mentioned much, would have pulled down. Surely Allah shall succour whosoever succoureth Him. Verily Allah is Strong, Mighty.
>
> They are those who, if we establish them in the land, establish the prayer and give the poor-rate and enjoin right and forbid wrong, and unto Allah is the end of all affairs.
>
> (xxii: 41)

The passage sums up in clear terms the aims and objects of qital in Islam. It is neither the acquisition of land, nor of power, nor yet of privilege. The Muslims were permitted to use force because their very existence had been made difficult due to persecution by the pagans of Arabia. They had been subjected to unspeakable tortures at their hands; beaten and insulted, and then driven away from their homes for no other reason than that they worshipped Allah. They had as much right to be in their native town and worship in the Ka'bah as the other Arabs, but nobody was tolerant towards them. The animosity of the Quraysh did not end even after having driven the Prophet and his companions out of their native place. The unjust men of Mecca had not only given no ear to the heavenly Message delivered by Muhammad (peace be upon him) but would not even let him live if he kept on preaching it. The pagan Arabs had evil design in their minds to pursue the innocent souls who left for Medina and to exterminate them even in their new abodes. If one were to reflect calmly over this state of affairs one would be convinced that the verdict of all religions and ethical philosophies, both ancient and modern, has been that under such circumstances war is not only justifiable but a basic necessity, and non-resistance is blameworthy and even immoral. There has been a practical unanimity as to the moral justification of self-defence when one nation is assailed by the ambition and cupidity of another.

Highest Ethics

Then the Qur'an also explains the function of war as a moral necessity. It is with the help of force that the ever-mounting evil in human life is curbed, for if it continues to spread unchecked, it would brutally shake the basis of moral order and justice in human society so much so that even the places of worship would not be safe at the hands of the wicked elements of the human race. It deserves to be noted that the Muslims have been asked to lay down their lives not only to save their own skins from the atrocities of the opponents, and to save their own mosques, but to save churches, synagogues, and cloisters as well. This means that Islam wants to protect the moral order vouchsafed to humanity through the Messengers of God at different stages of human history. The same idea has been expressed in another verse:

> And were it not for Allah's repelling people, some of them by means of others, the earth surely would be corrupted but Allah is Gracious unto the worlds.
>
> (ii: 251)

The above verse reveals that the rise and fall of nations is not a mere accident, but that it follows a definite pattern in the moral order of the universe. If some nations are swept out of effective existence, it is because they have been corrupted to the marrow of their bones and their dominance in the world is a terrible threat to the peaceful existence of the human race. They are, therefore, through the efforts of the other groups of human beings, thrown into an obscure background with a view to saving humanity from their corrupt and unhealthy influences.

The human society always contains a number of anti-social elements which need a check even though this check were to be exercised with the help of force. When the evil becomes parasitic upon the good, that is to say, it begins to nourish by preying upon what is good, it becomes the primary duty of humanity to restrain it with all the means at its disposal. "The philosopher", observes Joad, "cannot philosophize while his neighbour is abducting his wife, nor can the artist paint while the burglar is running off with his canvasses. In this sense, all civilized activity is dependent upon a minimum background of ordered security, and the maintenance of this background is a condition of its continuance." The use of the sword is, therefore, required to put a curb on the anti-social activities of the evil elements of the human race, as with individuals, so with nations. A rabid nation should no more be permitted to hold to ransom the humanitarian activities of peaceful men. The downtrodden people who are subjected to the tyranny and oppression of heartless tyrants are to be helped at all cost, and it is the bound duty of all God-fearing human being to rescue these helpless folk from the clutches of the enemies of humanity:

> And what aileth you that ye fight not in the way of Allah, and for the oppressed among men and women and children who say: 'Our Lord! Take us forth from the town whereof the people are wrongdoers, and appoint us from before Thee a patron and appoint us from Thee a helper'. (iv: 75)

It is significant that the war which is waged for upholding the cause of the oppressed is named by the Qur'an as "fight in the way of Allah". Then, in the succeeding verse a clear distinction is also drawn between the two types of war; the one which is fought for the sake of Allah and the other which is waged in the cause of evil:

> Those who believe fight in the way of Allah and those who disbelieve fight in the way of Satan. Fight then against the friends of Satan; verily feeble indeed is the cunning of the devil. (iv: 76)

A distinct and clear line of demarcation marks off the "just" from the "unjust" war. Those who fight for self-glorification, self-aggrandisement, or for the exploitation of the resources of the weaker peoples, are in the fact the friends of the devil; whereas the persons who raise arms in order to curb tyranny and oppression and to eradicate evil are the blessed souls who fight in the way of Allah. Thus, every war which is waged for personal or national glorification at the cost of others is a war in the way of Satan and is vehemently condemned by Islam. On the contrary, the war which is fought in defence of the oppressed, which aims at the eradication of evils and the suppression of those who spread them is a Holy War which is upheld by Islam for it is essential to strike at the very root of the supremacy of the wicked elements in order to establish peace and justice in the world.

> And fight them until there is no more tumult and oppression and religion should only be for Allah. So if they desist, then verily Allah is the Beholder of that what they do. (viii: 39)

This verse clearly defines the aims and objects of fighting in Islam. Muslims have been asked to raise arms not for any personal end but purely for the love of Allah, so that the rebels, who, by their evil designs, have made life intolerably difficult for the innocent souls, should be forcibly prevented from carrying on their nefarious activities and there should prevail justice, goodwill and fraternity in human society.

The war of Islam has been completely purged of the spirit of self-aggrandisement or that of national dominance. It is narrated on the authority of Abu Musa al-Ash'ari that once a man came to the Holy Prophet and said: "A person fights for booty, another fights with a view to winning fame and still another raises his arms in order to display his courage and bravery—who among these should be considered as fighter for the sake of Allah?" To the question the prophet replied: "He who raises his arm with the sole objective that the Word of Allah should become supreme is the one who fights for the cause of Allah."

Thus in Islam, it is not every war which is sanctified as jihad. It is the noble objectives alone which justify a Muslim to raise arms against the tyrants and the expoliters of the human race. Such is the importance of this objective behind fighting that Bukhari has assigned a separate chapter to it in which it has been clearly laid down that it is not feasible to assert with certainty whether a man killed in warfare, is a martyr or not; since martyrdom of a person depends upon the intention with which he participates in the battle and it is always hidden from the view of human beings.

Allah alone is, therefore, the right judge in this matter. The Prophet emphatically said:

> Allah knows fully well who strives in His cause and sustains injury for His sake.

It is narrated that once in an encounter with the enemies the Prophet had on his side a hypocrite who was known as Qazman. He fought desperately in the battlefield. The Muslims were all praising for his valour and one of them said in the presence of the prophet: "No one has proved himself to be so useful as this man has done." Upon this the Prophet remarked: "His abode is the Hell." Badr al-Din al-Ayni the famous commentator of Bukhari, has recorded that when this man was on the point of succumbing to the injuries which he had received, one of the companions of the Holy Prophet, Qutadah b. Nu'man cheered him up and gave him the tidings of martyrdom. Upon this the dying man disclosed the motive of his fighting and said: "By God, I did not fight for the cause of the faith. I was impelled to take arms for the glorification of my tribe and family."

Ibn Hajar al-'Asqalai, while elucidating the implication of relationship between this particular tradition and the section under which it falls in Bukhari, has made the following significant observations:

Nothing can be said with certainty, except through revelation, whether a man is a martyr or not and that refers to the address of 'Umar when he said: "You call those people martyrs who fight in the battles; I advise you not to make such explicit assertions and say -as the Holy Prophet said: One who lays down his life in the way of Allah or one who is killed for no fault of his own is a martyr." This assertion is authentic and corroborates the words of the Holy Prophet which have come down to us through another source (Abu Dharr). It is narrated that the Messenger of God once asked his companions: "Whom do you count as martyrs?" They replied: "One who is attacked with a weapon and as a consequence of that he succumbs to the injuries," whereupon the Holy prophet remarked: "How many persons receive injuries and die, but they are neither martyrs nor are their sacrifices laudable. On the other hand, many a man courts natural death in the bed but in the eyes of the Lord, he is a champion of truth and a martyr." These words of the Holy Prophet clearly bring out the fact that it is not appropriate to call anyone a martyr with certainty, but we should speak in a general way, as we have been instructed by the Messenger of Allah: "God alone knows the man who fights or receives injury for His sake," Imam Bukhari has recorded the tradition relating to the death of Qazman under the section: "None should be called a martyr with certainty", simply because the person concerned did not fight for the sake of Allah alone, but he had in his heart an absurdly extravagant pride in his race or tribe.

Such is the noble spirit which underlies jihad in Islam. It is not an act of aggression for the sake of material interest or a wanton display of national or tribal power, but it is a sacred duty assigned to every Muslim in the interests of humanity so that there should be peace and justice in the world. It is this war, which aims at the achievement of noble ends, that is given the name of 'fighting in the way of Allah'! This alone has been eulogised in the Holy Book.

It is interesting to note that a war which seeks to serve such a sacred objective, has not only been permitted by all other religions but has also been lavishly praised by them. The Christian teaching include precepts which, at the first sight, appear to rule out any kind of engagement in war as inconsistent with its moral ideals, but even a little bit of careful study would convince one of the facts that even the Christian Church does not stand for an unqualified condemnation of war. "The Council of Aries in one of its canons appears to have visited ecclesiastical censure on those who abandoned the army even in time of peace from conscientious scruples. Some even thought that the sword might be drawn in a holy war for the exterpation of idolatry. Ambrose eulogised the warlike courage which prefers death to bondage and disgrace and claimed the O. T. warriors as spiritual ancestors. He even adopted the classical maxim that one who does not defend a friend from injury is as much at fault as he who commits the injury. Augustine was forced to face the question by the havoc of the Teutonic migrations and the peril of the empire and his active mind fully explored the subject."

His observations are very significant:

The war is sometimes lawful on the Christian principles and the grounds are:

> (a) that it has been and may be waged by appointment of God; (b) that the case of wanton and rapacious attack by one nation on another falls under the same category as crimes of murder and burglary, and should presumably be similarly dealt with; (c) that John the Baptist did not require the soldiers to abandon the service, but only exhorted them to do violence to no man and be content with their wages. The implications of the Sermon on the Mount are most fully discussed in the Epistle to Marcellinus which was called forth by the pagan objection that the precepts of non-resistance were inconsistent with public policy and ruinous to the state. The precept to turn the other cheek to the smiter, cannot be taken literally. What it requires is an inward disposition of patient goodwill towards the aggressor, and it does not prescribe any uniform manifestation of the dispositions in act, as appears from the fact that Jesus at least protected himself against violence. We ought always to cherish the spirit of clemency, and be willing to render good for evil, but many things have to be done in which we have to pay regard not to our kindly inclinations but to the real interests of the others and their interests may require that

> they should be treated much as they may dislike it with a certain benignant asperity.

In the same way, Thomas Aqinas, explaining the view-point of Christianity with regard to war, says:

> Jesus said that he who takes the sword shall perish by the sword. But 'to take' means to use without warrant and the words only prohibit unauthorised or private persons from drawing the sword. (b) War is inconsistent with the command that we resist not evil (Matt, 5: 38) and avenge not ourselves. "But these injunctions are fulfilled by the cultivation of a placable spirit and cannot require us to do mischief by allowing wickedness to go unpunished. If the peace-makers are blessed, war-makers are accused. But war may be the best or the only means of attaining the end of peace.

Luther held that the Gospel presupposed natural rights and duties, and vigorously defended the Christian soldier. Calvin argued that the war is branch of the work of retributive justice which has been entrusted by God to the civil magistrate, and that it has the same moral justification as the police measures which protect the citizens against the criminal populations. In Calvin's own words:

> Whether it be a king who does it, or a scoundrel who does it on a small scale, he is equally to be regarded and punished as a robber. It is no breach of the command: 'Thou shalt not kill,' the slaying of the authors of the unjust war is an execution, the judge is God, and the fighting men who defend the right are merely God's instruments. If it be objected that the New Testament does not expressly permit Christians to fight, it is to be observed that NT does not undertake to legislate about civil policy, and that it presupposes the Old Testament in which the

greatest men of God, like Moses and David, were mighty men of valour in the service of God.

The views expressed by the famous writers of Christianity eloquently speak of the fact that "war is not always sin", contrary to what is commonly imagined by some of the ultrapacifist interpreters of the Christian faith. Such a view rests on a superficial view of the ethical system of Christianity. The doctrine of retributive justice—that wickedness ought to be punished and curbed— fills at least as large a space as the doctrine of non-resistance in the structure of Christian thought.

Since war need not be merely an impulsive outburst of fury and aggression, but can also be a means for the achievement of some lofty ends, it has been completely humanized by Islam. It is not allowed to degenerate into an act of savagery, but is required to be carried on as a noble struggle with human considerations, under the leadership of a responsible and God-fearing man, and directed to weeding out evil and enthroning goodness, charity and benevolence.

Even a cursory glance over the pages of history would reveal, on the other hand, that war has had in the past even as it has today an extremely horrible record. The countries invaded are ruthlessly devastated, the captured cities are sacked and destroyed, and neither age nor sex counts on immunity. Such has been and continues to be the general practice of warfare. If the practice is commonly less than the theory, this is probably due not so much to clemency as to the consideration that a ruined and depopulated country affords less opportunities of exploitation than the populated one. Islam is the greatest religion of the world which makes a strong plea for humane fighting and regulates the conduct of war in such a way that it ceases to be a sheer drive for power, a naked exaltation of the tribal passion for fighting an act of collective gangsterism, but becomes "a thoroughly reformative process."

> And fight in the way of Allah those who fight you, and transgress not the limits; verily Allah loveth not the transgressors." (ii: 190)

The Holy Prophet has clearly set the limits which may not be transgressed in fighting.

Firstly, the belligerents are divided into classes: combatants, who actually participate in the battle, and non-combatants, who do not or cannot take part in actual fighting or who are incapacitated to do so, for example, women and children, the aged and the infirm, the blind, the imbecile, the travellers, and the man devoted to monastic services. Islam has forbidden their killing altogether.

The following instructions of the Holy Prophet lay down the well-defined limits of warfare:

> Neither kill the old verging on death, nor children and babes nor the females. Do not steal anything from the booty and collect together all those things which fall to your lot in the battlefield, and do good. Allah loves those who do good.

It is narrated on the authority of ' Abdullah b. 'Umar that once the Holy Prophet saw the dead body of a woman who was killed in a battle. He admonished his men and warned them against killing women and children.

It is also recorded that the Holy Prophet (peace and blessings of Allah be upon him) once saw in battlefield that people had surrounded something. He sent one of his men to find out what the matter was. The man returned and told the Messenger of Allah that a woman had been slain and the people had gathered around her. Upon this, the Holy Prophet said: "The woman did not participate in the battle, then why was she made a victim of your sword?" The people replied: "Khalid b. al- Walid was in the vanguard of the army." The Holy Prophet sent a man to Khalid and instructed him not to lay hands on any woman or slave. The Prophet also issued a stern warning to his men against the burning of the enemies.

There is a tradition which has been narrated on the authority of Hamzah al Aslami that the Messenger of Allah once appointed him the leader of a battalion and said: "If you find such and such an infidel, kill him, but do not burn him, because it is the Creator of fire alone Who has the right to use it for punishing the wicked people."

It is recorded by Samurah b. Jundub that the Holy Prophet (peace be upon him) exhorted us to give charity and forbade us from mutilation of dead bodies.

It is said that once a news was brought to Abu Ayyub al Ansari that Muslims killed four prisoners after having tied them in their camp. The famous companion of the Holy Prophet listened to this with a sense of anguish and said: "I heard the Prophet forbidding us to kill our enemies in this way." He also added: "By God, in Whose hand is my life, I would never slay like this even if it were a hen."

This, in brief, is the teaching of the Holy Prophet with regard to dealing with the enemy on the battlefield. So great is the respect for humanity in Islam that it has forbidden wanton destruction of even the enemy's crops and property at the time of invasion or at the time of conquest. While describing the traits of the mischief-monger, the Quran explicitly tells us that:

> When he turns his back, his aim everywhere is to spread mischief through the earth and destroy crops and cattle. But God loveth not mischief and disorder. (ii: 205)

Islam has purged war of all base passions, so that the Muslims have been ordained to refrain from creating noise on the battlefield as far as possible, and only chant the glory of the Lord, the Creator of the universe. It is narrated on the authority of Qays b. Abd, that the companions of the Holy Prophet did not like taking loudly on the battlefield.

This injunction speaks eloquently of the sanctity of the occasion. War in Islam is not the wild expression of the baser elements of man, but a sacred struggle undertaken to achieve some definite noble ends.

The four righteous Caliphs followed closely the teachings of Allah and His Apostle in letter and spirit and did not deviate from the path shown to them by the Holy Prophet. The celebrated instructions which the first Caliph gave to his army while bidding them farewell on their expedition to the Syrian borders are permeated with the Message of Allah.

He said:

> "Do not commit treachery, nor depart from the right-path. Do not mutilate, nor kill a child, nor aged man, nor a woman. Do not destroy a palm tree, nor burn it with fire and do not cut any fruit tree. You must not slay any of the flocks or herds or the camels, save for your subsistence. You are likely to pass by people who have devoted their lives to monastic service; leave them to what they have devoted their lives. You are likely to find, likewise, people who will present to you meals of many kinds. You may eat; but do not forget to mention the name of Allah:"

It is said that once at the time of conquest a singing girl was brought to al-Muhajir b. Abi Ummyyia who had been publicly singing satirical poems about Abu Bakr. Muhajir got her hand amputated. When the Caliph heard this news, he was rudely shocked and wrote a letter to Muhajir in the following words:

> I have learnt that you laid hands on a woman who had showered abuses on me, and therefore got her hand amputated. God has not sought vengeance even in the case of polytheism, which is a great crime. He has not permitted mutilation even with regard to manifest infidelity. Try to be considerate and sympathetic in your attitude towards others in future. Never mutilate, because it is a grave offence. God purified Islam and the Muslims from rashness and excessive wrath. You are well aware of the fact that those enemies fell into the hands of the Messenger of Allah who had been recklessly abusing him, who turned him out of his home, and who fought against him, but he never permitted their mutilation.

Another letter written by 'Umar the second Caliph which is addressed to Sa'd b. Abl Waqqas, speaks eloquently of the noble spirit with which the Muslims have been exhorted to take up arms:

> Always search your minds and hearts and stress upon your men the need of perfect integrity and sincerity in the cause of Allah. There should be no material end before them in laying down their lives, but they should deem it a means whereby they can please their Master and entitle themselves to His favour: such a spirit of selflessnes should be inculcated in the minds of those who unfortunately lack it. Be firm in the thicket of the battle as Allah helps man according to the perseverance that he shows in the cause of His faith and he would be rewarded in accordance with the spirit of sacrifice which he displays for the sake of the Lord. Be careful that those who have been entrusted to your care receive no harm at your hands and are never deprived of any of their legitimate rights.

Exemplary Behaviour

Such in fact is the humane and noble attitude which Islam exhorts its followers to adopt on the battlefield when passions are generally let loose. It is an attitude the like of which is not to be found in the history of any other nation. Has the world any code of military ethics more noble and compassionate than this one? "The moral tone adopted by the Caliph Abu Bakr in his instructions to Syrian army was," says a Christian historian, "so unlike the principles of the Roman government that it must have commanded profound attention from the subject people. Such a proclamation announced to Jews and Christian sentiments of justice and principles of toleration which neither Roman emperors nor orthodox bishops had ever adopted as the rule of conduct."

Western scholars have indulged in a good deal of mudslinging on the question of the use of the sword in Islam. But if one were to reflect calmly on this point one would be convinced that the sword has not been used recklessly by the Muslims; it has been wielded purely with humane feelings in the wider interest of humanity. Utmost regard was, always shown to human life, honour and property even on the battlefield. That is why in all the eighty-two encounters between the Muslims and non-Muslims during the life of the Holy Prophet (peace be upon him), only one thousand and eighteen persons lost their lives on both sides. Out of this, two hundred and fifty-nine were Muslims whereas the remaining seven hundred and fifty-nine belonged to the opposite camp. One wonders at the audacity of these writers when one only compares the religious wars of Charles the Great, in which 4500 pagan Saxons were killed in cold blood, when one recalls the "famous answer by which the Papal Legate, in the Albiqennian war, quited the scruples of a too conscientious general, 'Kill all God will know His own',—when one recalls the Spanish Inquisition, the conquest of Mexico and Peru, the massacre of St. Bartholomew, and the sack of Magdeburg Tilly."

This ruthless criticism on the use of sword by Muslims is a matter of great surprise for us when we find that it emanates from those whose hands are soiled in the blood of countless innocent human beings, by those who exult in the techniques of homicide, who have depersonalized warfare to such an extent that millions of innocent men and women are put to death and numberless are thrown into concentration camps and flogged with steel rods and oxidized whips, and all this is done without any qualm of conscience. As human beings, we hang our heads down in shame when think of the horrifying atrocities which have been perpetrated by the modern civilized man. It is estimated that in the World War I, ten million soldiers were killed and an equal number of civilians lost their lives, and twenty million died on account of widespread epidemics and famines throughout the world as an aftermath of this war. Economic costs are estimated at $ 398,000,000,000 of which 186,000,000,000 were direct costs.

The losses in the World War II were staggeringly greater as compared with the first one. Twenty-two million persons were killed and thirty-four million were wounded. The estimated cost of war was $ 1,348,000,000,000 of which 1,167,000,000,000 consisted of direct military costs.

It is significant that in the Korean War, the first instance in which an international organization for establishing peace utilized military force to suppress aggression, more than one million persons were killed which added to the civilian deaths in Korea and totalled about five millions.

7

First Capital

After the social boycott of Banu Hashim came to a happy end, particularly on account of the Divine revelation concerning the boycott document, the holy Prophet (PBUH) had heaved a sigh of relief. But, unfortunately, soon thereafter Hazrat Abu Talib fell seriously ill with little hope of survival. He had fallen ill before also, and it is related that on one such occasion he had called his illustrious nephew by his bed-side and asked him to pray to Allah, whose Messenger he was, to remove his illness. The holy Prophet (PBUH) had prayed and Hazrat Abu Talib had recovered, whereupon he had told his nephew:

"God listens to your prayers".

"Allah will answer your prayers also if you obey Him."

It is narrated by Allama Qastalani in "Marvehebud Dunya" that when the notables of Quraish came to visit Hazrat Abu Talib during his illness, he addressed them thus:

"God will remain pleased with you, if you all respect Kaaba above everything else, do not deprive any one of his rights, do not oppress each other, do not give up looking after the needs of your kinsmen and keep the tradition of truth and trustworthiness.

"I also desire, as my last will, that you should deal with Muhammad (PBUH) in a befitting manner as he is the most trustworthy person among the Quraishites and the most truthful throughout Arabia. He is presenting a religion which appeals to the heart but some how it becomes difficult to proclaim its acceptance by mouth, because of the fear of violent opposition from other people. But, I believe, he will have an upper hand in future and the Quraishites will be deprived of sharing honours with him."

It is related in 'Tabaqat' that, shortly before he breathed his last, he called his relatives and expressed his will:

"You will always flourish if you follow Muhammad (PBUH) and obey him."

He also called his illustrious nephew close to him and said:

"My nephew! when I pass away, it would be better for you to go to your grandfather's maternal tribe Bani Najaar in Medina, as those people are known for providing protection to their kinsmen at all cost."

Hazrat Abu Talib died at the age of eighty, six months after the withdrawal of the boycott. His death gave a grievous shock to the holy Prophet (PBUH), as was quite natural, because it was this uncle of his who had left no stone unturned to extend protection and support to him and who suffered trials and tribulations and even the three-year boycott of his entire relatives only for his sake.

No sooner had the holy Prophet (PBUH) recovered from this shock that his loving wife, who cared for him more than for any one else and who was the first to 'believe' Hazrat Khadija passed away at the age of sixty five in the 10th year of Prophethood. The holy Prophet (PBUH) laid her dead body in the grave with his own hands at a place called *Hajoon*. This year was termed by the holy Prophet (PBUH) as the 'year of grief.'

After the demise of Hazrat Abu Talib, the idolaters of Mecca, realising that he was deprived of his protector, started hurting the holy Prophet (PBUH) in many ways. One day, while he was passing through a crowded market place, a ruffian from among the Quraishites threw dust on his head and face and the holy Prophet (PBUH) entered his house in that condition whereupon his daughters started weeping and comforting him. It has been narrated, on the authority of Hazrat Aesha, that the holy Prophet (PBUH) used to say that "as long as Abu Talib was alive, the Quraishites lay low". The same tradition has been reported by Baihaqa, on the authority of Urwa bin Zubair.

It has been recorded in Tabaqat that when excesses against the holy Prophet's (PBUH) person became too common, after the death of Hazrat Abu Talib, it was of all persons, Abu Lahb who stood up to protect the holy Prophet (PBUH) and asked him to carry on his missionary work in the same manner as he did before. Support from Abu Lahb who inspite of being the holy Prophet's (PBUH) uncle, was his greatest enemy astounded every one. When Abu Lahb chanced to see how Haris bin Qais was misbehaving with the holy Prophet (PBUH) once while the latter had come out of his house, he threatened Haris bin Qais of dire consequences. This fellow was so perplexed at this change in Abu Lahb's stance that he ran to the precincts of Kaaba and announced that Abu Lahb had renounced his ancestral faith. The notables of Quraish rushed to Abu Lahb's house to verify this, but the latter told them that he had not renounced his faith, but that he would provide the holy Prophet (PBUH) the same kind of protection as his deceased uncle, Hazrat Abu Talib had done. But, since fate had arrayed him on the other side of the fence, Abu Lahb gave up the patronage which he had extended, when pressed by Abu Jahl and Uqba bin Abi Moeet.

After the death of Hazrat Khadija, there was no one in the holy Prophet's (PBUH) house to look after his two daughters, Hazrat Umme Kulsoom and Hazrat Fatima. After giving it a serious consideration for quite some period, the holy Prophet (PBUH) sent his proposal of marriage with Hazrat Sauda bint Zamaa, who was of almost the same age as he himself and was considered quite capable of looking after his two daughters.

Hazrat Sauda had embraced Islam alongwith her first husband Sakran bin Umroo, and the couple had migrated to Abyssinia where her husband had died. Hazrat Sauda could not get a better offer of re-marriage and she immediately gave her consent and Hazrat Hatib bin Umroo, representing Hazrat Sauda, solemnised the marriage and she moved to the holy Prophet's (PBUH) house. In fact, it was Hazrat Khula, the same noble lady who had arranged the holy Prophet's (PBUH) marriage with Hazrat Khadija, who played the role of an intermediary in the marriage with Hazrat Sauda. The same lady, later, had arranged the holy Prophet's (PBUH) marriage with Hazrat Aisha. When she approached Hazrat Abu Bakr's wife, Hazrat Umme Rumaan, with the proposal, she responded positively but asked for time to consult her husband, Hazrat Abu Bakr. The latter had already given his consent to give Hazrat Aesha in marriage to Mutam bin Adi's son. He, therefore, went to the latter's house to ascertain whether the proposed marriage of Hazrat Aesha with his son was firm and final or not. But, as God had willed, Hazrat Abu Bakr came back without going back on his commitment to give his daughter in marriage to Mutam's son. It was Mutam's wife herself who, on the plea that her son will also renounce their ancestral faith after his marriage with Hazrat Aesha, broke off the marriage proposal.

Hazrat Abu Bakr, being thus free to marry Hazrat Aesha, elsewhere, immediately called the holy Prophet (PBUH) to his house and solemnised the marriage, though Hazrat Aesha went to her husband's house after his migration to Medina.

Since the holy Prophet (PBUH) had given up hope of gaining more converts in Mecca because of the continued ill-treatment meted out to him by the idolaters of this city, he thought of contacting the powerful and influential tribe of Bannu Saqif at Taif, which lies 50 kilometers east of Mecca. It was at the close of the 10th year of Prophethood that the holy Prophet (PBUH) set out for Taif on foot. He met there Abd Yaleel, Masood and Habib, the three sons of Umroo bin Umair, who wielded all the power and authority in that city. But their reaction to the holy Prophet's (PBUH) preaching smacked of arrogance, misconception and conceit.

They turned away and gave an insolent reply. One of them said:

"I will tear the curtains of Kaaba to shreds if God has sent you as His Messenger."

The other said:

"Did God have no other choice before deciding to appoint you as His Messenger?"

The third one said:

"I will not talk to you; because, if you are actually God's Messenger, it would be improper on my part to speak on this subject, and if you are not His Messenger then any discussion with you is purposeless."

Apart from this rude behavior, they incited the rogues and scoundrels of the city to stand in two rows along the path and pelt stones on the holy Prophet (PBUH) when he was departing from Taif. So, they not only shouted scornfully at him and indulged in booing and hooting but also threw pellets of stone on him with such ferocity that his feet got wounded badly and blood collected in his shoes and Hazrat Zaid bin Harisa, while trying to protect the holy Prophet (PBUH) from the rain of stones, received grievous injuries on his head. Whenever the holy Prophet (PBUH) tried to sit and take rest, the rowdies made him stand and walk through the barrage of stones being pelted on him. With great effort, he came out of the limits of Taif and sat resting against the walls of an orchard of grapes belonging to two chieftains of Quraish, Sheeba and Uqba, sons of Ah Rabeea. Both of them were there and saw the holy Prophet (PBUH). They sent a bunch of grapes in a plate to him through their slave Addas. Before eating the grapes, the holy Prophet (PBUH) uttered:" In the name of Allah the Most Merciful". Addas was taken aback and said:

"By God! No one in this country is conversant with these sacred words."

The holy Prophet (PBUH) enquired:

"Where do you come from and what is your religion?"

"I am a Christian of Ninevah;" he replied.

The holy Prophet (PBUH) then said:

"You belong to the city of Jonas, son of Mathew, one of God's pious servants".

The slave could not restrain his inquisitiveness:

"How do you know him?"

"He was my brother; he was an Apostle and I am also an Apostle," the holy Prophet (PBUH) explained.

Hearing this, the slave, in extreme ecstasy of reverence and regard, began to kiss the hands, the head and the feet of the holy Prophet (PBUH) and exclaimed:

"I bear witness that you are God's Servant and His Messenger. By God! when I had left Ninevah there were not even ten persons there who knew the name of Mathew."

Seeing this, the Sons of Rabeea said:

"This man has spoiled even our slave."

When Addas came back to them, they enquired:

"Why were you kissing the hands and feet of that man?"

"My master! There is none better than this man on the earth. He informed me of a thing which only an Apostle can know", the slave replied.

They advised him:

"Addas! Do not renounce your faith, it is better than his."

But Addas had turned a Muslim inwardly and nothing could shake his newly acquired faith.

Sitting under the shade of the boundary wall of the orchard, the holy Prophet (PBUH) cleaned his wounds and blood-soaked shoes. He looked ahead on the path leading to Mecca, where also people were equally unkind to him and treated his preaching with indifference. He turned to the Almighty and prayed with a voice choked with emotion:

"My Lord! I complain to you against my own helplessness and lack of resources as also against the disrespect and disregard with which I am being treated by these people.

"You are the Most Merciful, the Ray of hope for hapless and helpless persons. You Alone are my Master, my Allah".

"In whose hands are You leaving me—in the hands of those strangers who treated me cruelly or in the hands of those whom You have enabled to attain success in their conspiracies against me? If You are not displeased with me, then I do not care how any one treats me, as You alone are my best Supporter. I seek refuge under your Benevolent shadow. I seek refuge in the Light of Thy Being which drives away all darkness and brightens up everything. I surrender before Your Will; Your Holy Being is the Fountain-head of all power, the source of all strength."

The holy Prophet (PBUH) was suffering untold persecution only for telling the people that "he had received the revelation from Allah that He alone is to be worshipped and obeyed, that no one should oppress any one else, that there was no compulsion in religion, that Allah is One, has no partners, He rules over the entire universe and that he (the holy Prophet (PBUH)) was His Messenger sent to dissuade people from the worship of other than Allah and that he was just a man from among themselves deputed by Allah to guide them to the correct path, teach them to use their latent wisdom and thereby distinguish between good and evil and ponder over Divine portents in order to understand the role of Prophets whose obedience would lead to the obedience of the Almighty". The holy Prophet (PBUH) also told them that the Quran was God's own words and that every one would be resurrected after death for reward and punishment in the Hereafter which will be the eternal life."

While the holy Prophet (PBUH), accompanied by his faithful servant, Zaid bin Harisa (who had refused to leave him and go with his parents) was returning from Taif to Mecca, Zaid spoke to his master:

"How will you enter Mecca, as the Quraishites had already turned you out of that city"?

The holy Prophet (PBUH) responded:

"Whatever you see is known to Allah. He will certainly create conditions conducive to my mission as He Himself is the Protector of His religion and He will provide me the necessary support for my ascendancy over the non-believers".

The holy Prophet (PBUH) stopped, on way, at Nakhia and then went to Hera from where he sent message to Matam bin Adi enquiring whether he would extend his protection to him if he entered Mecca to which he responded in the affirmative and asked his sons to go to the Kaaba fully armed. Thereafter, the holy Prophet (PBUH) entered Mecca under Matam's protection, the latter escorting him on camel-back. Matam shouted aloud, on reaching the precincts of Kaaba:

"I have taken Muhammad (PBUH) in my protection."

The holy Prophet (PBUH) then circum-ambulated the Kaaba while Matam bin Adi and his armed sons stood guard. Abu Jahl enquired from Matam if he had adopted the holy Prophet's (PBUH) religion or merely provided him protection. On being told that he had only offered to protect the holy Prophet (PBUH), Abu Jahl said:

"No one can dare oppose you. If you have provided him protection then each one of us will also protect him."

The holy Prophet (PBUH) had sent the aforesaid message to Matam bin Adi through Abdullah bin Uraiqat who was respected by the people of Mecca. The holy Prophet (PBUH) and Hazrat Abu Bakr used to repose full confidence in this man as he never betrayed the secrets and, despite being a polytheist had great regard for the holy Prophet (PBUH). In fact, it was Allah, Who, in order to provide succour to His Prophet (PBUH) after his suffering at the hands of the people of Taif, created a soft corner for the Prophet (PBUH) in Matam bin Adi's heart and he signified his consent to provide full and unconditional protection to him, with complete liberty to preach his faith. But there was no change of heart in Abu Jahl and

Abu Lahb who kept on vilifying the holy Prophet (PBUH) and poisoning the ears of those among whom he preached Islam.

Since the Haj season was approaching and people from various tribes and regions of Arabia had started coming to Mecca, the holy Prophet (PBUH) visited the resting place of each tribe and contacted their respective chiefs and preached the tenets of Islam. Some of them were receptive to the preaching and some reacted adversely, but the holy Prophet (PBUH) kept up his proselytising efforts.

One day, the holy Prophet (PBUH) arrived at the resting place of the tribe of Banu Bakr bin Wael who had come from the central and eastern regions of Arabia and were famous for warfare, as they had repulsed a number of invasions made by the Persian army to annex their tribal belt bordering the eastern coast of Arabian peninsula. During his preaching among them, the holy Prophet (PBUH) had enquired from them regarding their capability to resist the armed might of Persia and being told in reply that they could not match their strength with that of the Persians, he said aloud:

"O, Bakr bin Wael! A day will come when you will have victory over them, marry their women and take their boys as slaves."

Abu Lahb, who was closely following the holy Prophet's (PBUH) movements reached the resting place of Bakr bin Wael, after the latter's departure from there, and spoke about the holy Prophet (PBUH) thus:

"This man once occupied a very honourable position among us but now he has come at his wits' end."

They also believed Abu Lahb's words, as they thought that what the holy Prophet (PBUH) had prophesied about the fall of the Persian empire was but mere idle talk and a figment of imagination, although, much later, they saw with their own eyes that the prophecy came true.

Accompanied by Hazrat Abu Bakr and Hazrat Ali, the holy Prophet (PBUH) visited a large camp at Mina where a number of chieftains were assembled. On enquiry by Hazrat Abu Bakr, it transpired that they belonged to the tribe of Bani Shaiban bin Saleba. Encouraged by Hazrat Abu Bakr, the holy Prophet (PBUH) started his preaching thus:

"I call you towards Islam. You have to bear witness that there is no worshipful being save Allah, Who has no partners and that I am His Messenger. So, I ask for your support and assistance to spread this faith, a duty that has been assigned to me by the Almighty, because the Quraishites have become united in opposing this Divine mission and are refusing to believe in my Prophethood."

One of them, named Mafrooq asked the holy Prophet (PBUH) to elaborate his mission, whereupon the latter recited the following verses from Sura Al-Anam:

"Say: Come, bring your witnesses who can bear witness that Allah forbade all this. And, if they bear witness, do not bear witness with them. Follow not the whims of those who deny Our revelations, those who do not believe in the Hereafter and deem others equal with their Lord.

Say: Come, I will recite to you that which your Lord has made a sacred duty for you: that you do not ascribe anything as His partner and that you do good to your parents and that you do not slay your children because of penury - We provide for you and for them—and that you do not go near lewd things whether open or concealed. And that you slay not life which Allah has made sacred, except in the course of Justice. This He has commanded you in order that you may discern."

Mafrooq and other chieftains, when they heard the recitation exclaimed:

"By God! these are not the words of human beings. Had it been the composition of soothsayers, poets and sorcerers, who could have discerned the difference better than us. Please tell us more about your faith."

In response, the holy Prophet (PBUH) recited verse 90 of Sura Al-Nahl:

"Allah enjoins justice and kindness, and giving to kinsmen, and forbids lewdness and abomination and wickedness. He exhorts you in order that you may take heed."

Hearing this, the chieftains were so deeply affected by the marvel of the holy Quran that they remained mute for a while, and then Mafrooq broke the silence:

"O, Qurashite brother! you have called us towards best conduct and virtuous and good deeds. Your own people are an ignorant folk that they reject you and have unitedly adopted the path of flasehood."

Another Chieftain, an elderly person, Hani bin Qabisa said:

"I heard every word that you recited. By God! Whatever you have said is absolutely true. But we can not renounce our old faith and become your followers, as a result of our present session, without consulting others of our tribe. It will not be appreciated generally. We will go back to our people and reflect on your teachings. So, you may have to wait till our decision is conveyed."

Another chieftain, Musanna, referred to two other obstacles in the way of their conversion, which arose from the geographical location of their tribal area. When asked by the holy Prophet (PBUH) to elaborate, he said:

"One is the mountaineous terrain of Arabia and the other is the Persian mainland and Khosro's canals therein. The Persian overlords have obtained a promise from us that we will neither start doing something new nor introduce any change in our status quo. Your call might conflict with the wishes of the Persian rulers.

We can support you in your effort against the Arabs but not against the wishes of Persians."

Then, the holy Prophet (PBUH) addressed them:

"You did well that you spoke the fact, as you perceive it. But the position is that any one who calls people towards Allah, does not pick and choose. He has to accept the call whole-heartedly and with complete surrender before Allah."

The tribesmen kept on looking at the appearance and bearing of the holy Prophet (PBUH)—so captivating and appealing that it kept them spell-bound. Then, the holy Prophet (PBUH) surveyed the gathering and said:

"You will see that the day is not far off when Allah will bestow upon you the lands and all the belongings of the Persians. You will have authority over their daughters. Will you then remember Allah with praise that is due to Him?"

Their faces brightened up and one of their chieftains, Noman bin Shank said:

"O, Quraishite brother! We accept your words".

Thus, came to end the long session with them and the holy Prophet (PBUH), accompanied by Hazrat Abu Bakr and Hazrat Ali, took leave uttering these holy words of verses 8 to 9 of Sura Al-Fath:

"We have sent you as a witness and a bearer of good tidings and a warner, so that you (mankind) may believe in Allah and His Messenger and may honour Him and revere Him and glorify Him at early dawn and at the close of day."

Tabaqat' contains the details regarding the holy Prophet's (PBUH) meetings with various tribes and what has been given above, in this book, is based on this source. During Haj season in the 11th year of Prophethood, the holy Prophet (PBUH) visited Aqaba where he saw the tents of Khazraj tribe. According to Ibne Ishaque, after their formal introduction with the holy Prophet (PBUH), they consented to listen to him and sat in a circle. They were extremely impressed by his preachings and recitations from the holy Quran and then said to each other:

"He appears to be that very Prophet, of whom the Jews have been warning us. We should take the lead before the Jews themselves accept his teachings."

Thus, they all embraced Islam on the spot and spoke:

"When we had set out from our homes, the condition of our people was deplorable. There was disunity in their ranks and they were enemies of one another. No wonder, your teaching might make them united again. The faith that we have accepted will be preached by us among them. And if Allah causes them to rally round you, then no single person in the whole of Arabia would be your equal in power and authority. God willing, we will meet again next year in Haj season."

The six persons of Bani Khazraj of Medina, who had embraced Islam, have been named in 'Tabaqat' as under:

Abu Imama, Asaad bin Zorarah, Jabir bin Abdullah bin Rubab, Aqba bin Aamir, Rafay bin Malik, Qutba bin Aamir and Auf bin Al Haris.

Medina is an ancient city of Arabia blessed with fertile soil, invigorating climate and peaceful environment. The Jews inhabited this place since ages. The cataclysmic deluge that inundated Yemen in olden days, whose traces are still to be seen there, had rendered thousands of Arab families homeless who migrated to various places in peninsular Arabia. Aus and Khazraj, the two brothers, who were also affected by the devastating flood in Yemen had migrated to Medina, and are the fore-runners of the two influential tribes of this place known after their names. Previously, these two tribes were settled on the barren tracts of Yathrib, while the Jews held sway over the fertile area. It was after a war fought by Aus and Khazraj tribes with the Jews that the latter were displaced from the fertile lands. After the advent of the holy Prophet (PBUH), the place came to be known as Medinatun Nabi (the Prophet's (PBUH) city) and the tribes of Aus and Khazraj as Ansar (Helpers).

In any case, the Jews of Medina enjoyed undisputed superiority over the tribes of Aus and Khazraj. The former were better off financially, were more cultured and better educated. It was from these Jews that the six tribesmen of Aus and Khazraj who had embraced Islam at the hands of the holy Prophet (PBUH), had learnt that a Prophet was expected to be sent by God.

After the conversion of these six Madinites, twelve more of them, including those five who had already met the holy Prophet (PBUH) earlier, visited Mecca during the Haj season next year. Of the other seven, who had not met the holy Prophet (PBUH) earlier, five belonged to the tribe of Khazraj and two to that of Aus. On this occasion, the holy Prophet (PBUH) obtained from them the oath of fealty which meant:

"That we shall not associate any partners with Allah; that we shall not commit theft, or adultery or kill our own progeny, level no false accusations against others; and that we shall not withold our support to the holy Prophet (PBUH) in implementing good deeds and obey him, whether we are rich or poor and whether the holy Prophet's (PBUH) commandments appear agreeable or disagreeable to us and even if some one else is accorded preference over us; and that we will not dispute any decision concerning administrative matters (except when they are manifestly heathenish); and that we shall speak the truth, wherever and in whatever circumstances we are; and that we shall not be cowed down by the calumny of those who will taunt us."

The oath ended with the promise of paradise for those who abided by it and a warning for those who violated any clause thereof, their fate to be decided by Allah, Who might punish or forgive.

City of Prophet

When these twelve new converts of Medina returned to their city, accompanied by Masaab bin Umair whom the holy Prophet (PBUH) had deputed with them to preach Islam, they worked very hard to propagate the faith and very soon Islam claimed a very large number of adherents and, barring a few families in Medina, the entire city embraced Islam, the credit for which goes entirely to the untiring efforts of the Ansar. But certain thought-provoking incidents, which are also of general interest, took place in Medina during the proselytising campaign launched by the Ansar.

One such incident relates to the conversion of the elders and other persons of Bani Abdul Ashhal. It so happened that Hazrat Asaab bin Umair, who had already embraced Islam sometime ago, entered an orchard in the company of Asaad bin Zarrah, and started preaching and reciting the holy Quran to a group of the tribe of Bani Abdul Ashhal. In the meanwhile, the two elders of that tribe Saad bin Maaz and Usaid bin Huzair who had seen the Muslims reciting the holy verses earlier in the orchard of Bani Zafar, chanced to see Asaab bin Umair and Asaad bin Zarrah preaching among the tribesmen. Saad bin Maaz asked Usaid bin Huzair to go and stop both of them from weaning the ignorant tribesmen from their ancestral faith. Saad would have gone there himself but did not do so because of the presence of Asaad bin Zarrah who was his maternal cousin. Usaid picked up his spear and approached the group in a threatening posture and asked the two Muslims preachers to disperse and never attempt to preach again. But, unruffled by this provocation, Masaab bin Umair received Usaid with due courtesy and requested him, very politely, to give him a patient hearing and in case his words offend him, no further preaching would be done among the people of his tribe. Usaid agreed to this fair and reasonable request and sat down among the group. Hazrat Masaab bin Umair started talking to him, in a very appealing manner, about Islam's notion of mono-theism, the holy Prophet's (PBUH) apostleship and his enviable character and conduct, about resurrection after death and the Divine plan of reward and punishment in the Hereafter and ended his speech with recitation of holy verses.

The marvel of Quran had worked on Usaid's body and soul, affecting him so profoundly that his face flushed and he completely softened up. When Hazrat Masaab bin Umair finished the recitation, Usaid could not help remarking:

"Indeed, what an elegant composition!"

"What is one required to do if he embraces this religion?" This was Usaid's query.

"He has to wash himself, wear clean clothes and then profess that Allah is One and Muhammad is His Messenger. Thereafter he has to offer prayer." This was the detailed reply of Asaad bin Zarrah and Hazrat Masaab.

Usaid lost no time in washing and wearing clean clothes. Thereafter, Hazrat Masaab formally converted him to Islam. Hazrat Usaid then, indulging in loud thinking, said that if only one man, Saad bin Maaz, could enter the fold of Islam, the entire tribe would be converted to this faith. So, he persuaded Saad bin Maaz to meet the group of Muslims, on whose hands he had embraced Islam. The latter did so and he too got converted, whereafter he addressed his tribesmen:

"O, Bani Abdul Ashhal! What do you think of me?"

"You are our chieftain and an extremely kind person, always giving good counsel." This was their unanimous opinion.

Thereupon, Hazrat bin Maaz told the gathering:

"I will not speak to the men as well as women of the tribe until you profess belief in Allah and His Messenger."

The sun had hardly set that day, when the entire tribe embraced Islam save one man, Sahibul Aseeram Umroo bin Thabit, who also became a Muslim just on the eve of the War of Uhud wherein he was martyred. According to the holy Prophet (PBUH), he will enter paradise in the hereafter.

While Islam was gaining a foothold quite rapidly in Medina, the heathens of Mecca continued opposing Islam and the holy Prophet (PBUH), despite the latter's kind treatment to their destitutes, orphans and the needy and spending whatever money he had on the general welfare of the poor and the hungry. The holy Prophet (PBUH) once said:

"I will not like to keep with me a heap of gold as large as the mountain of Uhud for a duration longer than three nights, except what I have to re-pay to my creditors."

He is reported to have also stated that "large heartedness and generosity are the real hallmarks of wealth and not the mere accumulation of money and material." These were not empty sermons. The holy Prophet (PBUH) acted upon these words. He used to spend in Allah's way whatever he earned. No one ever returned empty handed from his door. His 'companions' also acted similarly. They preferred to starve themselves than to see others starving. Hazrat Aesha relates:

"The holy Prophet's (PBUH) bed was of leather stuffed with barks of datepalm and his family members never ate bread of wheat to their full satisfaction for even three consecutive nights since his arrival in Medina till his passing away."

Contrasted with this, the well-to-do persons of Quraish loved money and its ostentatious display, as is the weakness of all men of wealth. Even their philanthropic acts were meant to show off their riches. They were prey to all kinds of vices that arise from accumulation of wealth—obscenity, lewdness, usurping the properties of relatives, amassing money in all manners right or wrong, looking down upon the less fortunate, indulging in drinking and gambling and so on.

All the Prophets who are sent to reform the society come across similar situations, as the forces of evil combine to oppose the truth. Even, a great Prophet like Moses, realising that he would have to face such adversities in preaching the true religion, prayed to the Almighty:

"My Lord! I fear that they will deny me. On this account, I shall be embarrassed and my tongue will not speak eloquently. Therefore send for Aaron" (Al-Shuara, verses 12-13).

Moses called for Aaron's help in accomplishing the extremely onerous responsibility of preaching a new faith among a wrong-doing folk. He wanted a helping hand so that he could devote his entire attention towards calling people to the right path. The Quran also mentions how Moses also prayed to God:

"My Lord! Relieve my mind

And ease my task for me:

And loosen a knot from my tongue

So that they may understand what I say"

(Ta-HA-Verses-25.28).

The holy Prophet (PBUH) did not have to pray to the Almighty for opening up his heart and mind as Prophet Moses had to do. The former had already been sent by God as "mercy for the worlds." When the holy Prophet (PBUH) went to Taif to preach the faith, after giving up hope of converting the people of Mecca, he was ill-treated, stoned and injured, as already described at length earlier. It has been narrated that while he was stopping at, a place called Qaruns Saahib, while returning from Taif, the holy Prophet (PBUH) saw a detached lump of cloud overshadowing him wherein Gabriel was clearly visible, who addressed him thus:

"Allah has taken note of all that which your people have told you in response to your call and that the angel who has authority over mountains is available to carry out your order, whatever it may be."

Thereafter, the Angel of the Mountains informed the holy Prophet (PBUH) that, as commanded by the Almighty, he could turn the mountains that surrounded Mecca up-side down and thereby crush that city, only if he so desired. But the holy Prophet (PBUH) replied that he hoped that the coming generations of the people of Mecca will receive the guidance and believe in monotheism. Had he willed, he would have, in retaliation of the brutalities which he had suffered at the hands of the people of Mecca, caused complete devastation of Mecca and its inhabitants. But, since he was sent as the last and the noblest Apostle of God he decided to forgive the sinners and not to wreak vengeance.

When the revelation regarding congregational prayer in the afternoon of Friday was received, the holy Prophet (PBUH) sent written instructions accordingly to Hazrat Masaab bin Umair to arrange for the weekly congregational prayer in Medina, as it was not possible to hold such prayers in Mecca because of the continued opposition of the polytheists.

Now that the majority of the people of Medina had embraced Islam and the time was ripe for setting up an Islamic polity in that city, the incident of Meraj, ('Ascension') took place at Mecca while the holy Prophet (PBUH) was extremely unhappy and despondent on account of the behaviour of the people of Mecca. He was consoled through Divine revelation in these words:

"Endure patiently. Thine endurance is only by the help of Allah. Grieve not for them, and be not in distress because of that which they devise. Indeed Allah is with those who keep their duty towards Him and those who do good deeds." (Al Nahl-Verses 127-128).

Again, the Almighty provided the much-needed solace to the holy Prophet (PBUH) in these words:

"Have We not caused thy bosom to dilate, (And eased thee of the burden.)

Which weighed down thy back:

And exalted thy fame?

But lo! with hardship goes ease" (Nashrah, verses 1-5)

Grand Entry

The holy Prophet (PBUH) was fifty three years of age and had completed twelve long years of Apostleship that the momentous event of Meraj took place. Although the date and year of this event are disputed, yet it is generally recognised that it happened in the night of 27th Rajab, long before the emigration to Medina. It is related that on that night, which the holy Prophet (PBUH), weary of preaching during the day, rested in the house of his paternal cousin sister, Hazrat Umme Hani in Shob Abi Talib, he lay down on bed after Isha prayers and had hardly gone to sleep that Gabriel aroused him, took him to the holy Precincts of Kaaba, opened his chest, washed it with Zam Zam water and enlightened it with Divine Light. Then Gabriel asked him to mount 'buraq', a heavenly steed, larger than a donkey and smaller than a mule, commanding it to behave as the rider was the most Illustrious person ever born. Gabriel also rode with him.

The opening verses of Sura Bani Israel describe this event thus:

"Glorified be He who carried His servant by night from the Mosque of Kaaba to the Mosque of Al-Aqsa (in Jerusalam) the neighbourhood whereof We have blessed, so that We might show him of our tokens. He, only He, is the Hearer the Seer."

This is all that the Quran mentions about the Ascension. The details appear in the 'traditions' of the holy Prophet (PBUH), there being 25 such 'traditions' concerning Meraj alone. According to these traditions, the holy Prophet (PBUH) stopped at Medina where he offered prayers and was informed by Gabriel that he would migrate to that place. Then Gabriel took him to Mount Sinai, then to Bethelhem where Prophet Jesus was born. The land journey ended at Al-Aqsa Mosque and Gabriel took him to Solomon's Temple where all those Prophets who had preceded him were present and they all offered prayer led by the holy Prophet (PBUH).

Thereafter, he was presented drinks in three different cups - one containing milk, the other alcohol and the third water. He picked up the one that contained water. Gabriel was pleased at the holy Prophet's (PBUH) choice of drinks and said that this was exactly according to the Divine Will.

Then appeared a ladder, by Divine order, spanning the earth and the heavens and the holy Prophet (PBUH) was led to the skies through this ladder. On the first sky, the man and the angel, i.e. the holy Prophet (PBUH) and Gabriel, stopped and the guarding angels enquired from Gabriel about the identity of the man accompanying him and when told that he was Prophet Mohammad (PBUH), who was summoned for an audience with the Almighty he was admitted in. No body saw how he was received in the presence of the Creator, the Omnipotent, Omniscient, Omnipresent Being, but, at least, the angels came to know that the 'light' in the form of Adam before whom they had prostrated themselves in

Primordium ('azal') had been granted the great honour of visiting the Creator Himself.

It is narrated, allegorically, in the Traditions that, on the first heaven, the holy Prophet (PBUH) was introduced by Gabriel to Adam, the precursor of mankind. Here the holy Prophet (PBUH) was shown an image of reward and punishment in the hereafter. The details of those observations are given in Hadith literature. The holy Prophet (PBUH) was conducted to various heavens where he met John the Baptist, Prophets Jesus, Joseph, Enoch, Aaron and Moses. On the Seventh heaven, where angels keep-on moving in and out of 'Bait-e-Mamour', "he met Prophet Abraham. Thereafter, the holy Prophet (PBUH) reached the 'last limit' beyond which even Gabriel could not proceed. The holy Prophet (PBUH) went ahead all by himself where he was granted the honour of audience with the Almighty. What transpired no one knows, but, according to hints available in the 'Traditions', prayers (originally, fifty times a day) were made obligatory and the verses 285 and 286 of Sura Baqra were revealed:

"The Prophet (PBUH) believes in that which has been revealed to him from his Lord and so do the 'believers'. Each one believes in Allah and His angels and His scriptures and His messengers—We make no distinction between any of His messengers—and they say:

We hear and we obey. Grant us Thy forgiveness, our Lord! To You is the journeying.

"Allah does not take to task a soul beyond its scope. For it is only that which it has earned and against it only that which it has deserved. Our Lord! condemn us not if we forget or miss the mark! Our Lord! Lay not on us such a burden as you laid on those before us! Our Lord! Impose not on us that which we have not the strength to bear! Pardon us, absolve us and have mercy on us! Thou, our Protector! give us victory over the disbelieving folk."

Also, it was indicated to the holy Prophet (PBUH) that, barring polytheism, all other sins can be hoped to be forgiven, reward for ten good deeds can be expected if only one good deed is intended and that an evil deed becomes punishable only when it is actually committed.

On way back, when Prophet Moses was informed by the holy Prophet (PBUH) about fifty times daily prayers, he advised that he should seek some remission from the Lord as based on his personal experience of the Jews, he could say that the followers of the holy Prophet (PBUH) would hardly be able to comply with such a heavy obligation. The holy Prophet (PBUH), therefore, represented to the Lord for remission and, ultimately, five-time daily prayers were fixed. On the return journey, as in the outward journey, he stopped at Jerusalem, where all the Prophets had assembled, and led the morning prayer. Therefore, he returned to Mecca riding the 'buraq'.

He spoke to Umme Hani about his heavenly journey and the observations. Although his cousin sister persuaded him not to talk publicly about this mysterious event, as it might provide the opponents yet another opportunity to falsify and vilify, the holy Prophet (PBUH) decided otherwise.

It was day-break and the Quraishites were coming to the precincts of the Kaaba. The holy Prophet (PBUH) arrived there and met Abu Jahl face to face. Tauntingly he enquired from the holy Prophet (PBUH) if there was something new or fresh to talk about. The holy Prophet (PBUH) merely said:

"Last night, I had been to the holy Land."

This startled Abu Jahl and he started shouting aloud to attract others' attention, and he told them about the holy Prophet's (PBUH) nocturnal visit to the holy Land at Jerusalem. When they all assembled, the holy Prophet (PBUH) narrated to them the entire incident of Ascension. But they all derided him. Abu Jahl, a cunning person that he was, went near Hazrat Abu Bakr and told him about the holy Prophet's (PBUH) Ascension. But the latter, instead of showing any surprise or hesitation, asserted that he believed in what the holy Prophet (PBUH) had narrated, as he knew that the latter received messages from the Lord in heavens. Hazrat Abu Bakr then rushed towards the holy Prophet (PBUH) who was surrounded by a jesting crowd of Quraishites. When, on his enquiry, the holy Prophet (PBUH) affirmed that he had narrated the incident of Ascension himself, Hazrat Abu Bakr expressed his belief in what he had said. Since, Hazrat Abu Bakr had visited the holy Land, he enquired about its prominent features which the holy Prophet (PBUH) described correctly, because the Almighty had enabled him at that time, to see Jerusalem again. Among those who were present at that time, there were a few others also who had visited the holy land. They were almost stunned to hear from the holy Prophet's (PBUH) mouth such a clear and correct description of the Land and in their heart of hearts, they believed that the holy Prophet (PBUH) had actually gone to Jerusalem overnight, but their intransigence stood in the way and they did not openly declare their belief in the holy Prophet (PBUH). It was only Hazrat Abu Bakr who kept on saying loudly, on hearing the detailed description of Jerusalem that the holy Prophet (PBUH) had spoken the truth. This earned him the title of 'Siddique' or one who acknowledged truth of the holy Prophet's (PBUH) version of Ascension although it, did not appeal to the sceptics. When the people of Mecca demanded further proof from the holy Prophet (PBUH), he told them that, on way to Jerusalem, he had seen a caravan carrying such and such goods and that one of their camels got frightened at the sight of the speeding 'buraque'. He further said that he had stopped beside a caravan, whose people were resting and fast asleep, at night and that he drank some water from their vessel and had left a tell-tale to remind them that some one had drunk water while they were asleep. When those caravans arrived, they confirmed the holy Prophet's (PBUH) words. But their mind still refused to believe the holy Prophet (PBUH).

It is a fact, beyond doubt, that the Ascension was physical as the very opening verse of Sura Bani Israel indicates, and that the Divine intention was to show to the holy Prophet (PBUH) some of His tokens, the greatest token being the nocturnal journey itself, during which the distance that could be covered in weeks from Mecca to Jerusalem was covered only in a few hours. Further, the journey in space from Jerusalem to the 'last limit' of the heavens, or galaxies, in a matter of hours and minutes, which was unthinkable then and is unthinkable even now when man has landed on the moon and is trying to travel after Mars and other planets, was the most astounding sign of Divine omnipotence. If God could create the entire universe just by saying 'let it be', He could, undoubtedly, make it possible for the holy Prophet (PBUH) to travel upto Him and return back to his abode on earth within a short span of night. In fact, it should be easier for today's man to believe in the Ascension because now that it is being considered possible to travel in space from planet to planet and galaxy to galaxy through harnessing the forces of nature, the question of the Creator Himself arranging for such a Journey for His Prophet (PBUH) should not be looked upon with doubt and suspicion.

For example, can human comprehension understand how the 'Companions of the cave' slept in a dark hollow place in a rock for well over a century. But this happened, as a few youths remained asleep for a number of years inside a cave while their dog waited outside. The Quran bears testimony to it. This relates to the period when the believers in Christianity were either burnt alive or stoned to death in the Roman empire. These youths had embraced Christianity and had made a public declaration of their faith in the city of Ephesus and had thereby incurred the wrath of the people and officials of the state. They were to be approached and punished. To escape this, they took refuge in a cave and supplicated to God " to bless them with His special care and set matters right for them." Their prayer was granted and conditions were made conducive for them to sleep in the cave for years on end. When they woke up, they asked themselves about the duration of their sleep. Some one thought that they slept only for a day or even less and then they themselves said that God alone knows how long they slept. Then they fell hungry and one of them went to the market, taking precaution that he would not be spotted by any one. He had a century-old silver coin to buy things which he offered to the shop-keeper in exchange for goods. His out-moded dress and the old silver coin aroused the shop-keeper's suspicion about his identity and a crowd collected around him and he was taken to the city official where he narrated the entire story of his sleep in the cave. During this period the Romans had embraced Christianity and given up idolatry. Therefore, no Christian was persecuted any longer in that city. According to the local legend about this incident, about two centuries had elapsed. When people went to the cave, the 'sleepers' saluted their Christian brethren and lay down whereafter they all expired. The Quran has neither specified the exact number of the 'sleepers' nor the period of their sleep. The following excerpt from the holy Quran throws light on the matter:

"Some say: They were three, their dog the fourth, and some say:

Five and their dog the sixth, guessing at random, and some say:

Seven, and their dog the eight. Say (O, Muhammad): My Lord is best aware of their number. None knows except a few. So, do not contend concerning them except outwardly and do not ask any one of them to say anything about them." (Sura Kahf - Verses 22).

Thus, the Quran clarifies that people will contend concerning their number but God alone knows best and also a few others who have not been specified.

Verse 25 of the same sura says:

"And they stayed in their cave for three hundred years and add nine."

The verse, immediately following the above one, says:

"(O, Prophet) Tell that God knows better how long they tarried in the Cave."

According to Hazrat Abdullah bin Abbas, the Quran does not mention that they lived in the cave for 309 years, but that it only refers to people's speculation about the duration of their stay and that the actual period is known only to God, just as people speculate about their correct number, the exact figure being only in God's knowledge.

The holy Quran also relates the incident of a pious man who, by God's command, came back to life after having been dead for a hundred years. This man may be either a saint or a prophet, who thought to himself, while passing by a devastated city whose population had been dead and houses demolished, how would God resuscitate this dead population. His soul was immediately taken by God's command and he remained dead for a century, whereafter he was brought back to life, by God's command, and he was questioned as to the period for which he remained dead. He answered:

"For a day, or even less, say, a few hours."

The Divine remark was conveyed to him:

"You remained dead for a hundred years. Now look at your food and drink which are still fresh. But, look at your donkey on which you were riding; even its skeleton has been eaten up by worms."

The saintly person must have felt perplexed at this extraordinary incident and when, by God's command, he saw his donkey being restored in its original condition, he exclaimed:

"Now I realise, God is capable of doing anything:"

Similarly, Prophet Abraham, who is the ancient ancestor of our holy Prophet (PBUH) too, once expressed his wish:

"My Lord! Let me see and observe how you enliven the dead."

"Do you not believe in life after death?" God asked him.

"I do believe my Lord! But my request stems from my earnestness to satisfy my heart and mind". - Prophet Abraham replied, whereupon he was asked to get hold of four birds and to train them like pets and then slaughter them and place a piece of the flesh of each of them on different hills and call them to come which they would do. He complied with the Divine instructions and saw with his own eyes of phenomenon of resurrecton of the dead, an experience which, apparently, defies all reasoning but which is an indisputable fact like the rising of the sun from the eastern horizon every morning.

All Convinced

Subsequent to the incident of 'Ascension', the polytheists of Mecca sent words to the holy Prophet (PBUH) that if he could come to them and answer satisfactorily a few questions, they would accept his faith. The holy Prophet (PBUH) went to meet them in the precincts of Kaaba, where the notables of Quraish, including Abu Jahl, Nazar bin Haris and Uqba bin Abu Moit, had assembled and looked over-whelmed with joy that they had, at long last, found a way to check mate the holy Prophet (PBUH), and were confident that they would have an upper hand, little realising that their fate had already been decided by the Almighty and they were doomed to fail in their nefarious endeavours to humble the holy Prophet (PBUH).

Addressing the holy Prophet (PBUH), they said that they had three questions to be answered by him. The first question related to the youths, who had disappeared a long time ago in history. The second concerned Hazrat Khizr and the third about that great traveller who had visited both the eastern and western fringes of the earth. The holy Prophet (PBUH) had never heard such questions before and he knew that these were prompted by people outside Mecca. In fact, the polytheists of Mecca had sent their representatives to the 'Rabbis' of the Jews who advised them to ask the aforesaid three questions, and if the holy Prophet (PBUH) answered them correctly then there was no doubt that he was a true Prophet of God. The holy Prophet (PBUH) promised to provide the answer the next day, hoping that Gabriel would tell him the correct answers. But, Gabriel did not turn up and the holy Prophet (PBUH) had no option but to procrastinate and ask for more time, to the utmost glee of the Quraishites. But Gabriel appeared on the third day which the holy Prophet (PBUH) was anxiously awaiting his arrival and counselled him not to promise, in future, that he would certainly do a thing but that he would do it if God willed. Thus, it was the Divine intention to instruct the followers of the holy Prophet (PBUH) that every work should be undertaken by pronouncing the words "God willing". Sura Kahf was revealed on this occasion which contained detailed answers of all the three questions and the holy Prophet (PBUH) recited this Sura before the notables of Quraish. The answer to the first question, concerning the 'Companions of the Cave,' has already been dealt with and discussed in the foregoing paragraph. The notables of Quraish were dumb founded and stunned when they heard the holy Prophet (PBUH) reciting Sura Kahf in his prophetic and appealing style which was a God given gift to him as to all other holy Prophets.

While reciting the said Sura, the holy Prophet (PBUH) read out the following verse whereupon the polytheists glanced in silence at each other as if they were life-less dummies:

"And be mindful of the Day (Resurrection) when He will say:

Call those partners of Mina whom you pretended. Then they will cry unto them, but they will not hear their prayer, and We shall set a gulf of doom between them."

The polytheists of Mecca, who were confident that only the Jewish 'Rabbis' knew the answers because only their religious literature contained these questions, were completely flabbergasted, particularly Nazr bin Haris and Uqba bin Moeet, as these were the two persons who had approached the 'Rabbis'. Further the same Sura describes the attitutde and entire outlook of the infidels in these words:

"Those who disbelieve contend with falsehood in order to reflect the Truth thereby, and take Our revelations and warnings as a jest.

"And who does greater wrong than the one who has been reminded of the revelations of his Lord and yet he turns away from them forgetting what his own hands have done for (the Day of Judgement). We have placed coverings so that they do not understand and in their ears is a deafness. And though you call them to the guidance, they can never be led aright.

"And thy Lord is the Forgiver and Merciful. Had He taken them to task for their deeds immediately, He would have hastened on the doom for them; but theirs is an appointed time from which they will find no escape."

Thereafter, in order to make the notables of Quraish take lesson from God's wrath that descended on the settlements of Sheba, Thamud, Madian and the people of Lot, the Divine revelation said:

"And all those townships! We destroyed them when they did wrong, and We appointed a fixed time for their destruction."

Education for All

About Khizr, the Divine revelation narrated:

"And when Moses said to his servant, I will not give up until I reach the point where the two rivers meet, even if I have to march on for ages. And when they reached the given point, they forgot their fish which, being free, took its way in the waters.

"And when they had gone further, Moses asked his servant to bring their breakfast, because the journey had been quite tiresome.

"The servant said: Did you not see when we took refuge on the rock, I forgot the fish, and none but Satan caused me to forget to mention it, and it plunged into the waters by a marvel.

"Moses said that that was the place they had been seeking. So, they retreated their steps again.

"There they found one of Our slaves who had been given mercy from Us, and who had been granted knowledge from us.

"Moses asked him if he could follow him to learn what he had been taught.

"That person said: You can not bear with me, because how can you bear with me when you can not comprehend my knowledge.

"Moses said: God willing you shall find me patient and I will not argue with you.

"He said: If you go with me, you will not ask me concerning anything until I myself mention of it to you."

The person about whom this narration revolves was Hazrat Khizr, as recorded in a Tradition on the authority of Hazrat Abdullah bin Abbas who heard it from Abi bin Kaab. According to this Tradition, once while Prophet Moses was preaching, he claimed that he was the "most knowledgeable person." This assertion on his part displeased the Almighty, Who indicated to him that he should set out in search of a person who will be present at the meeting point of two rivers. On further enquiry by Prophet Moses, regarding any particular sign to locate that person, the Divine instruction was conveyed to him that he should take alongwith him a fish which will disappear in water at the exact location of the person concerned.

When the two (Prophet Moses and Hazrat Khizr) started their journey together, the latter made a hole in the boat wherein they were crossing a river. Thereupon Prophet Moses uttered in surprise:

"You have drilled a hole in the ship so that all the folk and the ship get drowned. Indeed you have done a horrid thing."

Hazrat Khizr remarked:

"Did I not tell you that you can not bear with me?"

Prophet Moses entreated:

"Be not angry with me as I forgot and do not be hard upon me for my fault."

At the next stage of their journey, they came across a boy whom Hazrat Khizr killed. Prophet Moses could not restrain his horror at this act and he spoke out:

"You killed an innocent lad although he had not shed any one's blood. Indeed you have done something unreasonable."

Hazrat Khizr replied:

"Had I not told you that you will not be able to bear with me."

Prophet Moses assured:

"If I ask you after this concerning anything, you can part company with me. You have received an excuse from me."

The two journeyed on till they came to the folk of a certain township, whom they asked for food but they refused to be hospitable. There, the twain found a wall on the point of falling into ruin. Hazrat Khizr repaired it whereupon Prophet Moses said that had the former wanted, he could have taken payment for it.

This exasperated Khizr who told Prophet Moses:

"This is the parting between you and me. I will tell you the interpretation of that which you could not bear with patience."

As for the ship, Hazrat Khizr explained, it belonged to poor people working on the river and I wished to mar it as there was a king behind them who was taking every ship by force. As for the lad, his parents were 'believers' and I feared that he would be a source of oppression for his parents on account of his disbelief and rebellious nature in future. I thought that the Lord will give them a better substitute for the lad, who would be of good habits and full of kindness. Regarding the wall, it belonged to two orphan boys in the city and there was a treasure hidden underneath the wall. Since their father was a righteous person, the Lord intended that the boys, on coming of age, should bring forth their treasure as a reward from their Lord.

In the end, Hazrat Khizr said:

"I did nothing according to my own discretion, but on God's command."

Now, the polytheists of Mecca had received answers to their two questions and only one question relating to a globe-trotting traveller remained to be answered. The holy Quran disclosed the name of this traveller:

"They will ask you about Zul Qarnain; Say, I recite to you something about him."

Hearing this, the heart of the polytheists started sinking and their faces were filled with gloom, as the last weapon in their armoury to defeat the holy Prophet (PBUH) had also proved ineffectual.

Old Example

The holy Quran described Zul Qurnain as a powerful and resourceful person. To. start with his campaigns, he took an expedition to the West and reached the setting-place of the sun, setting in a murky sea. There, he saw a people regarding whom the Almighty authorised him to either punish them or treat them with kindness. Thereafter, he set out on another expedition till he reached the rising-place of the sun and found it rising on a people for whom there was no shelter therefrom. In yet another expedition, he came between two mountains where he built a barrier and a wall of molten iron and copper to protect the natives of that land from the raids and pillage at the hands of Gog and Magog.

Although the infidels of Mecca had heard the replies to their questions, yet they did not turn towards the faith and Divine guidance because of the covering that enveloped their hearts, and they dispersed quietly.

How unfortunate were these people who saw the glowing and beaming face of the holy Prophet, (PBUH) heard his angelic voice, knew his demeanour and polite behaviour, were aware of his high and honourable pedigree, had a first-hand experience of his selflessness, sacrifice, noble conduct and kindness towards all and had observed his steadfastness and unflinching faith in his mission, and yet they did not enter the fold of Islam; while others who came to him from far off places, declared allegiance to him at first sight!

Apart from the pressure on Banu Hashim and the persecution of the Companions of the Holy Prophet, a good deal of criticism was levelled against the Prophet's claim that he had received revelations from God—in fact against the very idea of revelation itself. This criticism was directed along four different channels.

Firstly, Muhammad was subjected to mental torture by suggesting other explanations of his religious experience than that it was revelation from God.

Secondly, the opponents could not believe that a human being who did not claim to possess any supernatural power could ever become the messenger of God.

Thirdly, if a human being were to be elevated at all to this exalted position, there were so many other persons who were richer and far more influential than Muhammad. Why was it, the sceptics argued, that God ignored all of them altogether and crowned the helpless Qurayshite orphan with prophethood?

Lastly, Muhammad had nothing extraordinary, nothing dramatic, to parade to substantiate his claim to prophethoood.

We will consider these allegations in the following pages and will note the way in which the Holy Qur'an repudiates them.

The Conspiracy

The commonest allegation against Muhammad was that he was a majnun, that is, possessed by a Jinn. They also suggested that he was a kahin, or soothsayer, a Sahir, that is, magician or sorcerer, and sha'ir, that is a poet.

It is significant to note in this connection that the common allegations which the Meccans levelled against Muhammad are repeated even to this very day. Professor Macdonald has attempted, though in vain, to explain Muhammad's prophethood in terms of epilepsy and psycho-pathology. He also believes that Muhammad was a genius. But this aspect is not well defined. The key to Muhammad is that "he was a poet" of the old Arab type without much of poetic skill, with all his being given to the prophetic side of poetry, and that he had a "strange jumble of Jewish and Christian conceptions" as material for his prophetic use.

The view of Macdonald that Muhammad was a poet is slightly different from that of Muir who ventures the suggestion that the supernatural influence, which appears to have acted upon the soul of the Arabian prophet, may have proceeded from the "Evil One" and his emissaries, yet the spirit in which the prophetic consciousness of Muhammad manifests itself is not the same. Macdonald asserts that just as Hassan the poet had his female jinni who overpowered him and pressed verses out of him, so Muhammad had his companion (qarin) who was the source of his inspiration. Muhammad, he continues, is not really a prophet in any exalted sense: "I know nowhere in the Semitic world any appearance like that of the great prophets of the Hebrew. "Rather, this first of all Moslem is in part a combination of 'soothsayer' adviser and admonisher, and a hurler of magical formulae against his enemies, although possessed of ideas which raised him above the common place and suggest that Muhammad a devout soul, if ever there was one and a mystic inspite of his creed—was adrift himself on that sea, and was nearing that shore."

Attempts of Revolt

I have given long excerpts from Macdonald's book in order to give an idea that inspite of the great difference of time there has been no change in the nature of the allegations hurled at the Prophet. The modern critics of Islam, like the Meccans of the olden days, believe that what the Prophet claims to be a revelation or the word of Allah is nothing else but the frenzied expression of the ecstatic state of his mind.

The Holy Qur'an has vehemently refuted this charge and has explained that the utterances of the Holy Prophet (peace be upon him) are the revelations of the Lord and their nature and contents provide a bold challenge to those who attribute his prophetic expressions to some base origin, at times to the mental throes of a dreaming reformer, at others to the effusion of a frenzied poet or the incoherent drivellings of an insane man. The Holy Qur'an categorically repudiates, for instance, the allegation that the Prophet is a poet: We have not taught him poetry nor is it meet for him." At another place the Holy Qur'an explains the reasons why it is absurd to call Muhammad a poet. A poet is commonly a mental rambler who tries to transform into beautiful verse his wayward whims and fleeting emotions. He is primarily concerned with abstract and remote issues and speculations which have no bearing on the practical problems of human life.

"As for poets, it is the erring who follow them. Hast thou not seen how they stray in every valley."

Thus, whatever the poet says cannot be consistent and closely knit. Being an expression of the fleeting emotions it is impossible to find coherence and harmony in the views expressed by a poet. Moreover, there is a world of difference between the practical life of a poet and his poetical utterances. His poetry merely expresses his emotional moods and therefore a poet is not required to transform his thoughts into living facts; "And how they (the poets) say that which they do not."

A prophet, on the other hand, is a practical reformer. He says what he means and means what he says. Whatever he professes is also transmuted by him into practical reality. In his great personality, the ultimate values which he preaches take flesh and blood.

Besides, there is complete harmony between the various components of the Prophet's teaching, each message being in entire unison with the whole of his revelation. There is nothing inconsistent, nothing superfluous.

Lastly, unlike poets, the actual impact of the Prophet's activity is the purification and enoblement of human beings. A spiritual Armageddon is fought out by the prophets on the plains of history. Humanity, rent with national antagonism and riven with class-conflicts and threatened by the tyranny of materialism, is freed by the prophets from the servitude of these evil forces and learns to live as the family of God. The Prophets restore peace amongst the different sections of the human race and bring harmony within man. The greed, selfishness, love for material gains, lust for power—all these base urges are purified and in their place human beings learn to live as self-less and God-fearing men whose uppermost desire to serve humanity and weed out corruption and tyranny from human society.

Can a poet achieve all this? Is he capable of expressing something which is consistent and is not in collision with any other aspects of his own preachings? The reply of history to this query seems to be conclusive and the attestation of human experience abundantly clear—and both of them in the negative.

The allegation that the Holy Prophet was under the influence of the evil spirits has also been categorically repudiated by the Holy Qur'an. How is it that a man who is controlled by a demonic being or a supernatural power of low grade, quite other than the Power that reigns over the universe, can set for himself the sublime purpose of destroying the spell of superstitions which had been interposed between man and his Creator, of restoring the rational and sacred idea of Divinity amidst the chaos of material and disfigured gods of idolatry and of effecting a moral regeneration of a society which had touched a low ebb of degradation, and of giving to humanity a superb code of conduct which does not guide man merely in the sphere of individual righteousness but also in the spheres of politics and economics, law, and morality. It is impossible for anyone who studies the life and character of Muhammad, who knows what he taught and how he lived, to feel anything but reverence for that noble soul—the greatest of the apostles of Allah. Can a person under the control of an evil spirit develop such deep consciousness of his inner self, and all its different aspects, the consciousness of God Almighty with His numerous attributes, the awareness of the sublimity of his mission, and the stern obstacles that stood in his way, the awareness of the qualities of his friends and the stubbornness of his foes—and yet perfect harmony within himself? Such rare qualities of head and heart are never to be found in those who are under the influence of evil spirits. History shows not a single example of such-like persons whose message created one of the most balanced and noblest civilisations of the world. The Holy Qur'an says:

> Shall I inform you upon whom the devils descend? They descend on every sinful, false one. They listen eagerly, but most of them are liars. (xxvi: 221-223)

Similarly, the Qur'an also vehemently repudiates the allegation that Muhammad speaks under the influence of the jinn. "Have they not thought them that their comrade is in no way under the influence of the jinn. He is but a plain warner." Here "comrade" stands for the Holy Prophet. The Qur'an exhorts the people to reflect if a man of such great eminence and wisdom, whose whole career was the faithful expression of a fine nature, free of every trace of self-seeking, vanity or affectation, a man of loving personality, of transparent candour and integrity, who successfully guided humanity not only in one aspect of life but in all sectors of life, could achieve such a spectacular success under the influence of the jinn. Never in history has a man, influenced by the spirits, been able to attain such glory as Muhammad did in the short span of twenty-three years of his prophethood. Coming from a land and a people who had no glorious past of which they could be proud, he elevated them to the heights of eminence, shattered the great empires, undermined the position of long-established religions, remoulded the souls of countless men and women and built up a whole new world—the world of Islam. How can any sane person conceive that this great revolution, which not only changed the map of the world, but also radiated morality and expanded the frontiers of knowledge, could have been brought about by a man who was under the spell of the jinn.

The fact that the opponents who brought forth such allegations were not unanimous in their accusations, is a clear proof of their falsehood. They were thoughtlessly slinging mud at the Prophet (peace be upon him) in the hope that some of it might stick. This is the reason why they could not follow any firm line of criticism. They said all sorts of things. Sometimes they said that he was a poet; at other times they declared his words to be those of a soothsayer or of a magician. It is indeed quite strange that a person who was unlettered, who had no knowledge of the ancient scriptures, should have been the one through whom the world received a book like the Qur'an which in its sublime composition and its incomparable literary excellence speaks for itself as an irrefutable proof of its Divine origin.

There was also the charge that the Prophet was just an ordinary person who walked in the bazaars, who had his wives and children, that there was nothing unusual or supernatural about him. The Holy Qur'an has discussed this point at some length and conclusively shown that prophets, who are sent to guide humanity to righteousness, are human beings and thus no Divinity should be attributed to them. Indeed, the Qur'an itself abounds in statements which stress that Muhammad was essentially a human being:

> Say: I am only a human being like you. My Lord inspires me that your God is only One God. (xviii: 110)

> Say (unto them O Muhammad): I am only a human being like you. It is inspired in me that your God is One God, therefore take the straight path unto Him. Seek forgiveness of Him. (xli: 6)

The Holy Qur'an has also mentioned the reason why a prophet should necessarily be raised from among human beings. The Prophet is sent to guide humanity, a function which can be performed only by a human being. He should live as a man, enjoying the pleasures and suffering the ills of human existence, so that those around him could follow in his footsteps. People should be able to see in his personality a living embodiment of virtue and piety. His life should be able to manifest the Attributes of the Creator. His love and concern for humanity should be sublime. He reflects the ideal pattern of human existence. This purpose can be achieved only if a prophet, as human being, exemplifies that pattern in his actual life. It is only as a human being that he could show the right path to the people and could inspire in them the religious devotion and piety.

There is a misconception under which people have been labouring since time immemorial that a person who claims no divine powers for himself cannot be deputed by God to reform and regenerate the human race. The Holy Qur'an has winnowed out this mistaken notion and has pointed out that the angels, who do not share human feelings and sentiments, cannot prove themselves to be good guides for humanity. Human beings can learn from the actions and practical wisdom of those alone who share human feelings and appreciate the different problems of human life. It is human beings alone, therefore, who have been deputed to deliver to humanity the words of God and to explain their practical implications by leading their lives in perfect accord with the behests of the Creator. Whatever the prophets say or do is ideal in every respect, because they live in constant fellowship with the Great Reality. The Holy Qur'an says:

> And naught prevented mankind from believing when the guidance came unto them save that they said: Hath Allah sent a mortal as (His) messenger? Say: If there were in the earth angels walking secure, we had sent down for them from heaven an angel as messenger.
>
> (xvii: 94—95)

These verses clearly show that a human being alone is competent to guide humanity because his life offers them a practical guidance. Since this world is primarily inhabited by human beings and it is for their regeneration that the prophets are sent, human beings alone can therefore successfully accomplish this great task.

At another place, the Holy Qur'an states that even if this task was assigned to the angels, they would present themselves before humanity in the garb of mortals, because it is only in the form of human beings that their lives can provide lessons for their guidance:

> They say: Why has not an angel been sent down unto him. If We sent down an angel, then the matter would be judged; no further time would be allowed them (for reflections). Had We appointed an angel (Our messenger). We assuredly would have made him a man. (vi: 8-9)

Another line of propaganda adopted by the opponents of the Prophet to ridicule his revelations was to assert that the revelations were completely human production, the work either of Muhammad himself or that of his human assistants or these were merely the stories of the past. The Holy Qur'an has repudiated this charge in the following words:

> Those who disbelieve say: This is naught but a lie which he hath invented, and other folk have helped him in it, so that they have produced a slander and a lie. And they say: Fables of the men of old which he had written down so that they are dictated to him morning and evening. Say (unto them, O Muhammad): He Who knoweth the secret of the heavens and those of the earth hath revealed it. Verily, He is Ever-Forgiving, Merciful. (xxv: 4-6)

The charge has been quoted repeatedly in other verses of the Holy Qur'an in different ways:

> And We know well what they say: Only a man teacheth him. The speech of him at whom they falsely hint is outlandish, and this is clear Arabic speech.
>
> Verily, those who disbelieve the revelation of Allah, Allah guideth them not and theirs will be a painful doom.
>
> (The Prophet invents no lie) only they invent falsehood who believe not Allah's revelations, and (only) they are liars. (xvi: 103-104)

Amongst the various attempts to deride the Qur'an, it was one of the most powerful charges. It is significant that it has been summarily dismissed by saying that it is nothing but a bare lie . The charge is so foolish and hollow that it hardly deserves any consideration.

The persons who have been referred to in this connection are Jabir, Yasir, Aish, or Ya'ish, Qais, Addas. They were the helpless slaves of powerful Arab masters. It is indeed strange hat these persons who had been allegedly teaching Muhammad (peace be upon him) the craft of prophethood and had been preparing him for this avocation by narrating to him anecdotes of the past should have been among the first to believe in the divine source of the Qur'an and should have been willing to suffer persecutions at the hands of their masters for this very belief.

Moreover, none of them was an Arab by descent. They were all aliens who had been sold as slaves in the markets of Arabia. It is indeed surprising that non-Arabs should have been able to produce a book like the Holy Qur'an which in respect of the elegance of its language, the superb structure of its words and sentences, in the peculiar style of its narration, in the extraordinary beginning and ending of its verses, in its flow of thought, in the introduction of parables and description of events, in the forms of its admonitions and warnings and in the manner of its reasoning and arguments, is unparalleled in the whole range of human history. The composition of the Qur'an, in spite of its concern with a variety of subjects, is remarkable. The Arabs were accustomed either to prose or to poetry. Their prose was divided into rhymed and unrhymed. The intellectuals practised in verse. As for prose, its use was for the common people. The Qur'an did not resemble either the prose or the poetry of the period, for the ending of its verses were different from the rhymes of poetry and the saj' of prose. The Holy Qur'an, in fact, introduced a new style of expression which was not within the reach of the common man.

Thus, every sensible man must acknowledge Muhammad's unalloyed sincerity in his claim that what he called revelation was not the secret learning from the Christian slaves, but that it came to him from God alone. "The Qur'an," observes Harry Gaylord Dorman, "is a literal revelation of God, dictated to Muhammad by Gabriel, perfect in every letter. It is an everpresent miracle witnessing to itself and to Muhammad, the Prophet of God. Its miraculous quality resides partly in its style, so perfect and lofty that neither men nor jinn could produce a single chapter to compare with its briefest chapter, and partly in its content of teachings, prophesies about the future and amazingly accurate information such as the unlettered Muhammad could never have gathered of his own accord."

Another line of attack was that Muhammad (peace be upon him) was not the sort of person to whom revelations should have come. He was not sufficiently competent for that. The Arabs in general could not imagine that a man who was a posthumous child and had been deprived even of the love of the mother in early childhood, who had lost the support of the important men of his tribe, who had no riches to display, could be elevated to the position of a prophet. They thought that prophethood should have been bestowed upon one of the wealthy chiefs of the tribes:

> And they say: If only this Quran had been revealed to some great man of the two towns (Mecca and Ta'if).
> (xiii: 31)

In refutation of this criticism, the Holy Qur'an points out that prophethood is a special favour of God and He knows well on whom it should be bestowed. No human being, therefore, has any right to question the choice of Allah and no one is entitled to dictate to Him whom to choose and whom to ignore.

> Is it they who apportion their Lord's mercy? (xiii: 32)

The unbelievers said that they would not believe in the prophethood of Muhammad unless they were also enabled to enjoy the prophetic experiences themselves:

> And when a token cometh unto them, they say: We will not believe until we are given that which Allah's messengers are given. (vi: 125)

The Qur'an spurns it as a fantastic demand and says that Allah is the best to decide correctly on whom His favour should be showered. Allah knoweth best whom to endow with His Message?

The Qur'an stresses this by pointing out:

> And thus have We inspired in thee (O Muhammad) a spirit of our Command. Thou knewest not what the Scripture was, nor what the Faith. But We have made it a light whereby We guide whom We will of our bondmen. And thou verily dost guide unto a right path. (xiii: 52)

Then in the chapter entitled Jumu'ah (Congregation) this point has been further elucidated:

> He it is Who hath sent among the unlettered ones a messenger of their own, to recite unto them His revolutions and to purify them and to teach them the Scripture and Wisdom, though heretofore they were indeed in error manifest.

> Along with others of them who have not yet joined them, He is the Mighty, the Wise. That is the bounty of Allah, which He giveth unto whom He willeth. (xii: 2-4)

The last group of opponents comprised those persons who expected revelation to have supernatural accompaniments observable by all. When they saw that Muhammad (peace and blessings of Allah be upon him) was no more than a person walking in the bazaars like all other human beings, procuring articles for his daily use, protecting himself against the cold blasts of the winter and the scorching heat of the summer, they were attempting to establish that a man who shared the life of other mortals and had nothing unusual about him, could not be a messenger of God. For them, a prophet was necessarily superhuman who had hardly anything in common with ordinary human beings. The disbelievers, therefore, expressed their doubts about the prophethood of Muhammad and said:

> What a strange messenger is he, that he eateth food and walketh in the streets, why is not an angel sent down unto him to be a warner with him?
>
> Or (why is not) a treasure thrown down unto him, or why hath he not a garden from whence to eat? And the evil-doers say: You are but following a man bewitched. (xxv: 7-8)

In the chapter entitled Banu Isra'il the demand for the supernatural signs in Muhammad (peace be upon him) are even more pressing:

> They say: We shall not give thee credence till thou causest for us to bubble up from the earth a spring;
>
> Or until thou hast a garden of palm and vine, and thou causest in the midst of it rivers to gush forth;

> Or until thou causest the heaven to fall upon us as fragments as thou hast said, or thou producest God and angels ascending;
>
> Or until thou hast a house adorned with gold, or thou ascendest into the heaven;
>
> Nor shall We give credence to thy ascent until thou bringest down to us a writing which we may read. (xvii: 90-93)

There is some variation in the precise nature of what is expected or demanded of Muhammad (peace and blessings of Allah be upon him), but underlying assumption is that a prophet should possess some supernatural powers by virtue of which he should be able to suspend or disrupt the working of the natural order whenever he desires. In answer to these demands, God commanded Muhammad to announce:

> Say: Glory be to my Lord! I am nothing but a human being (sent) as a messenger. (xvii: 93)

This verse beautifully explains the reason why the demand that the Divine can be manifested in time only through a serious disturbance of the natural order is foolish. Muhammad is only a warner and as such does not command the supernatural powers of the universe. The sudden bubbling up of springs from the earth, the gushing forth of rivers, the falling down of the sky and the abrupt appearance of a magnificent building made of pure gold, are not the essential accompaniments of a true prophet. On the contrary, the qualifications of a true prophet are his extremely pious and virtuous life, his perfect integrity, his shining and spotless character, his selflessness, his love for humanity and his unfailing and sustained devotion to the cause of Allah and His noble teachings.

The Holy Qur'an has explained this point at numerous places. In the first instance, it emphasises that the performance of miracles does not lie in the hand of the Prophet:

> And it was not given to any messenger that he should bring a portent save by Allah's leave but when Allah's commandment cometh (the cause) is judged aright, and the followers of vanity will then be lost. (1: 78)

The Prophet himself confesses his inability to perform miracles at his own sweet will, because it rests with the Almighty God. He says in very clear terms that the Prophet is only a messenger of God who honestly carries out the behests of his Master:

> Say (O Muhammad to the unbelievers): I say not unto you (that) I possess the treasure of Allah, not that I have knowledge of the unseen, and I say not unto you: verily, I am an angel. I follow only that which is inspired in me. (vi: 50)

> Say: For myself I have no power to benefit, nor power to hurt, save that which Allah willeth. Had I knowledge of the unseen I should have gathered abundance of wealth, and adversity would not touch me. I am but a warner, and a bearer of good tidings unto folk who believe. (vii: 188)

"It must be said," observes Ameer 'Ali "to the credit of the disciples of the Arabian Teacher that they never called for a miracle from their Master. They—scholars, merchants, and soldiers— looked to the moral evidences of his mission. They ranged themselves round the friendless preacher at the sacrifice of all their worldly interests and worldly hopes, and adhered to him through life and death with a devotion to human personality to which there is scarcely a parallel in the history of the world."

He further elucidates this point by adding:

> In an age when miracles were supposed to be ordinary occurrences at the back of the commonest saint, when the whole atmosphere was surcharged with super naturalism, not only in Arabia, but in the neighbouring countries where civilization had made a far greater progress, the great Pioneer of rationalism unhesitatingly replies to the miracle-seeking heathens—"God has not sent me to work wonders; He has sent me to preach to you. My Lord be praised! Am I more than a man sent as an apostle?"...No extraordinary pretensions, no indulgence in hyperbolical language, no endeavour to cast a glamour around his character or personality. "I am only a preacher of God's words, the bringer of God's message to mankind," repeats he always. From first to last no expression escapes him "which could be construed into a request for human worship" [The Qur'an, Ixii: 1-10]; from first to last there is unvarying soberness of expression, which, considering the age and surroundings, is more marvellous; from first to last the tone is one of simple, deep humility before the Creator.

The Prophet disclaims every power of working wonders and bases the claim for the truth of his divine mission entirely upon his teachings. He never resorts to the miraculous to assert his influence or to reinforce his warnings. It is recorded in Hadith that some of the Prophet's companions took the eclipse of the sun as a disturbance of the natural order on the death of his son Ibrahim. He plainly told his followers that the sun and the moon observed the commands of Allah and they had nothing to do with the death of his son. He emphatically remarked: "Indeed the sun and the moon are two out of the numerous signs of Allah. They do no eclipse due to birth or death of anyone. When you find them in this state, pray to Allah and celebrate His glory.

Instead of creating a halo of awe and mystery around himself, the Prophet appeals to the inner consciousness and credulity.

"Look around yourself (the Qur'an says in effect), this wonderful world, the sun, the moon and the stars, holding their swift silent courses in the blue vault of heaven, the law and the system prevailing in the universe; the rain-drops falling to revive the parched earth into life; the ships moving across the ocean, beladen with what is profitable to mankind; the beautiful palm covered with its golden fruit—are these the handiwork of your wooden or stone gods?"

"Fools! do you want a sign when the whole creation is full of the signs of God? The structure of your body, how wonderfully complex, how beautifully regulated; the alternations of night and day, and of life and death; your sleeping and awakening; your desire to accumulate from the abundance of God; the winds driving abroad the pregnant clouds as the forerunners of the Creator's mercy; the variety of the human race, and yet their close affinity; fruits, flowers, animals, human brings themselves—are these not signs enough of the presence of a Master Mind?"

The proofs of Muhammad's truth are not philosophically recondite. They do not require any great or profound speculative power to apprehend them. If they did, it would be extremely unfortunate for the masses of mankind—the common people who must of necessity be hewers of wood and drawers of water. To see and feel the force and cogency of some of these proofs demands to an extent the cessation of a strictly philosophic struggle with problems, and the exercise instead of what one calls "wise passiveness" along with the possession of sundry moral virtues such as reverence, candour, and openness of mind to evidence when it is presented ab intra, as well as ab extra. To the Prophet Muhammad, as to the seers of the past, it was not only through intellectual scrutiny that they could find "the secret of the universe" but through honest thinking and making use of a heart that watches and receives. The Holy Qur'an has beautifully expressed this state of mind in the following words:

> Say (unto them, O Muhammad): I exhort you unto one thing only: that ye awake, for Allah's sake, by twos and singly, and then reflect, (xxiv: 46)

But to all the exhortations of the Qur'an, the Quraysh turned a deaf ear. They were blind to the signs of God, deaf to the call of the Prophet towards righteousness and towards shunning corruption and abominations. In the language of the Qur'an they....

> "have hearts wherewith they understand not, and have eyes wherewith they see not, and have ears wherewith they hear not. They are as cattle—nay they are worse! These are the neglectful!" (vii: 179)

Then the Holy Qur'an also points out the fact that the demand of the unbelievers for miracles was not based on sincerity. The noble life of the Holy Prophet and the sublimity of his Divine message are sufficient to convince any sincere man that Muhammad is a true prophet of God. It is the vanity of the infidels, their grudge against his teachings and their inherited bias that prompted them to make such fantastic demands. Had they been sincere in their quest for truth they would have found ample proofs to believe in the prophethood of Muhammad:

> And those who have no knowledge say: Why doth not Allah speak unto us, or some sign come unto us? Even thus, as they now speak, speake those (who were) before them. Their hearts are all alike. We have made clear the revelations for people who are sure. Verily We have sent thee (Muhammad) with the truth, a bringer of glad tidings and a warner. (ii: 118-119)

In reply to the pressing demand for miracles, the Quran says that the extraordinary pious life of Muhammad and the wonderful Book revealed to him are themselves the two great miracles which testify to the truth of his claim. Is it short of a miracle that a helpless man, having no material resources, braves for many years the hatred of his people, without any selfish motive whatsoever, and when people rally round him, instead of making them his own bondsmen, he persuades them to bow down before Allah, the sole Master of the universe? Then this very person, who had no schooling whatsoever, presents to the people a Book, which is all wisdom, which contains a code of laws, a manual of prayer and ethics, and is reverenced to this day by a great portion of the human race, as a miracle of elegance of style, of sublimity of message and of truth. These are the great miracles; and miracles indeed these are. The Holy Qur'an stresses this point:

> And they say: Why are not portents sent down upon him from his Lord? Say, portents are with Allah only and I am but a plain warner.
>
> Is it not enough for them that we have sent down unto thee the Scripture which is read unto them? Verily, herein is mercy, and a reminder for the folk who believe. (xxix: 50-51)

In these verses, the Holy Qur'an is claimed to be the greatest miracle of Muhammad which pours forth in an inspired tongue "all the revelations of nature, conscience and prophecy. Ask you a greater miracle than this. O unbelieving people! then to have your own tongue closed as the language of that incomparable Book, one piece of which puts to shame all your golden poesy and suspended songs to covey the tidings of universal mercy, the warnings to pride and tyranny."

The Holy Qur'an further reveals that the advent of Muhammad is not unexpected. All the prophets and the revealed Books that preceded him proclaimed his glorious coming, sang his praise, exhorted their followers to obey him, prophesied extraordinary and unparalleled reforms and wonders to be worked by him, announced the sublimity and perfection of his teachings and declared themselves to be the simple harbingers of the final dispensation, destined for Muhammad:

> Is it not a token for them that the doctors of the children of Israel know it? (xxvi: 197)

> And they say: If only he would bring us a miracle from his Lord! Hath not there come unto them the proof of what is in the former Scriptures? (xx: 133)

The Qur'an also reveals the fact that the disbelievers were pressing for miracles, not because they were sincere in their demand, but because they wanted to subject Muhammad and his followers to mental torture by talking all sorts of foolish things. Amidst all kinds of doubts and misgivings, when they found themselves drifting to Reality, their obstinacy and self-interests stood in their way. They were unwilling to abandon their religion, because they knew that it would deprive them of so many sources of expolitation and self-aggrandisement. They realised that with the acceptance of Islam as their code of life they would be required to exercise so many restraints on their untamed lusts and surrender so many material benefits which they had been enjoying since long by unjust and immoral methods. They had been avoiding Islam purposely and had been trying to check its tidal wave and in this they actually had ulterior motives. Even if miracles were performed before them, they would attribute some low motive to them in order to belittle their value as a sign of Allah's power.

The Holy Qur'an is replete with examples showing that when miracles were shown by the Prophets, the stubborn amongst the unbelievers brushed them aside by telling people that they were nothing but feats of magic. For instance, when the prophet Moses performed miracles the unbelievers tauntingly remarked that they were merely magical tricks with the help of which he wanted to dupe them:

> But When our tokens came unto them, plain to see, they said: This is mere magic.

> And they denied them, though their souls acknowledged them, for spite and arrogance. Then see the nature of the consequence for the wrong-doers.
>
> (xxvii: 13-14)

In the same way, when miracles were shown at the hand of the Holy Prophet, unbelievers rejected them outright and said it was just a magic:

> Then turned he away in pride and said: This is naught else than magic fram the old. (xxiv: 23-24)

In this verse, Allah has also given the reason why unbelievers did not come to the fold of Islam. It was their arrogance and spite which kept them away from adopting the path of righteousness.

Such was the obstinacy of unbelievers that when the moon was split in twain by Allah at the gesture of Muhammad, they paid no heed to it and overlooked it altogether by saying that it was just an illusion.

> The hour drew nigh and the moon was rent it twain. And if they behold a portent they turn away and say: Prolonged illusion. They denied everything the Truth and followed their own lusts; and every affair is settled.
>
> (iv: 1-3)

The Qur'an further explains that since the unbelievers were fanatics and their vision were cramped and narrow, they could not, therefore, judge wisely between right and wrong. The portents and signs of God, however manifest, had no appeal for them, since their reasoning faculties had become almost dead due to arrogance which they had been constantly showing in their attitude towards the Messenger of Allah:

> Never came unto them a sign of the signs of Allah, but they did not turn away from it. (vi: 4)

The Holy Qur'an again points out their stubbornness in clearer words:

> Had We sent down unto thee (O Muhammad) a Writing upon parchment so that they could feel it with their hands, those who disbelieve would have said: This is naught else than magic. (vi: 7)

Apart from some of the above assertions, aspersions were cast on Muhammad's motives. The unbelievers tried to convince people, though vainly, that the religious mission of Muhammad, in respect of which he claimed to be actuated by the Command of Allah, had some material interests. He, with the help of these religious tactics, wanted to usurp power and prestige and gain pre-eminence over them. The Qur'an emphatically refute all such motives which were attributed to Muhammad and insisted again and again that he was only a warner that his function is simply to warn people and that he had no axe of his own to grind in this sacred cause:

> Say (O Muhammad unto mankind); I ask of you no reward for this, and I am no imposter. Lo! it is naught else than a reminder for all peoples. And ye will come in time to know the truth thereof. (xxviii: 86)

> Say (unto them, O Muhammad): whatever reward I might have asked of you is yours. My reward is with Allah only. He is the witness over all things. (xxxiv: 47)

The authentic records of the biography of the Holy Prophet show that it had occurred to the Meccan leaders to credit Muhammad with ambition. They, therefore, time and again plied him with temptation. One day some of the important men of Mecca gathered in the enclosure of Ka'bah, sent for Muhammad and addressed him in the following words:

> "We have seen no other man of Arabia, who has brought so great a calamity to a nation, as you have done. You have outraged our gods and religion and taxed our forefathers and wise men with impiety and error and created strife amongst us. You have left no stone unturned to estrange the relations with us. If you are doing all this with a view to getting wealth, we will join together to give you greater riches than any Qurayshi has ever possessed. If ambition moves you, we will make you our chief. If you desire kingship we readily offer you that. If you are under the power of an evil spirit which seems to haunt and dominate you so that you cannot shake off its yoke, then we shall call in skilful physicians to cure you."

"Have you said all?" asked Muhammad; and then hearing that all had been said, he spoke forth:

> I require none of the things that you offer me. I demand nothing, neither riches nor high status, nor kingship, in return for what I have brought for you. I have been sent to you as a messenger of God, a herald of glad tidings and a warning. I have performed my duty by delivering His message to you which has nothing but goodness for you. If you accept then I assure you the good of this world and the world to come. If you reject, I shall remain patient and watch for the verdict of Allah."

We do not find any trace of wavering or despair in the life of the Holy Prophet. A calm and lofty attitude was constantly maintained by him during all the years. The whole tenor of the revelation at this period was marked by a calm confidence, and therein lay the Prophet's strength.

This conversation between the unbelievers and Muhammad clearly brings out the reasons for the opposition of the Quraysh. "The grounds of opposition to Islam," remarks Montgomery Watt, "were thus, besides self-interest, fear of its political and economic implications and sheer conservatism. The situation which confronted Muhammad was a malaise which had social, economic, political, and intellectual symptoms. His message was essentially religious, in that it attempted to remedy the underlying religious causes of the malaise, but it affected the other aspects, and consequently the opposition had many facets".

8

Rights of Muslims

The historic chapter deals with the Laws which affect Believers only. For practical purposes the whole Charter concerns the Believers. However, there are some Clauses whose subject matter concerns Believers only, while there are others which affect those people who have not accepted Islam but will be working under the leadership of Believers. The heading of the Document, which also forms Clause I deals primarily with Believers clears all doubts about its nature and also that they are the people forming the Government of the state.

One of the significant points to note is that the Charter is addressed primarily to the people; the common man; the Believer whether a free man, a freed man or not free till then.

"This is a Document from Muhammad the Prophet (PBUH) between the Believers, Muslims of Quraysh and Yathrib and those who followed them and fought with them. They form one Ummah to the exclusion of others."

It includes others with a condition, otherwise the Believers Quraysh from Makkah and from Yathrib form One Ummah to the exclusion of the rest. This formation of Ummah was not to be confined to the Believers of these two places. Whosoever voluntarily

Believed in Allah and Muhammad (PBUH) as a Prophet which in practice meant that he lived in accordance with the Laws of the Quran and Sunnah, became a member of this Ummah.

There may have been similar Charters in other parts of the world. We have already referred to a Charter issued by a king of England in 1215 A.C., which is known as the Great Charter—Magna Carta. There are many differences but the first difference lies in the people to whom the Charter is being given. While the Constitutional Charter of Madina is given to the common man, the Magna Carta is given:-

> "To the archbishops, bishops, abbots, earls, barons, justiciars, foresters, sheriffs, stewards, servants, and to all his bailiffs and faithful subjects."

The subjects also formed categories and were at the mercy of the bishops and sheriffs and in practice held no social status unless they happened to be retainers of the categories enumerated above. The common man, the man in the street had no voice or weight until centuries later, when contacts with Islam is Spain and the Holy Land had brought about a certain amount of awakening among the Europeans, returning from Muslim lands.

The promulgation of a Constitution or Fundamental Law by a people or to them by the ruler signifies the commencement of organized life of that Millah. Organized collective life alone is most important characteristic of a human group from a herd of animals. Makkan life was the life of individual Muslims placed amidst unfriendly surroundings. Such a life could not last for ever. It cannot last even in the twentieth century. There are a number of countries today where Muslims find it impossible to live as Muslims. Hijrah of the Prophet (PBUH) was inevitable. Hijrah and the declaration of war by Quraysh created the situation where a Fundamental Law became essential to be promulgated. Islam became a living organization with the Charter controlling the collective communal life of those who had accepted Sovereignty of Allah and His Prophet (PBUH). Allah's Sovereignty was to control and direct the life of these individuals from hearth to the farm or the shop and would include the behaviour and inner feelings from the Mosques to the Battlefield.

It must be remembered that the Charter is being issued and promulgated by Muhammad (PBUH) The Prophet of Allah and not by Allah, although it is primarily for the people who have accepted Allah's Sovereignty. This fact reminds a Believer that he has accepted the Sovereignty of Allah, because, Muhammad (PBUH) has said so and the individual has accepted his Prophethood. It is the character, the conduct and the life of Muhammad (PBUH) although regulated, controlled and directed on the Right Path by Allah, which has made men believe in him, when he said, "Allah is the Creator, the Sustainer and Master of the Day of Resurrection." It is his statement that Allah the Merciful, the Loving, the Compassionate and Who has appointed him as His Last Prophet. Therefore, be it understood and remembered that when a Believer accepts the Sovereignty of Allah, he does not relegate the Prophet (PBUH) to a position of no consequence. It is the acceptance of his Prophethood which has prompted the Believer to Believe and have Faith (eemaan) in Allah. Therefore, as Law Givers, they both remain side by side. This is the explanation of repeated reminder of Allah regarding the position of Muhammad as a Law Giver and not one who as a result of applying himself to a problem, at hand, does Ijtehad and deduces supplementary law, under certain given conditions. Allah has repeatedly Commanded:-

> "Say: Obey Allah and the messenger". 3: 32

The preceding Verse is worth noting:-

> "Say: If ye love Allah, follow me".

Whereever the Command to "Obey Allah" occurs it is followed by "Obey the Messenger." Obedience to Him is given singly only in one Verse, where it is said "Obey My Command" (20: 90) and not the usual Word, "Obey Allah."

Source of Law

The position of Muhammad (PBUH) as a Law Giver in accordance with Allah's Own Commands is direct. His Commands take the place of Law directly and independently. Any reported Command of his, which does not fully support the Words of the Quran, can be rejected as Maudhu-Spurious, concocted and coined by some one and not merely as of a secondary nature, which, may or may not be applicable in all cases. He knew the place he held. He could not give an Order which would be contrary to the Dictates of Allah. Allah has said about him:-

> "By the Star when it setteth your comrade erreth not, nor is deceived, nor doth he speak of (his own desire)".
>
> 53: 1-3

The Quran and the Sunnah are complementary to one another. Neither can be understood except by studying the other. If Allah Himself has, in a dozen places bracketed His Rasul with Obedience to Himself then we must also give to his Commands an equally important position. It is Muhammad (PBUH) who has had to say that the Quran is not the result of his authorship. Who, except Allah and his own Conscience, was there to stop him from crediting himself with the authorship of the Quran Who was there, except Allah, his Creator and his own truthfulness to stop him from declaring himself as God in human garb? After all, there were many in Arabia, who, by the queer theory of Trinity, then prevalent, gave to Jesus Christ the position of the Son of God, and of the God who came to earth to be crucified for the sins of humanity. The Quran is the Word of Allah because, apart from the Quran itself, Muhammad (PBUH) has said so. Muhammad's command, therefore, must be believed and acted upon as eternal commands, in the same spirit as Commands of Allah.

The Clauses of the Charter dealing with Believers only are very few. As the Charter was addressed to the Believers initially the clauses dealing with Believers only precede all others. We have already dealt with Clauses I including the few words given above.

Clause 2: "Quraysh Muhajireen will continue to pay blood-money among themselves in accordance with the existing custom."

This Clause has thus laid down:-

1. The Principle of payment of blood-money will continue.

2. Its amount and manner of payment can be in accordance with the tribal custom.

3. Uniformity in the amount etc. is not demanded.

Quraysh Believers had migrated to a new place, the city of Yathrib, where there must have been local customs regarding the payment of blood-money. It was neither advisable nor in accordance with the Spirit of Islam, which was meant to cover the whole of the Globe, to lay down permanent laws regarding matters which should, preferably, be decided in accordance with local customs, conditions and requirements. Within Arabia itself there were different standards of payment of blood-money, in view of this it was decided and proclaimed that local and tribal practice, in the case of blood-money would continue to be followed in future.

Code of Conduct

Islam is the Last Revealed Way of Life. It has lasted for fourteen centuries and has to remain during the coming one thousand or one million centuries that will take this universe to reach its destination in the immeasurable void. A Way of Life which has to last for ever, and, to be applicable in all places at all times, cannot have eternal laws for situations which must undergo changes with change in time and place. Allah alone possesses the knowledge and the Wisdom and knows what aspects suffer change. He has, as a result, not Laws for problems, situations and matters which are likely to undergo changes. Those matters, which are of lasting nature, have been the subject of Laws given by Allah and His Rasul.

If the problem had been posed to a man, it would have been impossible to bring the permanent and the temporary, to reconcile. The permanence of Islamic Laws has been possible only because Allah and His Prophet (PBUH) have meticulously avoided to give Laws, for aspects of human life, which are of changing nature.

All men are equal. They will always remain equal. Hence Equality of man has been brought under Law. And yet the question of electing, selecting, nominating or appointing a leader of society. Khalifa or Imam has not even been touched because this is a purely social problem, the solution of which is subject to change with time and place. Uniformity is advisable but only where it is possible. Where uniformity is likely to create hardships Allah and His Rasul have left it to the Believers to come to a decision through discussion. The Prophet (PBUH) himself was Commanded to decide problems after consulting his Companions. But once a decision has been taken then all have to see to it, that it is suitably carried out.

Clause 3: "They will redeem their prisoners with kindness and justice common among Believers."

The word "they" cannot refer to anyone else but those to whom the Charter was being issued. It was a state of Muslims in which laws of Islam were to be administered. The Fundamental Law had included "those who followed them," but that was to be seen as to who were prepared to follow them and defend Yathrib along with them. Muslims of Quraysh and Yathrib were being given the Document and as such this Clause referred to them jointly. The subject is the redeeming of prisoners, which could be tackled at the level of the Federal Government of Yathrib and none else.

It must be noted that the, "redeeming of prisoners of war is being made a collective responsibility," of the Ummah. It is also worthnoting that the standard of sentiments involved in redeeming prisoners of war is "the kindness and justice common among Believers." The kindness and justice of Believers cannot be of any other kind than that of Allah Who is Most Merciful, and His Prophet (PBUH) who has come as "Mercy to Mankind."

Holy Prophet at the Helm

This Command of Allah's Messenger was not confined to the Believers of Yathrib only. It was the first Muslim state, which expanded within a century to cover two continents and had started influencing the third as well. This order did not merely apply to the subjects of the state of Yathrib. Although the Charter was given to the then existing Ummah, this order was and is applicable to the Ummah of Islam for ever. The present writer has no knowledge of this Order being amended, deleted, cancelled or replaced by any Quranic Injunction or an order by the Prophet (PBUH). The question arises as to what has the world of Islam done to redeem the Muslim prisoners of war in the hands of various victorious nations, who during the last three centuries have availed themselves of the weakness of Muslim peoples and while occupying Muslim lands have taken millions of Muslims as prisoners of war. These Muslims are kept as prisoners jointly and singally in these territories known as European colonies. Generation after generation has grown up and lived as slaves and the Muslim World elsewhere has not moved a finger even to redeem them. We have to admit that a greater part of Muslim World was, until few years ago, under the domination of one or the other Christian power, but nothing has been said regarding the redeeming of millions who, though in majority, in their homelands, are living as slaves and leading a life worse than the life of ethnic minorities. This Clause of The Constitutional Charter of Madina is still operative and I, as, an humble individual, and a student of Muslim history, would submit, that, it needs further thought by the intellectuals of Muslim World.

Until the issue of this Charter there was no question of redeeming prisoners of war. The armies in those days did not belong to the nation. There was no notion of an Ummah.

They used to belong to the kings and when a king was killed in war and was defeated the personnel of that Army had no one else to look to. If they were taken prisoners they were made slaves. If they escaped they became robbers and highwaymen. Very few managed to reach their homes. Yathrib was not a country or a state in the normal sense of the word. It was a place, a piece of land, where the Muslim Ummah, the Believers in Allah and His Rasul (PBUH) had commenced a communal life and were beginning to demonstrate the New Way of Life granted by Allah. Ummah which was then coming into existence was completely new. Those who were to fight the battles of this Ummah were the Army of the Ummah and not of the land comprising the territories of Yathrib. Hence he Ordered that the Ummah will redeem their prisoners of war, and not only that, but they will do so with love and justice which is a hall-mark of Believers in Allah and His Prophet (PBUH) and Mercy to Mankind.

This order was so new and unique, that, the moment the Prophet (PBUH) had dictated it and the scribe had written it, there must have been a demand from "The others", who were present, that this Law should be applied to all. Hence Clause 5. There were some who were not even satisfied with the words "all parties will redeem their prisoners with kindness and justice common among Believers." Their names had to be inserted that such and such tribe and so and so group, "will be governed on the above lines." The demand was placed a second time and names of four more tribes had to be included for the fulfilment of this humane responsibility which was to take ten centuries for other parts of the world like Europe to emulate.

Clause 8: "Believers will not fail to redeem their prisoners or fail to pay blood-money on behalf of one of them."

This Clause is to emphasize Clauses 2 and 3. It has been brought in particularly because Clause 2 had mentioned Quraysh only. This Clause emphasizes the contents of both Clauses mentioned earlier and reminds the Believers of today that contrary to the expectations of the Prophet of Allah, they have failed to redeem their prisoners for centuries.

Clause 9: "A Believer will not make the freedman of another Believer as his ally against the wishes of the other Believer."

The relations between the master and slave are of personal nature. When a master frees a slave new relations are formed. The trust or lack of trust a person places on his freedman is known only to him. His good points, his weaknesses and his idiosyncrasies are also known to a freedman. Relations of allies are on a different level. A Believer giving protection to a freedman is undertaking certain responsibilities in respect of a person not really intimately known to him while Believers are like brothers to one another. Therefore, when a Believer takes a freedman of another Believer as ally, and gives him protection, it is in their common interest to have the blessings of the other Believer. This order was being given to maintain internal peace of the community.

Clause 10: "The Believers who fear Allah, will oppose the rebellious elements and those that encourage injustice or sin or enmity or lack of cooperation among Believers."

It has to be kept in mind that the Believers were to defend Yathrib. It was, therefore, essential that the best of relations existed among them. There were people within Yathrib who were likely to create mischief and create situations detrimental to internal security. The factor which had to be kept in mind was that every Believer had, until then, persons closely related to him, who had not yet embraced Islam. It was possible that some such person was found guilty of injustice, sin, or enmity to Islam or of creating trouble between Believers. On such occasions. Believers were being told that their duty lay with law and order and their loyalty lay with High Command's policy and decision and not with the kindred, however dear they may have been. It was a very delicate situation and the Ansars deserve all the credit for having come out of this very severe test successfully. The leadership provided by the Prophet (PBUH) and the minor circle of his Companions deserve equal praise for steering the Millah with patience, love and tact, through this most difficult period. "Believers who fear Allah", is the key factor in the shaping of an Islamic society. Love of family ties can over-ride all other situations, except that of men and women, who fear Allah, and as a result of fear of Allah are prepared to sacrifice family interests and affiliations. When the object is to create a flawless Muslim society in which no Believer can be thought of committing a sin, rebellion, injustice or create dissension, then every Muslim is expected to oppose such sinful elements even though they may be his close relations. A country or a state can be defended only if there is peace and harmony within the boundaries of that state.

Such a society can only come about if individuals fear Allah and have firm belief that they will have to answer for their actions on the Day of Judgement.

Clause 11: "If anyone is guilty of any such act all Believers will oppose him, even, if he be the son of any one of them."

This Clause is more or less a corollary to the foregoing Clause. It was being laid down firmly and without any ambiguity that injustice, sin and rebellious acts would not be permitted in that society, which was being created in accordance with the Code of Law Revealed by Allah. This was after centuries that a society was taking shape on the principle of Sovereignty of Allah. This society was to prove to humanity, for all times, that a people, a nation, an Ummah, observing in their day to day life, the Sovereignty of Allah prove in actual practice that their objective was to achieve three things:

(a) A happy and contented individual who has patience, for-bearance and steadfastness and these individuals show love for each other in their normal day to day dealings.

(b) These happy and contented individuals bring into existence a happy and loving society.

(c) They do not fall prey to the temptation of committing aggression or transgression against other nations even though as a result of being a happy, contented and united people they have gained strength and have the capacity of over-running their neighbours. In addition such an Ummah does not engage in any war unless they are attacked first. But whenever they are attacked they punish the aggressor to an extent, that he does not repeat it again.

Such a happy and strong society can come into existence only if its individuals observe law for themselves and for all who may be near and dear to them. This Clause draws the attention of Believers to the injunction of the Quran:-

> "O ye who believe! Be ye staunch injustice, witnesses for Allah, even though it be against yourselves or (your) parents or (your) kindred, whether (the case be of) a rich man or a poor man, for Allah is nearer unto both, (than ye are). So follow not passion".

Clause 12: "A Believer will not kill another Believer for the sake of an un-Believer."

This Clause was a further explanation and an illustration of Clause 11.

Family ties held strong loyalties in Arabia as in all tribal societies. If a member of a family was killed, his kith and kin were expected to avenge that death or be satisfied with the usual blood-money. These prejudices were very deep rooted. The Prophet (PBUH), however, was creating an Ummah, the members of which were to be above all such ties, prejudices and loyalties. He was stressing on Believers and un-Believers alike that the only loyalty in Islam is loyalty to Allah and this is exhibited by obedience to His Laws. The Law of Allah is clear on the subject that a Believer cannot kill another Believer unless by mistake. He ceases to be a Believer if he kills another Believer wilfully.

> "Whose slayeth a believer of set purpose, his reward is Hell for ever".
>
> 4: 93

The society was, as yet, a mixed society but laws had to be promulgated, which would gradually develop the society into a society of love, peace and justice all round. This could only be achieved by having strict laws and meticulous observance of those laws. Believers and their un-Believers relations were being told categorically, that no Believer, should be expected to avenge the death of a relative killed accidentally or otherwise by another Believer.

Islam had to step out of Arabia and spread to far off lands. It was to declare, from the beginning, as to where did the loyalties of new-Muslims lie immediately after becoming Muslims. The Code was strict, unusually difficult to observe but the choice of observance of loyalty was between the Sovereignty of Allah and worldly ties. Allah had to be given preference by those who claimed to have accepted Him as their Lord and Master.

Clause 13: "No Believer will help an un-Believer against a Believer."

This Clause in conjunction the foregoing sets a standard of behaviour for Believers in a mixed society where Believers are placed in a non-Believer majority, even though general relation may be on the best of terms. Believers must remain united among themselves, if they desire to possess weight, as an Ummah, however small their number may be.

This Clause could be used as precedent and for relations between Muslim states, so that inter-state relations between Muslim states are kept at friendly level and instances of acute differences between them do not arise. It would then coincide with the directions given in the Verse quoted below:-

> "Let not the believers take disbelievers for their friends in preference to believers." 3: 28

Disobedience of Clause 13 and the Verse quoted above have brought about the situation, that vast areas populated entirely by Believers have fallen prey to un-Believers and millions of Muslims are forced to live as atheists. It is punishment for having rebelled against both the letter and spirit of the Quran and the Charter.

9

Rights of Non-Muslims

The Jewish tribes of Yathrib were rich and had fairly large number of members prominent in business. They, however, had no political or social status among the Arab population. They appear to have migrated from Syria during one of their exodus resulting from Assyrian invasion. Some writers are of the opinion that they were settled in Yathrib even before the Arabs. This does not appear likely. The theory, that they were Arabs who had been converted to Judaism also does not appear plausible. They were, at the time of Prophet's Hijrah, adherents of one or the other of these Arab tribes (Aus and Khazraj). They had, however, preserved a sort of intellectual ascendency, owing to their being in possession of the Scriptures and their fame for the occult sciences, the pagan Arabs consulting their rabbies on occasions and paying heed to what they said."

Special Concessions

The Prophet (PBUH) gave them a privileged position in the Constitutional Charter, provided they followed the Believers loyally and fought alongside with them. They possessed strong forts just outside the main city of Yathrib and each tribe was independent in every respect, each having a separate fort. They had all the weapons of the period and boasted of their prowess as fighters. When the Quraysh were defeated at Badr, one of their tribes, Banu Qainaqa, in reply to the Prophet's advice of good behaviour, they boasted of their strength and rebelled. They are a people of the Book. The way in which the Prophet (PBUH) was laying the foundations of bringing humanity on one platform would have benefited the Jews in the long run, but they were short sighted and did not avail of the special position, they could have enjoyed under the terms of the Charter. In spite of the behaviour of leading Jews of Yathrib the Prophet (PBUH) continued treating them with kindness and until a Jewish tribe did not commit an act of treason or outright rebellion he did not take any action against them. He pardoned two of the rebellious tribes, when they surrendered.

Those terms of the Charter, which were of general nature and those in connection with defence of the state, were applicable to Jews as well. There were, however, some Clauses which referred to the Jews only. The Clauses of general nature included the heading (Clause 1) in which it was laid down that those who followed the Believers and fought alongside with them will form one Ummah with them. This was a great attraction for the Jews. They were being elevated to the status of equality with Arabs and in some respects they were becoming superior to them, because, they were becoming equals of the ruling party of Yathrib, the Believers. Clauses like Clause 5, which laid down that "All parties will redeem their prisoners with kindness and justice according to practice among Believers," are being studied elsewhere. In this Chapter only those Clauses will be brought under discussion, which pertain to Jews exclusively.

Clause 16: "Those Jews who follow us, will be helped and will be treated with equality."

We have touched on this Clause very briefly, under Laws pertaining to defence. As the Clause mentions Jews particularly, we feel that it must be due to some special reason, that the question cropped up again, although it had been touched upon in Clause 1, where it referred to "those who," followed them. The only reason, for the mention of Jews specifically, could be that they had, during the dictation of the Charter, asked a direct question about the subject.

Clause 15 had spoken of "Believers are all friends to each other to the exclusion of all others." The Jews and 'the others' were being denied the friendship and equality with Muslims, which had been promised in Clause 1. The Jews must have felt that their position, in respect of equality with Muslims, needed to be clarified. They must have asked a specific question, "What about us." The answer came in the form of Clause 16 that "Those Jews who follow us will be helped and will be treated with equality."

This Clause shows their keenness to gain an equal socio-political status with the Believers. As yet they knew very little about Islam. They may have been still under the impression that the Prophet (PBUH) will announce himself as a sect of Judaism, and not as final shape of Islam, the Way of Life, preached by Ibrahim and Musa (Alaihi-ssalam). The Prophet having sensed the worries of Jews dictated the next Clause.

Clause 17: "No Jew will be wronged."

Jews had been persecuted all the world over to such an extent that it was rare to find a place where they could live an honourable life. It may have been, that the Jews themselves have followed a policy of persecution in respect of communities which happened to be weaker than them. It could also be that whereever they happened to be in a minority, they took recourse to mischief and intrigue, which invited persecution against them. Centuries of such mischievous and selfish behaviour gave them a reputation that they attracted hatred merely by the mention of the word Jew, where-ever they went. The only person in authority, throughout history, who has shown compassion and kindness to them through the enactment of a Law is Muhammad (PBUH) the Prophet of Allah. This historical Clause placed the Jews on a pedestal of honour, respect and safety which they had not enjoyed under their own kings. This assurance of safe and respectful life was independent of the Clause giving them equality with Believers if they fought alongside them on the Path of Allah.

It is clear that the Clause governing their status of equality must have been the result of their volunteering to take part in the defence of Yathrib against an attack by the Quraysh of Makkah. It could be because according to Yaqubi, the famous geographist, they were from an Arab stock. He says that "Jews of Madina were basically local Arabs and were Judaised by immigrants who fled from Palestine after the Roman invasion.It could also be through Jews who migrated earlier. In any case, they had not only adopted the Law brought by Moses but had also imbibed the universally adopted national character of Jews based on miserliness, cheating and mischief mongering, and had, as a result lost their status as honest citizens, as in other parts of the world." The history of the scattered tribes of Jews has been a history of fraud, criminality and cunning; sabotage and destruction", but he being "Mercy to Mankind," could not refuse a request of a down-trodden people even though they may have deserved such a behaviour in the past. The Jews, however take their roaming around the world as a boon from above. They call it, "A beneficent protection, which God has instituted in the life of the Jews is, that He has dispersed them all over the world".

The Prophet (PBUH) was giving them equality because they were a part of mankind, created and fashioned by Allah. To a Muslim, equality has become a second nature, as a result. "A barefooted Beduin, in a ragged cloak, would walk upto a king, shake him by the hand and wish him good morning, completely disregarding horror of the whispering courtiers".

It may appear strange that the Jews were accepting to live under Laws of the Quran and the Commands of the Last Prophet of Allah as loyal citizens and fight for the safety of the New Deen in a chance, for receiving the status of free citizens of Yathrib. It may be because in this way they were becoming co-rulers along with Arabs, as their equals. It speaks of their urge for living an honourable life of equality with the high born in Arabia and be subject to Laws, which gave equal status to men, irrespective of their ethnic or geographical origin. They were proving the dictum that, "The most obvious and recognized characteristic of just laws is that they are equal",for all concerned. Justice has been recognized as the central theme of Islam. It is based on the principle of equality of men in the eyes of Allah. When human beings, irrespective of the colour of their skins, the language that they speak and the creed they prefer to follow, are treated as equals before law, there is no possibility of injustice prevailing. "Injustice arises when equals are treated unequally and also when unequals are treated equally". This was the first time, that Jews were being treated as equals, and were to enjoy complete freedom. "Closely related to the value of equality is that of freedom. These two values are often defined in terms of the other. Freedom is most often defined, in terms of absence of restrictions, which we see as one way of defining equality.

Freedom as a value calling for absence of restrictions or restraints is laden with contradictions. Society can exist only if human behaviour is predictable and controllable to some extent Unconditional freedom could result only in chaos in all areas of activity".

It appears that Jewish mind has always wanted uncontrolled freedom. Movements like Socialism and Communism have been supported by Jewish intellectuals with greater zeal than thinkers of other schools of thought. The treacherous behaviour of Jews in different parts of the world, at various periods of history is the result of unbridled thought of their thinkers and intellectuals. They have a history which abounds in rebellious conduct even under their own rulers. The number of occasions, when anti-Jewish communal disturbances have taken place are too numerous to be mentioned in an essay of this nature. A few instances may, however, be mentioned.

Jews massacred in Alexandria (216 B.C.).

Antiochus killed 40,000 Jews in Jerusalem (170 B.C.).

Titus killed 11,00,000 Jews and destroys the Temple (70 A.C.).

Desolation of Judea (135 A.C.). Rebellion of Jews. Romans killed 580,000 (136 A.C.).

Rebellion of Jews at Alexandria. Jews massacred (415 A.C.).

Omar took over Jerusalem not a single person was killed (655 A.C.).

No more Jews killed in the Middle East. Jews banished from England (1020 A.C.). Jews returned to England (1060 A.C.). Jews massacred in London on Coronation day of Richard I.

Christian priests joined in the massacre. (1189 A.C.).

Jews besieged in the castle of York. (1190 A.C.).

They cut each others throats. Hunderds killed.

Jews of both sexes imprisoned in England.

Their eyes and teeth pulled out.

A large number butchered by king John. (1204 A.C.).

700 Jews slain in London (1262 A.C.).

Statute that no Jew should enjoy a freehold (1269 A.C.).

Jew moneylenders forced to hang a plate on their breast or quit England. (1274 A.C.).

267 Jews hanged, accused of clipping coins. (1278 A.C.).

All Jews 16511 banished from England. (1290 A.C.).

Jewish fate in France and other countries of Europe during 14th and 15th centuries is a grim story.

Several hundred thousand banished from Spain.
(1492-1494 A.C.).

Addicts against Jews rescinded·by Pope Sixtus V Cromwell permitted them to return to England. (1650 A.C.).

These instances of persecution of Jews speak of the manner they have been hunted from place to place. Their own laws of war and peace are primarily responsible for introducing cruelty during and after war.

According to their own history books, the behaviour of Jewish personalities of note has not been praise-worthy either. "Edom and Jeshurun were rivals and great were the cruelty of the Hebrew arms in their countries. When David was king, his sister's son Jacob went down and killed Adonites in the Ghrov twelve thousand men and Jacob's brother Abishai killed eighteen thousand of them... Other ten thousand taken captives, he brought to the top of the rock, and there he made them the king's tumblers, casting them headlong down together, by the sharp rocks, that they were all broken in pieces".

There have been numerous occasions during 20th century in Europe and particularly in Germany when great atrocities have been committed against Jews because they had captured the economic life of these countries. Efforts have been made to get rid of them. Israel has been created for this purpose, but the Jews have not left either Europe or America. Christianity appears poised to start a fresh campaign to annihilate them during the 21 st century of the Christian Era, while Muhammad (PBUH), gave Yathrib a Charter in 7th century, which said:-"No Jew will be wronged."

Professor Sergeant has tried to prove, that the Charter is not one Document but a collection of eight different documents. He, however, admits the authenticity of the Document, and does not deny the existence of the Clause "No Jew will be wronged." This guarantee of safety was being given to a people, who did not hold the status of nationals of that city and were living at the mercy of the tribes, which had given them protection.

Muslims have always shown magnanimity to the Jews. When they were banished from Spain between the years 1492 and 1494 A.C., "it was to Turkey that the persecuted Spanish Jews fled for refuge in enormous numbers." The persecution of Jews by Christians appears to he natural justice, after a lapse of centuries. They persecuted, in their time, those who fell into their hands. "The Jews used to bum their prisoners alive and most barbarously mutilate the slain".

Yathrib was witnessing a change. A new order was being established by Muhammad (PBUH) who has been sent by Allah, as "Mercy to mankind." All barbarities, all prosecutions, all wrongs to humanity were being made as illegal. All men were being declared as equal. Even the Jews, the downtrodden of East and West were being promised, that no harm will come to them as long as they committed no sin or crime. They were being given a place in the Charter, which was being offered without any pressure. Centuries later king John of England gave a Charter, at a time when "The capital was in rebel hands, the whole administration was at a stand still. Without his exchequer, John had no revenues. He had to yield. The king agreed to meet the barons on the meadows of Runnymede, between Staines and Windsor, and there signed the Great Charter". It would be interesting to read the Great Charter, and compare it the Charter of Madina and see which Charter gives more freedom, equality, justice and human rights.

Jews have had a chequered career throughout history. They have invited this fate because of their internecine warfare. They butchered one another, whenever and whoever had the upper hand. Their final self-inflicted blow came when, "After the defeat of Bar Cochba, in A.C. 135, much of Judea was left a desert and some towns of Galilee were also ravaged".

They seem to have a rebellious nature. If they were not quarrelling among themselves, they would rebel against authority, however benign it may have been. They rebelled against Nebuchadnessar and "resolving to settle the Jewish problem once for all, as he thought, he recaptured Jerusalem, burned it to the ground, destroyed the temple of Solomon, drew Zedekia's sons before his face, gauged out their eyes, and carried practically all the population of the city into captivity in Babylonia."

During one of their marches in captivity and when their women were ordered by their guards to sing for them, they are supposed to have composed a song, bemoaning of their separation from Jerusalem. The words are:-

> "By the river of Babylon, there we sat down,
>
> Yes, we wept, when we remembered Zion,
>
> We hanged our harps upon the willows in the midst thereof.
>
> For there, they that carried us away captives, required of us a song.
>
> And they that worked us required of us mirth.
>
> Saying, sing us a song of Zion.
>
> How shall we sing the Lord's song in a strange land"

In later days, Jews have suffered only at the hands of Christians because of their having had a hand in the supposed Crucification of Jesus Christ. We have given a list of well known instances of persecution of Jews but did not include the migration of Jews to Babylon during the sixth century when Justinian withdrew citizenship from all those who were not members of Orthodox Church. Jews, as a result, chose the kindlier atmosphere of Babylon, which, at that time was under the Iranians. When the Iranians reconquered Syria, at the beginning of the 7th century, the Jews, who had been left behind, sided with the invaders. They paid heavily for this when Emperor Heraclius reconquered the country. During the "early period of Arab rule they prospered. The Jewish towns and villages remained Jewish, paying taxes to Muslims, instead of Christian rulers, but otherwise continuing their normal life".This kind of treatment by Muslim rulers was in the spirit of the Constitutional Charter of Madina, which had categorically made it highly illegal to do any wrong to the Jews. The only other people who have been kind to the Jews are the Iranians. Yazdgard I was most kind to them. His "married to a Jewess, was so well disposed to them, that they called him "The Christian King".

The Prophet (PBUH) was so kind to the Jews that, he, made it illegal for everybody to harm the Jews, unless they were guilty of a crime. Also he laid down that —

Clause 18: "The enemies of Jews will not be helped."

Both these Clauses were independent of the Jews following the leadership of Believers otherwise. These concessions were given to them as ordinary citizens of Yathrib. This was a great step forward towards freedom, equality and basic human rights of man considering that this legal Document was being dictated verbatum in the year 622 A.C.

In the normal course of events, this is not much of a concession to a group accepted as free citizens of a state. It becomes a great concession when no civic duties are imposed on that group. It gives the impression that although their Arab Haleefs were giving them protection yet they were on friendly terms with the enemies of the Jews previously. They were now being told that their enemies will not be befriended.

Equal Opportunities

These two Clauses give a clue to the consistently good treatment of minorities by Muslim rulers. These two Clauses have served as a Sunnah of the Prophet (PBUH) indicating the manner in which, minorities living under Muslim rule should be treated, Muslim rulers have never persecuted people on whom they may have had to rule. Persecution of the weak appears to be a part of the European race and Muslim, in their earlier period, were fortunate to have escaped European influence. Even during the present civilised century Europeans have prided themselves on their superior strength to dominate other people. A German writer of early twentieth century, Ludwig Welliman, "affirmed as early as 1903, that, the race is called upon to dominate the earth, to exploit nations' treasures, and the physical strength of man, to make the passive races simple subaltern organizations for the evolution of its nation".

When Germany overran France, during the Second World War, it set about to depopulate France, so that France was not able to provide itself with adequate manpower during any future war. "The annual total of French births which did not exceed six hundred thousand in 1939, would be halted or worse, since there would also be economic difficulties and privations skilfully organized and maintained by the victor".

Jews, though a mislead people, have been unfortunate throughout history. They have been persecuted in all lands except where Islam reigned. We know how they suffered in the Middle East and England. Their fate in Germany during twentieth century has been worse. To persecute them for having particular religious views has been highly unjust. It appears, that Europeans are too narrow minded, to permit others to hold views, which differ with their own views, and yet nearly all European nations pretend to be secular. One of those who have suffered at the altar of their Secular Christianity writes, "Christian Missionaries, who came from secular states of Europe, with public funds, introduced education on the Western pattern, which spread all over the country. Admission to these Christian schools was conditional on accepting Christianity". In some cases and particularly after independence "they were baptised forcefully, at the Victory College Chapel". The writer goes on to say, "What is most essential for the dignity of man and social progress is freedom of thought, the very freedom, which the Churches have striven for, through centuries of religious wars and persecution to destroy". The Last Way of Life, sent to mankind, through Muhammad (PBUH), happens to be the only Way of Life, with the school of thought that there will be complete freedom of thought and has forbidden use of force in "Deen."

"There is no compulsion in religion." 2: 256

Clause 29: "The Jews will contribute towards the war when fighting alongside the Believers."

The last Clause dealing with the subject of Jews was in relation to their enemies not being helped. Immediately after that Clause matters of defence were taken up. As a result the Jews must have asked about contribution towards the war, in case they also took part in it. It was logical for them to come forward and share the expenses of the war. This, however, was a general statement and Jews under the protection of Arab tribes must have wanted, that their names be specifically mentioned in the Charter. It had been dictated earlier that those Jews who fought alongside the Believers will be considered as part of the Ummah. When they had accepted to share at the cost of war at the time of joining in Jehad on the Path of Allah, they were entitled to become a part of the Ummah on by the Jews would have gradually brought humanity on to the same platform. Mankind is destined to become one Ummah eventually, when they will be following the same Law. Clause 28 already dictated says, "When you differ on anything the matter will be referred to Allah and Muhammad (PBUH)." Reference to Allah means the Dictates of the Quran and reference to Muhammad (PBUH) signifies his Sunnah. It meant that the mode of worship was to remain separate but the Law governing the society was to be that of Islam. Orientalists have failed to comprehend the significance of Prophet's approach to forge an Ummah in which all People of the Book, should live as One Ummah. Muir accepts that "No expression regarding either the Jewish or Christian Scriptures ever escaped the lips of Muhammad (PBUH) other than of implicit reverence". And yet on the same page he writes: "In his later years Islam diverged rapidly from all sympathy with the Bible". He has given no proof of this divergence. He, however, has realised that, "It was the opposition of the Jews, and the martial superiority of Islam that imperceptibly led to the exclusive authority of Muhammad (PBUH) and the Quran".

If Muir had read the Charter carefully, he would have realised that exclusive authority of Muhammad (PBUH) and the Quran had been established from the beginning of Islam in Madina. The Jews failed to perceive, and so has Muir missed the point that unity of human race was the object of the Final Way of Life being Revealed to Muhammad (PBUH). It was the Jews who sabotaged it and it is Christian Missionaries and the Zionists who are still on the path of war with Islam the Deen of Peace. Allah has said:-

> "Mankind were one community". 2: 213

Differences arose and people forgot the true Faith. Messengers were sent to guide them back to the right path. Some listened and some did not. Although many Messengers were sent the main theme remained, as the Sovereignty of Allah. When the Last Messenger came, he tried to bring people on to the same platform. A beginning was made, but when people of the Book laid stress on their own separate identity and ignored the Sovereignty of Allah, the experiment failed. The present writer feels that, the result was that for the future the order came, that, who ever accepts Islam must submit completely.

> "O ye who believe Come, all of you, into submission (unto Him)". 2: 208

Clause 31: "The same applies to Jews of Bani Al-Najjar, Bani Al- Harith, Bani Saeeda, Bani Jasham, Bani Al-Aus, Thaliba and the Jaffra and the Bani Al-Shuraiha".

Clause 34: "Those in alliance with the Jews will be given the same treatment as the Jews."

The Jews were accepting the responsibility of joining in the defence of the state. They had allies abroad. As the Jews had promised to become a part of the Ummah, it was only fair to consider and treat their allies in the same manner as the Jews.

Clause 37: "The Jews bear their own expenses and the Believers bear their expenses."

The subject matter of defence continues. The question of payment has arisen again. This refers to expenses connected with each ethnic contingent of the Army. Each was to pay for its own contingent.

Clause 43: "The Jews must pay with the Believers."

This was to refer to expenses of general nature like blood money or other damages, in which both parties had to share the expenses.

Clause 47: "The Jews of al-Aus, including their freedom have the same standing as other parties to the Charter."

This Clause speaks for itself. Late-comers were being accommodated.

These were Clauses in respect of Laws binding and giving rights to Jews. Irrespective of what status they had possessed prior to the Hijrah of the Prophet (PBUH), they were to be governed and treated in accordance with the dictates of this Document. It is incumbent on all students of Seerah and early history of Islam to bear in their minds the contents of the Charter. Without reference to this important Document no opinion can he formed on the behavior of one or the other party.

10

Treaty for Peace

The Prophet (PBUH) once in Medina in the very first year of Hijrah considered in the fitness of things to enter a contract with all the ethnic and religious parties around him so that despite differences racial and cultural unity may be maintained and in civilization and culture there may be spirit of cooperation.

Some select terms of this contract are as under:

1. This is a document from Muhammad (PBUH) the apostle of Allah among the Muslims, Quraysh or citizens of Yathrib, with those who are associated with them (Muslim) and their partners in day-to-day affairs of the administration and maintenance of peace.

2. In spite of the differences in their identities, they will be regarded one nation (people of a country).

3. The Judaic people of Bani 'Auf are one nation with the Muslims.

4. And whoever starts hostilities with these entrants of contract, one and all will oppose him en masse. The Muslims shall come to their aid.

5. The relations of the contracting units shall be based on mutual well-wishing and benefiting and not harming and sinning against.

6. During the wars, the Jews will be contributors in expenditure of war.

7. The rights of the nations friendly to the Jews shall be on a par with the Jews.

8. No one will start any move hostile to his ally of contract.

9. The oppressed shall be supported and helped.

10. Bloodshed on the soil of Medina shall be strictly prohibited to all the partners of the contract.

11. The neighbours too will be deemed on a par with the partners of contract.

12. If something happens among the partners threatening violence, the decision will rest with Allah and His apostle Muhammad (PBUH).

When signatures of all the Madinite communities were taken on this charter of rights, the Prophet (PBUH) wanted to include the tribals of the neighbouring areas also in this agreement, having in view two advantages:

1. To put an end to the tribal mutual clashes and unnecessary bloodshed (of the guilty and innocent alike).

2. The Quraysh of Mecca shall not be able to instigate the tribes that have entered the contract against the Muslims.

   (a) With this intention, the Prophet, in the first year after migration from Mecca travelled upto Waddan (between Mecca and Medina) and included Bani Hamzah, bin Bakr bin Abd Munaf of tribe in the agreement mentioned above. It was signed by 'Amr bin Fehshi Al-Sakhri.

(b) And for the same purpose, the Apostle of Allah went to Razwi in the month of Rabi I, 2 A.H and brought into the agreement the people of bawat mountain.

(c) And in the same year (2 A.H.) in the month of Jawadi II the Prophet went to Zil 'Ashirah, situated somewhere between Medina and Yanbu,' and after signature of Banu Mudlaj on the contract he returned to Medina.

If he had had sufficient time for extending this agreement further, the world would have become conscious of the fact that the Apostle of Allah, Mercy for mankind had come not to draw sword but to bring peace to humanity.

The Background

The Quraysh of Mecca in thier aminosity to the Prophet and the Muslims had gone so far that even after their migration to Medina 300 miles from their town they were not at ease and did not let them live in peace. Earlier on the migration to Abyssinia, they had tried to detain them and on the second occasion went in pursuit of them to Abyssinia in an attempt for their extradition. And as we have seen earlier they miserably failed in these attempts. And now when they had come to Madmah, they followed them there too and intended to attack them.

As a preliminary, they had written to Abd-Allah bin Ubai that they had given protection to their man (the Prophet). So they were duty bound to fight against him or compel him to leave their town. Or else they have resolved under an oath to attack Medina, murdering your young men and taking your women as slave girls.

On receiving this letter Abd-Allah bin Uba'i decided in favour of giving the Prophet and his Muslim followers a fight. The Prophet (PBUH) got scent of this conspiracy and personally going to the hostile group talked to them directly.

The Prophet said to them: "The Quraish have played this trick upon you so that if you are taken in by them you will come to much greater harm than in violation of their terms. For, if you were to fight against the Muslims you will be slaughtering your own sons. In case you are confronted by Quraysh, it will be waging war against aliens."

This brief talk of the Prophet had such an affect on their minds that the entire gathering got immediately dispersed.

After failure in the first attempt, the Quraysh secretly started their conspiratorial moves with the Judaic community of Medina. And when they were perfectly in league with them, with full confidence in their success they sent the following message to the Muslims of Medina:

"Do not be proud of your safe arrival from Mecca, and do not gloat over your success against us. We are capable of your ruin even there—your safe refuge, your asylum. After this challenging message they started vexing them.

The Assaults

In Rabi I, 2 A.H. one of the tribal chiefs from Quraish, Kurz bin Jabir, Al fahri came to Medina and drove away the cattle of Madinites grazing out of the town and made his escape good, as if to impress upon them that they could strike at them from a distance of 300 miles whenever they pleased.

Then in the month of Ramadan 2 A.H., Abu Jahl gave it out falsely that the Muslims are going to waylay our caravan laden with rich goods. This baseless propaganda against the Muslims was aimed at instigating all those who had a share in trade or their men formed the trade caravan or all those nursing hatred against the Muslims, may come together ready to fight against Muslims en masse. And they succeeded in this mischievous plan of theirs.

With a vast army of one thousand venturesome, valiant, fierce fighters with seven hundred camels and those hundred horses as mounts, Abu Jahl came out of Mecca. The caravan (had not been engaged in attach on its way by the Muslim army and it had reached Mecca safely, but Abu Jahl continued his movement towards Medina and the Muslims were now dead sure of his evil design to attack them.

The Prophet (PBUH) had consulted the companions in this behalf. The muhajirs (migrants) came out with a satisfactory answer (to lay down their lives against the invading army). He repeated his query and they firmly assured him of their faithful obedience. When he put the same question a third time, the Ansar (old residents of Medina) took it that he was waiting for their response. Sa'd bin Mu'az said, "Perhaps you have taken it on principle that Ansars do not regard it their duty to stand by you and their Muslim brethren if it comes to an encounter outside Medina. On behalf of Ansars I assure you that we are with you under all conditions whether you enter an agreement or reject another. You can take as much from our goods as you please and leave for us as much as you please. That taken by you would be preferable to us than that left with us. We shall obey you, order us what you are pleased. We shall gladly follow you if you take us to the 'Imran spring, we will follow you. And if you order us to enter an ocean, we will enter with you." Miqdad said: "O apostle of Allah! we are not like the people of Moses to say "Go thou, and thy Lord, and fight ye two, while we sit here (Q. V: 24), for we are with you everywhere, right, left, in front and behind, ready to fight."

The Muslims were not in a state of perfect readiness (most of them had come out to intercept a caravan of a few highly armed guards of Quraysh and not fierce fighting forces). There were 313 persons in all, muhajirs and Ansars combined.

Muslims had not been so far permitted to enter wars even in the face of strong opposition and persecution, for Islam is the religion of peace avoiding armed struggle if peace can be maintained without it. That is why, they put up with oppression quietly and moved out of Medina, leaving behind their birth place, houses and wherewithal to abstain from contention. And they overlooked vexation even after getting out of the way of their opponents. But now things had come to such a pass that clash was inevitable, for even survival of Islam dearer to Muslims than even their lives. After annihilation of this handful of devotees engaged in Allah's clarification and propagation of Divine Faith, none would have been left to take it up. 'Isa (PBUH) had also, at the end of his brief mission of less than three years, compelled by necessity, had ordered his disciples to purchase arms even if they had to part with their clothes, cash and other belongings: Then set he unto them, but now he that hath a purse, let him take it, and likewise his scrip: and he that hath no sword, let him sell his garments, and buy one. Luke 22: 36. So it was this pressing need of self defence and protection of their Faith that Allah in His Infinite Mercy, permitted them to take to arms in emergencies like the present, after they had very patiently preserved with oppression and tyranny, excesses, loss of life and property, insults and difficulties in living up to the dictates of Faith.

Below is given the first permission as revealed in the Quran:

> To those against whom war is made permission is given (to fight) because they are wronged and verily Allah is most Powerful for their aid. (They are) those who have been expelled from their homes in defiance of rights, (for no cause) except that they say, "Our Lord is Allah." Did not Allah check one set of people by means of another, they would surely have been pulled down monasteries, churches, synagogues and mosques, in which the name

> of Allah is commemorated in abundant measure. Allah will certainly aid those who aid His (cause) for verily Allah is full of strength, Exalted in Might, (able to enforce His will).
>
> —Q. XXII: 39-40.

The Quran, as every body can see for himself, points out the reasons behind this permission, which also brings out clearly the nature of this war— defensive and not aggressive as the wars of the ungodly."

1. The first reason given here is oppressed condition of those fighting in defence of self and their Faith, which the people of our age have termed right of self-determination; justifying even armed struggle in its defence.

2. The second reason is their expulsion from their homes and hearths, deprivation from their wherewithal and that too on the basis of difference of creed.

   The so-called peace-loving King Edward VII, in his message to his Indian subjects on the occasion of 50th anniversary of the British rule in India in a tone of great pride among other things, that "during these fifty years no one has ever been harmed on grounds of the difference of creed, when it is no secret that all these Muslims were those who had been tortured, deprived of rights, jailed, exiled, hanged and shot for their only crime that they asserted strongly. "Our Lord is Allah."

3. The third reason pointed out by the Quran is not of exclusive advantage to the Muslims but very wide in its scope, almost universal, covering the two major faiths of the world, Judaism and Christianity, whose protection has also been thus ensured, Mosques of Islam and Muslims finding the last place on this list, probably out of courtesy shown to even these enemies of Allah. Moreover, Muslims had entered an agreement with these

> two religious communities in Medina and this was out of regard for maintaining friendly relations with them. However, the Muslim community was of the greatest importance, since it were they who pledged and actually laid down their lives in defence of the right of self-determination for humanity at large. Without their waging wars through the ages, there would have been no party of selfless, righteous justice-loving party in the world for the defence of the charter of human rights and the world would have never heard of them.

All these factors made it imperative for the Muslims to check them on the way to Medina, in spite of their extreme paucity of arms, mounts and rations they had decided upon total confrontation.

During the month of Ramadan 2 A.H. the Apostle of Allah as the head of the Muslims started from Medina. An idea of their military equipment can be had from the fact that they had only two horses and sixty camels.

Shall we call it a matter of chance that the participants in the battle of Badr were just the same in number as those of the army of Taloot (Saul) against Jaloot (Goliath).

On arriving at the battle field of Badr, the Muslim witnessed the enemy's fighting force three times their own number and in the matter of equipment they stood no comparison with the enemy.

A day ahead of the battle, the Prophet inspected the battle field, pointing out with precision that Allah-Willing such and such men of the opposing force will fall dead at such and such places on the battle ground.

On Friday, the 17th Ramadan the two fighting forces confronted each other. The Prophet (PBUH) entreated Allah for success in the battle against the enemy, saying that if these handful of Muslims get killed, there will be no one left to proclaim the message of Thy Unity. The Muslims also prayed earnestly.

With the aid of Allah, the enemy was defeated at the hands of the Muslims. Seventy of their fighters were killed and another seventy taken prisoners. Abu Jahl was killed exactly at the site pointed out by the Prophet (PBUH) to his companions the previous day. It was he who had brought the hosts (to wipe out the Muslims). Out of the fourteen tribal chiefs who had come together at Dar-al-Nadwah for deliberations on the theme of the Prophet's (PBUH) murder, eleven lay dead on the battle field. The three survivors had at last embraced Islam.

In keeping with (a) the accepted law of war (b) the passion of the oppressed Muslims for revenge (c) the need of over awing the other tribes of Arabia with horror of war, the situation demanded the killing of the prisoners of war, but the Prophet of Mercy freed them all on payment of ransom. The ransom for the freedom of the literate prisoners was literacy of the children of Ansar.

The trial of strength of the two parties of the battle of Badr proved true to the prophecy of the Quran while permitting the Muslims to fight against the invader:

> "Allah will certainly aid those who aid His (cause), for verily Allah is full of Strength, Exalted In Might (Able To Enforce His Will)." —Al Quran XXII: 40.

That is why, this battle has been termed Yaum-al-Furqan (the day of evidence or proof), since the Muslims and the people of the Book had been provided with evidence on the true nature of the Islamic Faith. Allah has elsewhere mentioned this incident, the Battle of Badr, in the following words:

> Allah had helped you at Badr when ye were helpless: then fear Allah: thus may ye show your gratitude.
> — Al Quran III:123.

A few days after the battle of Badr, Safwan bin Umayyah, whose father was killed in Badr and 'Umair bin Wahab whose son was a prisoner in the hands of Muslims, came together in a desolate spot outside Mecca and talked about the Prophet (PBUH).

Umair said to his associate: "If I was not indebted irredeemably, and I had not been worried about the helplessness of my family in my absence (death) I would have myself gone to Medina and would have made short shrift of Mohammad (killed him)."

Safwan blurted out: "I shall clear thy debts and support thy family during my own life-time."

'Umair, assenting, said to him: Settled. But this secret of ours should not be allowed to leak out." Then he got his sword sharpened and poisoned and started off on his mission.

On arrival in Medina, he was making his camel sit in front of the Prophet's mosque when the camel started gurgling. 'Umar Faruq (R) saw and recognizing him, it occurred to him that this devil has come with an evil intent. And so he approached the Prophet (PBUH) informing him that 'Umair bin Wahab was coming and was fully armed. The Prophet said: "Let him come to me." 'Umar (R) got hold of the hilt of his sword and holding his neck took him to the Prophet who asked 'Umar (R) to free him, and asked 'Umair to come to him. 'Umair coming before him greeted him formally. The Prophet asked him: "What brings you here? He said in reply: "I have come to see my son a prisoner here." The Prophet further enquired: "And how about this sword of yours." He tauntingly remarked: "Of what use is this sword? And what have our swords achieved when pitted against you?" The Prophet (PBUH) said to him: "Be honest and come out with the truth 'Umair repeated his reply. The apostle of Allah said: "Look here, you and Safwan had gone to a desolate spot in the hills outside Mecca. Safwan has taken upon himself relieving thee of my debts and support of thy family, and thou hath promised him my head with which intent thou art here. 'Umair, thou did not care to think that Allah Himself is my Protector."

On hearing this much from the Prophet, he was confounded. He submitted: "Now I am satisfied that you are certainly the Prophet and a Messenger of Allah." It was easy for us to falsify you about heavenly realities and revelations and were engaged in it with impunity. But I have no explanation for this secret that was strictly between Safwan and me. No third person could have got wind of it. I must be grateful to Allah Who made it (the disclosure to you of our well-guarded secret through super natural means) the cause of my embracing Islam.

The Prophet said to the companions: "Teach your brother his Faith, make him memorize the Quran and free his son." Umair said: "O Apostle of Allah! Kindly be so good as to permit me to go to Mecca and call people to Islam. And now I intend to vex and torment the idolaters in the same way as I did to the Muslims before this."

After 'Umair had left for Medina, Safwan used to say to the elite among the Quraysh: "Just wait. Shortly there is going to be good news from Medina which will relieve you of the shock of Badr."

But when Safwan learnt that 'Umair had embraced Islam, he was shocked and he viewed not to speak to him for the rest of his life, nor allow any benefit to go to him if it can be helped.

'Umair came to Mecca. He used to proclaim the message of Islam and many people embraced Islam through his efforts.

After the disgraceful defeat at Badr, Abu Sufyan, now the outstanding leader of Quraysh, had under an oath denied himself a change of clean clothes and bathing his body, until he had avenged himself and the community of Muslims. So he came out of Mecca with two hundred mounted men and on approaching Medina he detached himself from them and in the darkness of the night entered the town all alone (by stealth) and met his friend Salam bin Mashkam a Jew and spent the night with him in a drinking orgy of sorts. Probably in their mutual consultation, it was decided that the time was not appropriate for an attack. So during the last part of the night he came out and setting fire to fruit laden trees of Muslims and murdering a Muslim and his ally, returned home.

On receiving information, he and his retinue of too hundred men were given a hot pursuit upto Qarqarah-al-kadar. So this pursuit of the invaders has come to be called 'Ghazwah' (Expedition) of Qarqarah-al-Kadar. On the return journey, the contingent of the Abu Sufyan dropped their tiny bags of parched, ground barley and therefore this is also known as Ghazwah-al-Saweeq.

Next year, the Quraysh of Mecca attacked Medina once again. This time, they had collected funds from the citizens in general. The poet Abu 'Uzzah in his campaign in Tahawah had reconciled Banu Kananah to come to the aid of Makkans in their strife against Madinite Muslims. Fifty thousand Mithqal of gold (about 225 kilogram) and a thousand camels from Syria, the collective property of Makkan traders, was also donated by common consent generously to war fund. In short, an army of five thousand blood thirsty fighters of various tribes, comprising three thousand camelry and two hundred strong cavalry and seven hundred armoured infantry men, came to attack Medina. The Prophet was in favour of the defence of Medina from inside. But the young zealots (who had remained deprived of participation at Badr insisted on confrontation with the enemy outside in the open. And the issue was decided in favour of the majority. With true democratic spirit, the Prophet did not insist on his own and that of older men's nature and wiser opinion nor the decision once taken was changed (when on second though the younger lot repented and requested revision). So the Muslims came out to the mount Uhud, about three miles from Medina and confronted the enemy from Mecca.

The Muslim fighting force comprised one thousand men. But at the nick of the moment and most critical juncture, the arch-hypocrite, Abd-Allah bin Uba'i bin Salul played foul and betraying the Muslims left with his three hundred misguided and hypocritic companions. The burden of facing the enemy hordes, five thousand strong (furious with passion of revenge) came to the shoulders of the remaining seven hundred. The Muslims had inflicted defeat on such a powerful enemy with numerical superiority and much more and better equipment, and twelve of their standard bearers were killed (eight of them at the hands of 'Ali Murtaza alone). But the Muslim contingent of archers stationed by the Prophet (PBUH) to guard a mountain pass, the only vulnerable position for the Muslim ranks, was deserted by them (under the erroneous nation that the battle was over and they too were free to collect booty from the defeated, fleeing army). They misunderstood and disobeyed the Prophet (PBUH). The clever enemy took advantage of this error on the part of Muslims and taking a round surrounded the Muslim from both sides. (Khalid bin Waleed, yet in the opposite camp, with his cavalry attacked the Muslim, through the vulnerable and now unguarded pass and created havoc. Causing great loss and dispersing the greater part of the rest).

Among the companions of the Prophet (PBUH) the following 12 were with him: Abu Bakr, 'Umar, 'Ali, Abd-al-Rahman bin 'Auf, sa'd bin waqas, Talha bin Abdullah, Zubair bin-al-'Awam, Abu'Ubaidah bin Jarah, and four others, Allah be pleased with all of them, never left him alone (to fend for himself). The enemies threw stones at him. That thrown by Ibn Qumayyah wounded his forehead and that by Ibn Hisham his arm. Utbah's stone broke four of his teeth. Again, he had fallen into a deep pit and it was erroneously given out that he has been killed. Honourable woman from Medina rushed to Uhud. Once in the battle field, Fatimah (R) washed her father's wounds, and stopped haemorrhage with burnt mat (ash). 'Ali Murtaza (R) brought water in his shield and 'Ayeshah Siddiqah (R) and Umm-e-Sulaim (R) took up small leather water bags and brought water to the wounded lying on the battle field. Seventy companions of the Prophet (PBUH) were war casualties.

The heaviest loss in this battle field was the fall of Mus'ab bin 'Umair who had come to Medina as an ambassador of Islam, a connecting link between Mecca and Medina and whose sermons converted the tribes of Aus and Khażraj to Islam, was martyred here. His wife, Hanmah bint Jahash had received news of the martyrdom of her brother and maternal uncle and had quietly recited the Quranic words of resignation to the Will of Almighty Allah. "Verily to Allah do we belong and it is to Him that we are destined to return" and prayed for their forgiveness. After that, she was told of her husband's martyrdom, on hearing which still gave out a loud cry of anguish and grief. The Prophet remarked: "See, how much she loved her husband."

In this battle, the prophet's uncle, Hamzah (R) (lion of Allah and His Apostle) also got martyred. His dead body was desecrated by the unbelieving lady Hindah. After the war was over, Safiyah, mother of Zubair (R) came to see the dead body of Hamzah, her brother. Zubair tried to stop her but that brave lady insisting on seeing it, saying: "I know that my brother's dead body has been mutilated and desecrated. But this is something to be proud of for us. My dear son, I am neither going to cry over it nor scream but only to pray for him."

Great Warriors of Islam

Anas bin Nadhar too had been martyred in this battle. This valiant soul noticed certain brave and courageous Muslims who, throwing away their arms were sitting crest fallen and in great grief. He asked them: "What is wrong with you?" They said to him "The Apostle of Allah has passed away." Anas said to them passionately: "When the Apostle of Allah laid down his life, we too should sacrifice ourselves for the same noble cause. What use is living after him." And entering the thick of the battle he fell on the enemy in a rage, received seventy wounds of deadly weapons and entered heaven.

Sa'd bin Rabi' was another martyr in this battle of Uhud. After the battle was over, the Prophet sent out his men to search his deadbody. One of them saw him in pangs of death lying among the wounded and dying. When asked about his condition, he replied: "Take me for dead now. But have the goodness to convey my respects to the Prophet of Allah. And also say to him pray to Allah that He may reward him with a reward greater than any given to any prophet for his guidance to his people. And convey from me this message to the Muslim community that so long as there is a single eye among them that winks if the enemy is allowed to get to him, they will have no excuse to offer to their Lord for that negligence."

A companion of the Prophet (PBUH) has stated that he went to see Abu Bakr (R). Sitting on his chest I found a small girl whom he was kissing and fondling. I asked him about that child and was told that she was the daughter of Sa'd bin Rabi'. He was superior to me and on the Day of Reckoning, he will be among the heralds of the Apostle of Allah.

'Amarah bin Ziyad too was one of the martyrs of this battle. When in the pangs of death he had dragged himself somehow to bring his cheeks in contact with the feet of the Prophet, dying the most peaceful death.

All these valiant supporters of Islam had performed deeds of extra-ordinary temerity and valour in this battle. 'Ali (R) had single handedly killed eight opponents as mentioned earlier. Talhah had used his hand as the shield to protect the Prophet from the enemy's arrows. This hand of his had become palsied and crippled for ever.

Exemplary Conviction

A lady of Banu Dinar tribe had lost her father, a brother and husband (having probably heard the false rumour about the Prophet (PBUH) Medina) came to the scene of action and enquired about him. People told her that by the Grace of Allah he was all right. But she wanted to make sure and he was pointed out to her at a distance. Thus assured she exclaimed showing her satisfaction:" Now that the Apostle of Allah is among us, any grief, however tormenting has become bearable."

Overlooking Faults and Forgiveness by the Prophet (PBUH) and his Prayer for the Pagan Oppressors.

Some companions of his suggested to him to curse the pagans (when he himself was badly wounded by them). The Prophet, however, said to them in his usual mild tone: "I have not been sent to curse but to call (mankind to Allah and His Faith) and as Mercy to them. 'O my Lord, guide them (to the right path) for they know me not."

After the battle of Uhud, the enemies of Islam and Muslims, adopted various methods of harming Muslims. So in the 4th year after Hijrah:

> Seven persons of Adal and Qarah communities were instructed by the Quraysh and sent to the Prophet (PBUH) with the request that since their tribes were ready to embrace Islam some preachers should be sent with them to teach Islam to them. The Apostle of Allah sent with them ten companions of his as preachers of Faith with 'Asim bin Thakit leading this party. When these companions (on a mission of preaching) with their treacherous guides had come in their range to become easy targets, two hundred armed men came out and wanted to arrest them alive. But the companions confronted them and eight of them fell fighting. Two of the

party Khubaib bin 'Adi and Zaid bin Wathnah (Allah be pleased with all the ten of them), were however arrested by these barbarian, and sold out to the Quraysh of Mecca.

The Quraysh kept them confined without food and water for a few days in the house of Harith bin 'Amir. One day, a child of Harith playing with a household knife approached Khubaib. Out of love with little children Khubaib lifting him up placed him on his thigh and taking the knife from his hand put it aside. The child's mother noticing that her child with a knife was with the prisoner who had been starved by them. So out of fear of safety to the child a loud scream left her lips. Khubaib, however assuringly remarked: "She mistakenly is under the impression that I can kill her child, not knowing that a Muslim is not guilty of perfidy. And they are very kind to every one, particularly children.

The tyrants of Quraysh took him to the cross offering him his freedom on condition of rejecting Islam. Both the prisoners said in reply: "What is life worth after rejection of Islam?" They then asked him: "If you have any desire, let us know." Khubaib as their spokesman said to them: "Permit us time for two raka'ats (units) of prayer if you can." They were permitted. They said the desired prayer, not taking much time and saying: "We could have spent longer time in our prayer but we did not like to be misunderstood that it was out of fear of death." They hard-hearted tyrants, put them on the cross and asked the lance bearers to keep piercing every part of their body constantly.

How firm was their belief in Islam and Pleasure of Allah and eternal bliss in life to come can be inquired by the fact that they patiently persevered with all sorts of calamities without complaint!

Holy Prophet above All in the World

One of the spear-bearing tyrants asked him after giving Khubaib a painful prick: "At this stage you too must be wishing all this for Muhammad and your own redemption." Khubaib replied in a passionate tone: "By Allah, I would not like that even a thorn may prick him for my deliverance."

He also recited some lyrics of his depicting the position of a true Muslim. Last of all, he prayed to Allah that he had conveyed the Message of His Faith to these people and entreat Thee that Thy Apostle may be informed of our plight and the beastly treatment of the pagan opponents.

Abu Bara' 'Amir also played the same trick, the same dirty game. He came to the Prophet (PBUH) and requested him for the services of some preachers of Islam for the education and guidance of Najd. He wanted to take them with him. 'Amir's nephew was the ruler of Najd. 'Amir had given assurance of protection to them. The Prophet assigned this duty to Munzir bin 'Amr Ansari at the head of seventy others, all well-versed, select in religious knowledge. When they reached Bi'r-Mannah, the homeland of bani 'Amir, Haram bin Malham was deputed to see Tufail the ruler with the letter of the Prophet. This herald was killed by the ruler. He was pierced with a spear going from the back through the chest. Falling on the ground, he had proclaimed his view of life and wealth, uttering: "By the Lord of Ka'bah, I have achieved felicity."

These words of the dying person had such a magical effect on the murderer that he went to the Prophet and embraced Islam. The ruler got the rest also killed. Ka'b bin Zaid saved his life getting behind those being killed and getting back he informed the Prophet of what had happened.

In the 8th year after Hijrah, the Muslims had to besiege Mecca during the month of Ramadan under an emergency. The reason behind it was that one of the terms of Hudaibiyah Treaty was that:

For ten years, there will be no war. The communities wishing to ally with the Prophet's community may do so and others who prefer to join Quraysh are free to do so. So Banu Khuza'ah allied with the Prophet and Banu Kananeh went with the Quraysh. Hardly two years, had elapsed when Banu Kananah attached Banu Khuza'ah and the Quraysh too came to their aid with arms. 'Akramah bin Abu Jahl, Suhail bin 'Amr (he had signed the treaty), Safwan bin Umayyah (the well-known elite of the Quraysh with their followers, all under cover fought against Banu Khuza'ah).

These people (Khuza'ah) requested for clemency, took refuge in Ka'bah as the safest asylum, but they were mercilessly put to the sword. When these oppressed people appealed to them for mercy in the name of Allah (For Allah's sake) they, (the Makkan pagans) most blasphemously turned on them with loud proclamations of "Allah is nobody today (—is mere nothing)."

Forty of them that had somehow escaped the blood thirsty swords of Banu Kananah and Quraysh came to the Prophet (PBUH) with their tale of woes.

For reasons of 1. Abiding by the terms of treaty 2. Re-dressal of grievance with full justice 3. Future protection of allies and tribes bound by treaty. The Prophet was forced by the demands of justice and fair play, to take immediate strongest action against the offenders, he, like the previous emergency of Badr (in the month of Ramadan) started with a ten thousand strong force for Mecca also in the month of fasting. They had hardly covered two days journey when Abu Sufyan Al-Harith bin Abd-al-Muttalib and Abd-Allah bin Abu Umayyah met him on the way. They were men who had tormented the Prophet very much and had left no stone unturned in wiping out Islam. The Prophet sighting them turned his face in the other direction. Umm-e-Salmah submitted that Abu Sufyan was his first cousin and Abd-Allah is also the first cousin, the son of 'Atikah, his real paternal aunt. Such close relations should not remain deprived of merciful affection.

At the instance of 'Ali (R) they came to the Prophet and asked for his forgiveness in the words of the erring brothers of Yusuf (PBUH).

By Allah! Indeed has Allah preferred thee above us, and we certainly been guilty of sin —Q. XII: 91 The Apostle of Allah said in reply:

This day, let no reproach be (cast) on you Allah will forgive you. And He is the Most Merciful of those who show mercy!—Al Quran XII: 92.

The Apostle of Allah wished to take the Makkans by surprise. (They should not get wind of his arrival. And so it did come to pass that when he with his companions had camped outside Mecca and to strike terror in their hearts he had ordered lighting of fires not only for cooking their food but also big fires to make the mountain side ablaze. The thousands of these fires gave the Makkans an idea of their helplessness and not to even think of disturbing peace by taking to arms. The Apostle of Allah, Mercy for mankind, had aimed at a bloodless victory, an entirely peaceful revolution.

Declaration of Truce

The next morning, the Apostle of Allah ordered the army to enter the town by different routes and observe strictly the following rules:

1. Whoever throws away his arms should not be killed.
2. One entering Ka'bah should also be spared.
3. One confining himself to his house should not be pursued.
4. Whoever chooses Abu Sufyan's house for safety should be left alone.
5. And so also those entering the house of Hakeem bin Hizam.

6. Those absconding should not be followed to be brought back.

7. The wounded and the disabled shall not be killed either, nor

8. The captives should be treated as free person for reckoning.

The only contingent that entered the town under the command of Khalid bin Waleed experienced some resistance but the Makkans to their heels. The others entered without the least resistance. In the confrontation two Muslims and 28 opponents lost their lives. When on 20th Ramadan, the chosen Apostle of Allah entered Mecca, his head was bowed and he was reciting Surah Al Fatah (Q. XLVIII) and mounted on a camel was going to the House of Allah, when riding this camel along with him was Osaman (R) son of Zaid (R) his freed slave. Once there he cleansed the house of Allah of the pollution of all sorts of idols 360 in number. He was bringing down each one of them with the end of his bow or his stick and was reciting the Quranic verses:

1. Truth has (now) arrived and falsehood perished: for falsehood is (by its nature) bound to perish.

   —Q. XVII: 81.

2. The truth has arrived, and falsehood showeth not its face and will not return. —Al Quran XXXIV: 49

After this iconoclastic activity was over, he called 'Uthman bin Abi Talha. His family had been the bearer of the keys of Ka'bah since long. During the early days of his prophethood, the Prophet (PBUH) had asked him ('Uthman) to open the Ka'bah and he had refused to oblige. And the Apostle of Allah had prophesied: "All right, you will see on some future day that these keys will be in my hand and I shall entrust them to whomsoever I like." And 'Uthman had asked him whether all the males of the Quraysh would have been brought low and annihilated. And the Prophet (PBUH) had replied: "No, they would be much more honoured and dignified.

The Prophet taking the keys from him opened the door of Ka'bah and entering made every corner of it resound with loud cries of Allah-u-Akbar (Allah is the Greatest), and then in prayers of thanks laid his forehead on the ground as the most devout and grateful servant of Allah the Greatest and the Exalted in Might.

During this period, all those elite of Mecca had come together who:

1. Had slain many Muslims or got them killed in other ways.
2. Had expelled hundreds of Muslims from their homes and hearths.
3. To destroy the Islamic Faith and wipe out Muslims had undertaken journeys to Abyssinia. Syria, Najd and Yemen.
4. Who had not let the Muslims live in peace after they had left for (Medina) three hundred miles off.

All those who had done all in their power to annihilate their Muslim adversaries with the power of money, might, strategy and deceit, and for twenty one years had made it their only concern.

The Apostle of Allah, mercy for Mankind, when he came out after thanks giving for Allah's Graciousness, 'Abbas (R), his uncle, submitted that the key be now entrusted to Bani Hashim. But the Prophet did not agree with his suggestion saying: "This is the day of generosity and one of gifts and donations. And calling 'Uthman he handed over the keys to him, saying: "Whoever tries to snatch them from you will be a Usurping tyrant."

Historic Address

After this act of great generosity to one who, in the light of his past conduct, hardly deserved it, he turned to the crowd of those tyrants, murderers and barabrious bereft of civility and sense of justice, who could go to any length in opposition. He addressed them thus:

"O ye the community of Quraysh! This day Allah has brought you down for your haughtyness based on Jahiliyah and pride of ancestry when the truth is: All of us are the progeny of Adam and Adam was fashioned out of clay. Then he recited the Quranic verse:

> O mankind! We created you from a single (pair of a male and a female, and made you into nations and tribes that ye may know each other (not that you may despise each other). Verily the most honoured of you in the sight of Allah is (he who is) the most righteous of you.
>
> (Q. XLIX: 13)

Then he said:

> This day let no reproach be (cast) on you. Allah will forgive you and He is the Most Merciful of all those who show mercy. —Al Quran XII: 92

Then the Apostle of Allah taking his seat at the Safa hill, took Bai'ah (oath of allegiance and fealty) from those coming to embrace Islam. On this occasion, Umar Farooq (R) was presenting them one by one before the Prophet (PBUH). Those entering this contract (Bai'ah) had to affirm the following terms:

1. I shall not associate any one with Allah in His Person, Attributes, His worthiness of being worshipped and worthiness of being invoked for aid.

2. I shall not steal, fornicate (commit adultery), commit unauthorized murder, neither be guilty of female infanticide, nor slander any one.

3. I shall to the best of my ability obey the Apostle of Allah in all matters relating to Truth and Justice.

The women had, in addition to the above, were to affirm:

In mourning for the dead they will not slap their faces nor pinch them (with the nails of their fingers). Neither tear the hair of their heads nor tear their garments to pieces, nor wrap themselves in black clothes (as a sign of mourning even to the extent of a black band on the arm), nor yet sit over the graves in mourning.

The procedure adopted here was that the Prophet (PBUH) used to immerse his hand in a basin full of water and each pledging female individual would come and immerse her hand in the water after the Prophet had taken out his own hand. On other occasion in pledging loyalty to Islam (obedience to Allah and His Apostle (PBUH)) it was deemed sufficient to a verbal affirmation (without any symbolic formality).

The next day after the conquest of Mecca, the Prophet was circumambulating Ka'bah when Fudalah bin 'Umair intended to murder the Prophet. With this evil intent when he approached him, he said: "Is Fudalah coming?" Fudalah said: "Yes it is Fudalah." The Prophet asked him: "What were you intending to do a little earlier?" Fudalah said: "Nothing was remembering Allah." On hearing this (falsehood), the Prophet (PBUH) laughed and said to him: Make your peace with Allah (entreat Him to forgive you for your evil intent of a heinous crime and falsehood). And saying this he placed his hand on his (Fudalah's) chest.

Fudalah later stated: "With his hand on my chest I had a strange experience of mind. After that no one was so dear to me as Muhammad (PBUH)"

"From there, I started for home. On the way I met my beloved girl, with whom I associated and passed my time. So she requested for a brief chat. She had an important thing to say to him.

I replied to her offer saying: "Allah and His Apostle prohibit such things." (This immediate change of heart on conversion is amazing indeed! And this is not an isolated example. The early Islamic history is replete with them).

Let us here mention briefly the incidents of forgiveness of certain specific heinous crimes of the outstanding enemies of Islam in Mecca on this occasion as an important part of Seerah.

As we have seen, the fighting men had been ordered to desist from attacking and killing people (general Amnesty), except four men and two women who, due to the nature of their crimes were liable to Qisas or punishment like for like under the Divine Law.

It was proclaimed that they should be killed.

Out of the four men only Ibn Khalal was killed. He had embraced Islam but he had killed his slave for delay in preparing food for him. After this, he had escaped, fleeing to Mecca. The other three, Ikramah bin Abu Jahl, Hiba bin-al-Aswad and Abd-Allah ibn Abi Sarah were left off.

1. Ikrama not only because of his alliance with his father Abu Jahl in atrocities against Islam, even armed struggles, he had recently against the allies of Muslims, banu Khuza'ah, he being the main culprit in the tribes annihilation.

2. Hibar had wounded Zainab, the daughter of the Prophet, with his spear causing abortion and consequent death.

3. Abd-Allah ibn Sarah had given out that revelation (in fact) came to him and Muhammad (PBUH) on hearing from him get it set down in writing.

Could these culprits expect mercy from any save the Mercy for Mankind?

Among the two women, the one guilty of intentional murder was killed under the Islamic law of 'Qisas', equal for equal.

Among those forgiven was Hindah, wife of Abu Sufyan. Mad with wild rage, she had arranged murder by artifice of Hamzah the uncle of the Prophet, in a secret arrangement with Wahshi, and after his death, she came to the battle field, took out Hamza's liver, tried to chew it and mutilated his body cutting his nose and ears had made a wreath for herself to put it round her neck.

Wahshi too was forgiven who had killed Hamzah by deception and then had desecrated his dead body by mutilation together with Hindah.

So it is evident like broad day light that the army of Muhammad had not conquered Mecca but conquered the hearts of the Makkans, through the civility and unlimited mercy and forgiveness of Muhammad (PBUH).

After the bloodless conquests of Mecca and most of them embracing Islam, there was no question of taking possession of their goods as booty as customary in battles, the Muslims who had been robbed of every thing they had there in Mecca had been taken by the pagans both forcibly and voluntarily (to remove the hitch in migration). It was all over now, some of them, however, claiming the houses they had left behind and now in possession of Makkans.

The Prophet (PBUH), however did not agree, meaning that whatever they had left in the way of Allah, they should not even think of getting back.

The Consequences of the Makkan Conquest: The Reasons of Entry to Allah's Religion in Crowds. According to the revelation a little later, people entered Allah's religion in crowds after victory with the Help of Allah. (Q. CX: 1-2). There were several reasons for it:

1. Many tribes had alliances and pacts with the Quraysh and their entry to the fold of Islam would have meant violation of trust.

2. Many tribes were too weak to act independently but were related to or allied with the Quraish. They feared severance of these relations and wrath and revenge of Quraysh which was too much for them.

3. There were some others who were waiting for the Muslims to dominate Quraysh which alone would be proof of their belonging to Allah's party, since through the centuries many attempts of powerful invaders had failed, bereft as they were of Allah's Help. Abraha Ashram, conqueror of Yemen, coming for mention in the Quran (companions of the Elephant- Q. CV: 1) was annihilated sixty-years before the conquest of Mecca (8 A.H.) by Allah's own forces, the natural agencies, having come with the intent of demolishing Ka'bah. There were some persons alive having witnessed it. So to some, the Prophet's getting the better of his own people was the true criterion of his being a true Prophet of Allah and they were waiting for conquest of Mecca.

Therefore, after the easy bloodless, perfectly peaceful take over of Mecca the former pacts disappeared into this aid, the influence and pressure of the Quraysh was no more of any consequence, and Muslim's position as aided by Allah was also made clear to the doubters so far.

And lastly, the resistance to the preaching of Islam had dissipated. The preachers could preach freely and the listeners (audience) listened unhindered and without fear, the charm of the True Faith drew crowds automatically.

After the conquest of Mecca, Hawazin and Thaqif tribes having a common border with Makkans thought to themselves that if they were to defeat the Muslims, all the groves and other properties of the Makkans in Ta'if shall become theirs without any risk. And they shall have avenged for their iconoclasm.

They brought the Bani Madar and Bani Hilal tribes also to their side as allies and with an army of four thousand strong they started for Mecca, coming down in the valley known as Hunain. Under the advice of their chief, Malik bin 'Auf, they had also brought their women, children and cattle and other goods with them. The advantage of this measure pointed out by him had been that nobody could even think of desertion of all those to save his own life.

On receiving this information, the Prophet (PBUH) who did not like to be engaged in a battle adjacent to Ka'bah and within the sacred precincts, also advanced towards the invading army.

An addition of two thousand fighting men comprising also the freshly converted to Islam was made aside the idolatrous allies under protection, thus making the Muslim army twelve thousand strong. They were feeling proud of their numerical strength to some extent and hence had become a little mindful of their usual alertness and precaution. It is borne out by the Quran:

> And on the day of Hunain: behold! your great numbers elated you, but they awaited you naught: the land for all that it is wide, did constrain you, and you turned back in retreat. —Al Quran IX: 25

The enemy lay in ambush in a narrow pass with a party of archers. When the advance guard of the Muslim army (comprising those devil-may-care-type of young men who were hardly armed or not, at least, the requisite arms) reached the enemy's range of shooting. They rained down so many arrows on them that they were forced to fly in panic. Only about a hundred on them that they were forced to fly in panic. Only about a hundred companions of the Prophet firmly held their positions in the battle field. The Prophet (PBUH) when he saw the enemy advancing and his own army running away for safety, displayed unique valour and perseverance. He got down his mule and said:

"I am a Prophet, there is not a shade of doubt about it I am the son of Abd-al-Muttalib."

What he meant to convey was that success or failure in an armed conflict was not the criterion of his position as a true Apostle of Allah. Rather it lay in his own identity and personality.

At this stage of confusion, Abbas (R), the uncle of the Prophet, started calling them by their distinguishing features as Muhajirs (immigrants) and Ansar (the helpers) and they responded to this call like a flight of pigeons without delay. Now the army was arranged in a totally different order, with muhajirs and Ansars in the forefront. With the renewed attack in this order, the enemy took to flight, getting divided into two groups:

1. The leader of this group, Malik bin 'Auf with this fighting men took refuge in the fort at Ta'if.

2. The other group comprising their women and children alongwith their goods went into concealment in the Autas gorge.

The Prophet (PBUH) ordered siege of the Ta'if fort, and to take vigilant care of Autas gorge he appointed Abu 'Amir Ash'ari, who on getting there took possession of the families and goods of the enemy. When the Prophet learnt about performance of Abu 'Amir at Autas, he ordered lifting siege of the Ta'if Fort, since they were faced with the calamity of losing their most precious assets, wives, children and goods. There were 24,000 camels, 40 thousand goats, four thousand oqiah (about 420 kilogram) silver and six thousand women and children in all.

The Prophet had stayed very close to the battle field, where six chiefs of the Hawazin tribe came to him appealing for mercy. Some of these men were those who had rained stones on him when he was visiting Ta'if on a preaching mission, and Zaid (R) had lifted him unconscious to carry him to safety.

The Prophet (PBUH) said to them: "Welcome! I had myself been waiting for you. Two weeks have elapsed and the booty has not yet been distributed. In consideration of your request I can release prisoners coming to my share and those of my family. And if there were Muhajirs and Ansar alone with me (as fighting men) I could consider their shares also. But as you can see for yourself, I have here with me even those who are yet unbelievers. So we will have to tackle this problem in this way: come to me tomorrow morning after the early morning prayer (Fajr) to present your request in the presence of the assembly of common people. Let us see if a solution can be found." He concluded saying: "choose for yourself your good or your families since the invading army cannot be reconciled to total deprivation. (They must get something as return for their (taking) pains)."

Next morning the same representatives presented themselves on the scene and in public gathering repeated their request for the release of their prisoners to the Prophet.

Great Amnesty

The Prophet of mercy said to them: I hereby release the prisoners, my own and those of Banu Abd-al-Muttalib free (without demanding any ransom for them). The Ansar and Muhajirin with one voice declared that they too were releasing those coming to their shares.

Now it came to Bani Saleem and Bani Fuzava. It was something strange to them that the invading enemy, luckily vanquished also, should be shown such mercy and generosity. So they did not proclaim their prisoners released. The Prophet called them and after deliberation, 6 camels was settled as the equivalent of one prisoner and the Prophet paid it to them, and the remaining prisoners were also set free. He also donated one changes of clothes to all the prisoners at parting time.

Among these prisoners was also Shima' bint Harith the daughter of the Prophet's wet nurse Halimah. The Prophet recognized this foster sister of his and spread out his sheet on the ground to sit on. He said to her: "It would be much better for you to stay here with me. However, you are perfectly free to go back home if you please. She wanted to return home and was sent away to her own people honourably.

The booty was distributed on the spot. The largest shares were awarded to those who had recently embraced Islam. The most sincere, Ansars, received nothing. He consoled the younger lot showing dissatisfaction saying would they not be pleased taking him with them while others take some petty goods. They were very much pleased. Some of them were moved to tears of joy on hearing these words from the Prophet (PBUH). It had afforded them much greater pleasure than those receiving booty.

Some poet has expressed the Prophet's generosity in the following verse:

To me Khaiber and Hunain stand witness (to the fact)

That you most generously give away what you win through conquests.

Breach of Faith

Yehudi, as a matter of fact, should be the name of the offspring of Yehuda, the third son of Yaqub (Jacob) only. But somehow the progeny of all the twelve sons of Jacob came to be called by this name and now the Israelites are usually termed Yahudi or Jews a denomination which due to their transgression and evil traits of character had become the most detestable among the nations of the world. They, in their vain glory and self-conceit, claim to be the chosen of God, worthy of exaltation and rule over the rest of the world, Here and in eternal bliss Hereafter when the rest of humanity is fit only to be the fuel of Fire of Hell, the horrible pit. Of all that tall talk and braggadocio only this much is true that they are the progeny of a long line of Prophets and so many high ranking prophets were raised from them through the ages and they were really a fine people chosen by Allah in a particular period for a sacred mission borne out by the Quran also and for some time they proved worthy of it too. "But long ages passed over them and their hearts grew hard" (Q. LVll: 16) and through shameful breach solemn covenants, persecuting their prophets, even killing them, calling Allah "close fisted" "Allah is indigent and we are rich", saying to Moses, their great benefactor, "Go you and your Lord and fight, we are sitting here," and many worse blasphemies which brought Allah's wrath and they were deposed from leadership of humanity, cursed and dispersed.

Their own and last of the Israeli line of prophets, 'Isa (PBUH), kind-hearted as he was, but witnessing their despicable conduct, had called them (venomous) vipers and their progeny and had also prophesied that the kingdom of God (leadership and guidance of mankind) shall be taken away from them and entrusted to another community that may make it blossom, coming into full bloom.

When the appointed time for this prophecy came true (materialized) and Muhammad the Apostle of Allah, Muhammad (PBUH) (called Ahmad in another prophecy by 'Isa the son of Mary):

> 'O children of Israel! I am the messenger of Allah (sent) to you confirming the Turat (which came) before me and giving gladtidings of a messenger to come after me, whose name shall be Ahmad. —Al Quran LXI: 6),

The Jews finding them conflicting with their self-devised independent views about 'Isa whom they almost handed over to the Roman governor to be crucified, they were very much annoyed and in their rage finally decided to vex, tyrannize and get him out of their way if possible as they had earlier done with his predecessor 'Isa ibn-Maryam.

Although the Jews in the very first year of migration had entered an agreement of peace for all the communities of Medina yet their inherent evil nature and diseased mentality could not remain hidden for long and eighteen months after signing the contract they had entered with the Prophet and the Muslim community mischiefs one after the other were witnessed.

When the Muslims with the Prophet (PBUH) had gone to Badr, a Muslim woman went one day to the locality of Banu Qainuqa' to sell milk. Some Jews played a mischief and stripped her in the market place. Hearing the screams of the woman, a Muslim rushed to the scene and in a rage murdered the mischief mongering culprit, Jew. The Jews gathered together on the spot of murder and they killed the Muslim creating a tumult. On his return from Badr, the Prophet called the Jews to enquire about this riot. They returned the signed copy of agreement with the Prophet to him and the Muslims and appeared bent on a war against the Muslims.

Things had now come to an insurrection and the Jews were punished in as much as forcing them to leave Medina and go to Khaibar to settle down.

Chain of Misdeeds

As stated earlier, the Quraysh had written to the unbelievers of Medina after migration to fight against the Prophet but due to the sagacity and clever handling of the situation it came to naught. After defeat at Badr they again wrote, but this time to the Jews of Medina:

"You are a powerful community, economically well off, in possessions of properties and forts. Fight against Muhammad or else we shall do such and such with you, taking off even the ornaments adorning the ankles of your women." On receipt of this letter, their Banu Nadir tribe was determined on violation of the agreement with the Prophet as well as deceitfully harm him.

It was in 4 A.H. that the Prophet went to the locality of Banu Nadir to collect a national subscription (it was probably to pay the blood money in connection with a murder). They seated him beneath a wall and planned that (the accursed) Ibn Hajash going upon the wall would let fall a heavy stone over him and thus end his life.

After sitting there for some time, he was informed by supernatural means (Allah's own special agencies) of the impending danger and left the place in time.

At last Banu Nadir were punished with banishment from Medina to get settled at Khaiber. They loaded all their goods, even the doors and windows of their houses they had themselves razed to the ground, on six hundred camels and settled in Khaiber.

The Third Conspiracy of the Jews, The General Insurrection Resulting in the Battle of Ahzab (Confederates) or Battle of Trench

The outstanding feature of the 5th year A.H. is battle of Ahzab. Banu Nadhir did not sit idle even after their banishment to Khaiber. They resolved to make a united effort for the total annihilation of the Muslims, involving all the tribes and religions of Arabia. They should participate with their select seasoned swordsmen. They selected twenty chiefs to induce all the tribes of Arabia to come together in a aggressive war against the Muslims. Their efforts were fruitful. In the month of Ziqa'dah 5 A.H. a formidable army of ten thousand strong including idolaters and Jews with some others, invaded Medina. The Quran calls it the Battle of Ahzab (the confederates).

1. Quraish, Banu Kananah, under the command of Suiyan bin Harb

2. Bani Fazarah under the command of 'Uqbah bin Husain

3. Bani Murrah under the command of Harith bin 'Auf

4. Bani Ashja' and Najdis commanded by Mas'ood bin Dakheelah

When the Muslim found themselves incapable of facing them in the open, they acted at the instance of Salman Farsi's (of Persia or Iran), an outstanding companion of the Prophet, they decided to dig a trench (for the first time in Arabia) and started work on it with great enthusiasm. Each team often persons had dugged out forty yards. While at it, the companions recited the following verse:

We are those who have taken an oath of fealty

At the hands of Muhammad to adhere to Islam forever

The Prophet himself helped the companions in the digging operations, breaking hard rock and removal of earth. In this strenuous labour, his chest was covered with dust. He undertook work where others failed.

The battle worthy Muslims were three thousand in all. They came to the battle field in such a manner that the trench was in front of them and Sala' mount at the back. Banu Quraizah the Jewish tribe, resident in Medina and under obligation as signatories of the agreement that we can call Medina charter of Human Rights, the chief of the Banu Nadir, Hai bin Akhtab visited them in the darkness of the night and insisting on them to violate the agreement made them join the invading hordes. The Prophet repeatedly sent his heralds to them to bring them round and desisting from breach of faith, but they flatly refused to listen to them saying: "Who is Muhammad to us that we should listen to him? We are not bound to him by any bond whatsoever."

Afterthat Banu Quraizah started disturbing the peace of the town. The lives, honour and property of Muslim women and children was imperilled. In this helpless situation, a detachment from this non too big a number had to be sent back to Medina to guard it, and maintain peace if breach was wickedly created by the Jews. Banu Quraizah were under the impression that the ferocious attack of ten thousand from outside and we inside the town creating lawlessness, can make life miserable for Muslim, they will be totally wiped out leaving no trace behind.

Since the Prophet was by nature peace-loving and anti-war, he held consultation with the companions on an offer of peace on the term of payment of one third of their produce (of duties). But the Ansar preferred war. Sa'd bin Mu'az (R) and S'ad bin 'Ubadah (R) speaking on the resolution submitted: When we were polytheists and idolaters, we never gave them anything (under pressure). Now that Allah has honoured us with Islam, how can we give them one third of our produce. For them we have nothing but our swords.

The invading army besieged them (Muslims) for twenty days. A few occasional single handed combats were also witnessed. 'Umar bin Abdand who boasted of equality with thousand men in combat was killed easily by 'Ali Murtza (R) in one such single combat. And Naufal bin Abd-Allah bin Mughira too was killed in an encounter. The Makkans offered ten thousand dirhams for the dead body of Naufal. The Prophet (PBUH) told his men to hand over the dead body. Nothing in return was needed.

When they could not confront Muslims during this period of siege, they were dejected and left one night bag and baggage surely grieved.

Last Act

After getting rid of this troublesome affair, the Prophet called Banu Quraizah to explain their position face to face (show cause for their dastardly conduct). Now Banu Quraizah in a state of self imposed siege in their fort woefully prepared for a trial of strength. At this stage, the Muslims came to know that the Banu Nadir chief Hai bin Akhtab was still with them in the fort.

This role of a trouble maker was not the first instance on the part of Banu Quraizah. At the time of Badr, they had strengthened the position of Quraysh with war material and arms. But then the kind hearted Prophet (PBUH) had forgiven them.

Now that they had taken refuge in their fort, the Muslims had no other cause left open to them but to have a go at them. They were factually besieged now by an invading army in zi-al-Hijjah, which lasted 25 days. The siege now becoming intolerable and sick of it they contacted the Muslims of Aus tribe with whom they were on terms of friendship since long and reconciled the Prophet to agree to the arbitration of Sa'd bin Mu'az (Aus chief) in their (Banu Quraizah's) affair and his arbitration should be acceptable to him.

Banu Quraizah came out of the fort and their case was entrusted to Sa'd bin Mu'az. What high hopes Aus and Banu Quraizah might have been nursing after Mu'az was accepted arbiter by both the parties? But this manly arbiter and God fearing Muslim after necessary investigations gave the following verdict:

1. The combat-worthy males of banu Quraizah be put to sword.

2. Women and children be taken as prisoner of war (slave).

3. Their goods be divided as booty.

In the materialization of this arbitration, what we learn from a report in Bukhari by Abu Sa'eed Khudri, that able-bodied combat-worthy men were killed. But the tradition has nothing to say about the women and children being taken as prisoners (slaves). It must also be kept in mind that the arbiter of their own choice, had pronounced for them the same punishment which they inflicted on their criminals and prescribed by their Shari'ah.

We have reasons to believe and precedents to show that Banu Quraizah had left their case in the hands of the Prophet (PBUH) the greatest punishment that would have been pronounced could be their banishment from Medina to settle in Khaiber. The cases of Banu Qainuza' and Banu Nadir are two precedents before us. The Prophet (PBUH) had mercifully exempted some of them (Banu Quraizah) also from the pronounced punishment. For example Zuhair (Jew) had received pardon from him with wife, children and his goods. And Rifa'ah (Jew) had also been spared his life.

11

Victory at Last

Medina was agog with stories of mass conversion of the people to Islam. There were converts in Mecca as well but the infidels outnumbered them. While, during the 'Ascension', the holy Prophet (PBUH) was given various guidelines, it was indicated to him that he would have to emigrate for the ultimate victory of the Faith.

Verse 80 of Sura Bani Israil points to this, where the holy Prophet (PBUH) was advised to pray:

"My Lord! Cause me to enter with a firm incoming and go out with a firm outgoing; and grant me from your Presence a sustaining power."

According to Ibne Abbas, this verse contained the Divine command for the holy Prophet (PBUH) to migrate from Mecca.

Conquest of Mecca

Twelve years of Prophethood had elapsed in Mecca and, despite his best efforts to convert the polytheists of that city, the holy Prophet (PBUH) continued to face their opposition and persecution.' He would look towards the heaven, sometimes, and pray to God to turn their hearts towards Islam, so that the people of Mecca, for whose reformation he was initially sent, could be saved from the final doom. The holy Prophet (PBUH) was fully conscious of the Quranic edict that "if some one saved someone else from a catastrophe, he almost saved the entire mankind. But the Divine knowledge encompassed who would receive the guidance and who would not.Therefore, the holy Prophet (PBUH) was advised not to feel depressed at the attitude of the people of Mecca:

"But if they are averse, We have not sent you as a warder over them. Thine is only to convey the message." (Al-Shura-48)"

Further, knowing that the holy Prophet (PBUH) had a soft corner for his own people of Mecca, the Divine command came:

"Therefore, O, Prophet! Do not treat them with favour, as you are not to blame at all."

This was by way of consolation to the holy Prophet (PBUH) that he had done his duty, and if the polytheists of Mecca did not listen to his preaching, he should leave them alone;

"Leave Me to deal with those who falsify thy preaching. We shall lead them on by steps from whence they do not know.

And yet I bear with them, but My scheme is firm".

(Qalam 41-45)

Again, Allah tried to explain to the holy Prophet (PBUH) in Sura Muzammil:

"Leave Me to deal with the deniers who are enjoying ease and comfort (of this life) and give them respite awhile"

The holy Prophet (PBUH) was now fully conscious of the fact that the last warning from the Lord had been served on these unlucky folk, as had happened earlier in the case of the deniers of the Prophets of God, but his attitude was quite different from that of the other Prophets. For example, Prophet Noah appealed to God, in similar circumstances:

"O, Lord! Do not leave even a single of the infidels safe on this earth."

Thus, the entire nation of Prophet Noah was drowned in the deluge, including his own son who belonged to the group of his detractors.

Similarly, Prophet Hood warned his people that if they failed to respond to his call, God would impose some other people over them. And this is exactly what happened, as those who had accepted the Prophet's message were saved and the rest perished.

Again, the people of Thamud, who were a wicked lot, were completely destroyed when they did not listen to the preaching of Prophet Saleh, who was sent to reform them.

General Amnesty

But, in identical conditions, when the people of Mecca made it almost impossible for the holy Prophet (PBUH) to live with security and when the people of Taif behaved brutally with him, he stayed the Divine punishment as he was sent as a "mercy for all mankind."

It was in the 13th year of Prophethood, during Haj season, when people from all over Arabia had assembled in Mecca, that four Muslims of Medina, who had not seen the holy Prophet (PBUH) before, were very eager to have a glimpse of him, and after great secrecy and caution lest the infidels of Mecca do them harm, enquired about the holy Prophet's (PBUH) address from some one who was, perhaps, a Muslim. They were Uwaim bin Saeda, Saad bin Khasima, Maan bin Adi and Abdullah bin Jubair. They had not seen the holy Prophet (PBUH) before, but recognised him at first sight because of his special prophetic features and captivating appearance and bearing. Picking up courage and collecting their senses, they saluted the holy Prophet (PBUH) which was duly acknowledged. Thereafter, they enquired:

"When will your goodself meet the people of Medina?"

The holy Prophet's (PBUH) uncle Hazrat Abbas, with whom he was staying at that time, enquired from the Ansar:

"Have the polytheists of Medina also accompanied you people?"

They answered in the affirmative. They were advised to keep the meeting a guarded secret until the pilgrims started journeying back after Haj. The holy Prophet (PBUH) fixed the slopes of Aqba as the meeting place and night fall as the time of the meeting.

The holy Prophet (PBUH) also advised them not to awaken any one who might be asleep and not to wait for one who might be absent. He had given similar instructions to Baraa bin Maroor and Kaab bin Malik when they had met him in the precincts of Kaaba.

At the appointed time and place, 71 men and 2 women of the Ansar of Medina, one by the name of Nasiba bint Kaab Umme Ammara and the other a courageous lady Asma bint Amroo, met the holy Prophet (PBUH).

It may be pointed out here that when the false prophets like Musailma Kazzat, during the caliphate of Hazrat Abu Bakr, raised their heads, Umme Ammara and her son, Abdullah took part in the campaign against Musailma and she lost one arm and suffered twelve grievous injuries. Prior to this Musailma had chopped off one limb after another of her son, Habib, who refused to acknowledge Musailma as a true prophet.

The holy Prophet (PBUH), accompanied by his uncle Hazrat Abbas, was already there at Aqaba when the Ansar, who were extremely eager to cast a glance at the holy Prophet (PBUH), arrived there. The holy Prophet, (PBUH) at the outset, advised them to be brief in expressing their views, as the detectives of the polytheists might be on their trail. Then, his uncle addressed the 73 Ansar in a low voice:

"O, people of Khazraj! I need not tell you in what high esteem we hold Muhammad (PBUH) and the entire clan of Banu Hashim has been at his back to protect him from his enemies. But now he has decided firmly to migrate to your city. Therefore, if you can fulfil your promise and can support him against all odds, then he can go with you, otherwise you may leave him alone."

A representative of theirs undertook to discharge all possible responsibilities in respect of the holy Prophet's (PBUH) protection and offered to declare it on any kind of oath.

Then, the holy Prophet (PBUH) verses from the holy Quran and spoke:

"I obtain your oath of fealty that you will protect me in the same manner as you would do your own children."

Therefore, Bara bin and Abul Haisan bin AlTihan stood up and assured the holy Prophet (PBUH) of full protection the way he wanted, but Abul Haisan, at the same time posed the question:

"O, Prophet of God! Should we rule out the possibility of your deserting us and joining your people of Mecca when you get the upper hand and become victorious?"

The holy Prophet (PBUH) smiled and assured:

'Never, never will it so happen. I shall live and die among you. I am yours and you are mine. Whoever is your enemy is my enemy and whoever is your friend is my friend."

This assurance cheered them up and all of them took the oath of fealty at the holy Prophet's (PBUH) hand. This was the last oath of fealty at Aqba.

Hazrat Bara bin delivered a very impassioned speech on the occasion pledging all support for the cause of Islam.

It may be borne in mind that the Ansar of Medina were not providing a kind of refuge to the holy Prophet (PBUH) taking him as a helpless displaced person but recognising him as their leader for whom they could lay their lives if the occasion arose. In fact, they considered it a great honour to play host to the holy Prophet (PBUH).

According to the 'Tabaqat', the holy Prophet (PBUH) asked them to elect 12 representatives from among them who should be dependable and responsible persons in their respective tribes and according to Ibne Ishaque, the holy Prophet (PBUH) cited the example of Prophet Jesus's helpers. Out of the twelve representatives, who were unanimously elected, nine belonged to the tribe of Khazraj and three to Aus.

Hardly had the 73 Ansar who had taken the oath of fealty at Aqba, retired to their camps that the polytheists of Mecca got wind of it and they contacted the Ansar in their camps and protested against their offer of refuge to the holy Prophet (PBUH) in Medina. The polytheists of Medina, who had no knowledge of this oath of fealty denied that any such offer had been made, and by daybreak they left for 'Medina'. The polytheists of Mecca went in hot pursuit after them and succeeded only in getting hold of Saad bin Ibada, who also got free shortly afterwards and returned to Medina. These 73 converts of Medina broke all the idols in their city, except a few.

End of Idolatory Days

At that time, Ba'alma's Chief Umroo bin Jamoo, who wielded great influence in Medina was lying prostrate before the beautifully carved wooden idol of Manaat in his house, as the night before this idol had been removed from its pedestal and dumped on garbage outside his house. He had, somehow, succeeded in recovering this 'desecrated' idol the same night; but when he went to the idol's chamber in his house, the next morning he found the idol missing again and he discovered it again lying on the heap of litter outside his house. He again restored it to its pedestal and hung an unsheated sword in its neck supplicating it to defend itself against the intruder. But the next morning, the idol was again missing and was found in a dry well with a dead dog tied to its neck in place of the sword. In the meanwhile, came his son Maad bin Umroo, who had turned a Muslim, accompanied by youths of his tribe, who explained to him the monotheistic message of Islam, driving home the point that if a life-less idol could not protect itself, it was sheer folly to expect of it any kind of help and assistance.

The disconcerting news of the spread of Islam in Medina had unnerved the polytheists of Mecca and they intensified their persecution of the Muslim converts of Mecca, making it impossible for them to continue living in their place of birth.

Among the heart-rending incidents of their oppression is the tale of Hazrat Umma Salma wife of the holy Prophet's (PBUH) aunt Barra bint Abdul Muttalib. She and her husband had decided to migrate from Mecca to Medina alongwith their children. Hardly had they mounted the camel with their belongings loaded on it, that Bani Mughira, to which tribe Umme Salma belonged, forced the wife and the girl child to dismount. They took both of them back to their tribe. Learning of this, the tribesmen of the husband appeared on the scene and took away their son just as the wife's tribesmen had taken away their daughter. Hazrat Umme Salma was so badly aggrieved that she spent most of her time in Mecca lamenting her separation from the husband and the son. One day, one of the notables of Bani Mughira chanced to witness the wailing and mourning of Hazrat Umme Salma and he was so affected by it that he prevailed upon his tribesmen to let Hazrat Umme Salma go to join her husband and she, accordingly set out for Medina and got united with her husband at Quba, on the outskirts of the city.

According to Ibne Ishaque, the holy Prophet (PBUH) permitted all the Muslims of Mecca to migrate under the circumstances, and soon family after family set out for Medina severing all connections with their native place and leaving their hearths and homes.

But the persecution was not restricted within the confines of Mecca alone. The polytheists even raided the approaches to Medina and arrested the emigrants whenever they could. One such case pertaining to the arrest of Hazrat Ayyash whom Abu Jahl and Haris bin Hisham arrested through deceit and brought him to Mecca lashed on camel back scorning and jesting and inciting the people of Mecca to follow suit.

But the distinctive way in which Hazrat Umar migrated from Mecca was eminently different from that of others. He openly sought the holy Prophet's (PBUH) leave, circumambulated the Kaaba, offered prayers there and declared aloud that he was migrating-to Medina and if one had the courage or strength to stop him from doing so, he should come forward. None did so, and he left in a procession of twenty riders in day light accompanied, among others, by his brother Zaid bin Khattab, brother-in-law Sayed bin Zaid. According to their plan, Ayyash bin Ali Rabeeya and Hisham bin Aas bin Wael had to meet them at a place ten miles away from Mecca; but Hisham was caught on way and Ayyash succeeded in reaching Medina. However, shortly, thereafter, Abu Jahl and Haris bin Hisham reached Medina and, through a perfidy, returned to Mecca, despite Hazrat Umar's advice to the contrary. Hazrat Ayyash was the cousin of Abu Jahl and Haris. How the two behaved with him after bringing him to Mecca in chains, like a prisoner, we know.

The holy Prophet (PBUH), Hazrat Abu Bakr and Hazrat Ali stayed on in Mecca:

Hazrat Abu Bakr, when he sought leave to migrate, was advised by the holy Prophet (PBUH) to tarry a little as he hoped that he would himself be given Divine permission to migrate. Hearing this, Hazrat Abu Bakr's joy knew no bounds. It is related, on the authority of Hazrat Ali, that Gabriel had informed the holy Prophet (PBUH), in advance, that Hazrat Abu Bakr would be his companion and comrade during migration.

The Meetings

The notables of Quraish were upset at the situation in Mecca and were holding secret sessions in the 'house of consultation' - Damn - Nadwa. They anticipated that in case the holy Prophet (PBUH) also left for Medina, he would be able to secure a strong foot-hold there, gifted as he was, with the power of persuasion and ability of guidance and organisation. What they apprehended most was the danger that the nascent Muslim power in Medina, which lay on the trade route for Mecca to Egypt, Syria and other Roman possessions, would pose a serious threat to their trade with these countries. At the instigation of Abu Jahl, they decided that each tribe should select one youth and they should jointly attack the holy Prophet (PBUH) and kill him. In that case, the holy Prophet's (PBUH) tribe will not be in a position to avenge his death and they will have no option but agree to accept ransom money for the death of the holy Prophet (PBUH). The proposal was adopted with extreme secrecy and the executants of this nefarious plan had also been selected. But nothing could remain hidden from Allah, Who revealed their secret plot to the holy Prophet (PBUH).

According to Ibne Ishaque, the holy Prophet (PBUH), hooding his face, came to Hazrat Abu Bakr's place at an un-usual time of mid-day and disclosed to him that he had been permitted by the Almighty to migrate and also that Hazrat Abu Bakr would be his companion during the journey. Hazrat Abu Bakr had already made arrangements of two dromedaries for the journey, one of which was purchased by the holy Prophet (PBUH) then and there from his companion despite the latter's protestations to the contrary. The holy Prophet (PBUH) promised to pay the actual price of the she-camel to Hazrat Abu Bakr.

Thereafter, the holy Prophet (PBUH) sent for Abdullah bin Alariqat, who was known for his expertise as a guide in the desert. Though a polytheist, he was a dependable man. This is the fellow whom the holy Prophet (PBUH) had sent to Matam bin Adi' as his personal envoy on return from Taif. Both the she-camels were made over to Abdullah bin Ariqat with instructions to reach the appointed site whenever advised.

Only Hazrat Ali had to stay on in Mecca and that too for returning the things deposited by the Makkans as trust with the holy Prophet (PBUH). He had to leave for Medina thereafter.

The polytheists had deputed detectives around the holy Prophet's (PBUH) house to keep an eye on his movements and advise the killers of the opportune time.

While the holy Prophet (PBUH) was busy preparing with a heavy heart to leave his home for good and be away from Kaaba for almost an uncertain time, he approached Usman, the key-bearer of Kaaba, a sworn enemy of Islam and an opponent of the holy

Prophet (PBUH). He requested him to open the door of the Kaaba for a short while so that he could have a last look at it.

Usman, who had persecuted his cousin Masab bin Umair most inhumanly, was not the type of person to oblige the holy Prophet (PBUH). However, the holy Prophet (PBUH) left Kaaba saying to Usman:

"Remember, a time will come when I will entrust this key to a person from whom no power can ever withdraw the key."

And, the day dawned after the conquest of Mecca when Usman was standing in front of the holy Prophet (PBUH) hanging his head in disgrace. No one anticipated to whom the holy Prophet (PBUH) would entrust the keys of Kaaba. But, what a surprise, when the holy Prophet (PBUH) entrusted the key to the same Usman who had not only been always disrespectful to him but one of the worst enemies of Islam. Usman was so swayed by emotion that he fell on the holy Prophet's (PBUH) feet and embraced Islam.

On the day, the polytheists had planned to assassinate the holy Prophet (PBUH), he did not come out of his house. This assured them that the holy Prophet was inside his house. So, they surrounded his house near Safa. The holy Prophet (PBUH) sent for Hazrat Ali and gave him his green cloak advising him to wrap himself up with that sheet of cloth and sleep on his bed so that the enemies might be under the impression that their quandary was in the house. He also instructed Hazrat Ali about the details of the articles held by him in trust and to return them to their owners.

After nightfall, the holy Prophet (PBUH), reciting the opening verses of Sura Yasin, came out of the house and went unnoticed by the would be assassins who stood around his house with their weapons of death. He took Hazrat Abu Bakr alongwith him and crossed the limits of Mecca before day-break.

In the morning, the killers peeped into his house and discovered that it was Hazrat Ali who was lying on the holy Prophet's (PBUH) bed. They got hold of Hazrat Ali and enquired about the holy Prophet's whereabouts. But since the former did not actually know where the holy Prophet (PBUH) was at that time, he could not tell them anything.

They beat him and locked him up in the precincts of Kaaba. But when they learnt that the articles kept in trust with the holy Prophet (PBUH) by many of them were in Hazrat Ali's custody, they released him.

The polytheists searched and searched on the routes leading to Medina but could not find any trace of the holy Prophet (PBUH), who had taken refuge in the Cave of Thaur which falls in the west on way to Yemen. None of them suspected that he would have travelled to Yemen.

According to Ibne Hisham, the polytheists, in sheer disgust and great anger reached Hazrat Abu Bakr's house, led by Abu Jahl and enquired from Hazrat Asma bint Abu Bakr about her father's whereabouts, and finding no satisfactory reply, Abu Jahl slapped her on the face.

The holy Prophet (PBUH) stayed in the cave of Thaur for three days, looking towards Kaaba which was built by his ancient ancestor, Prophet Abraham with supplication to the Almighty to send a Prophet in Arabia from his progeny. Hazrat Abu Bakr had first closed the various holes in the cave and cleaned it and then asked the holy Prophet (PBUH) to set his foot inside. On one of the holes, he put his heel to keep away serpents or other creeping animals from harming the holy Prophet (PBUH).

It was a dark night, and two holy persons, the holy Prophet (PBUH) and Hazrat Abu Bakr, were trudging along continuously in the hilly terrain in the dim light of the stars. Sometimes, Hazrat

Abu Bakr walked ahead and sometimes behind the holy Prophet (PBUH), to protect him from any one cither attacking him from the front or from the rear. Hazrat Abu Bakr had already instructed before hand his son Hazrat Abdullah, after disclosing him in confidence that they would travel via Yemen and take rest in the Cave of Thaur to keep an eye on the movements of the polytheists in day and inform him about their plans and activities by visiting the cave at night. At the same time, he had instructed his freed slave Hazrat Aamir to bring the goats for grazing near the cave so that the holy Prophet (PBUH) could get milk regularly.

One day, while still in the Cave, they heard the voice and sounds of footsteps close to the cave. These belonged to the polytheists of Mecca who had succeeded in tracing their whereabouts with the help of experts of foot prints of men and camels.

Hazrat Abu Bakr whispered to the holy Prophet (PBUH):

"O, Messenger of Allah! If any one of them would look below his feet, he might he able to locate us."

The holy Prophet (PBUH) consoled him:

"We are not two of us here. Allah is the third Being with us."

In the meantime, the voices grew louder. The expert of foot-prints, Alqama Khazai, was telling the pursuants that no foot-prints were discernable beyond the cave. Some one suggested:

"Let us enter the Cave and see".

But Umayya bin Khalaf laughed at the idea saying:

"There is a large spider's web on the mouth of the cave which is perhaps, there from before Mohammad was born."

Thereafter, they all went back. This was purely Divine power that misled them and they returned unsuccessful.

The holy Quran refers to this incident in these words: (Tauba: 40) "If you did not help him, Allah still helped him when the disbelievers drove him forth, the second of the two, when they two were in the cave, when he said to his comrade: Grieve not as Allah is with us. Then Allah caused His peace of reassurance to descend upon him and supported with hosts you can not see and made the word of the disbelievers low while it was Allah's word that became uppermost. Allah is Mighty, Wise."

End of an Era

These few words sum up, in a nutshell, the history of Islam's victory over the whole of Arabia. This verse, according to the various authorities on Quran being a part of Sura Tauba, is believed to have been revealed in Zeeqad of 9th A.H. the period when the holy Prophet (PBUH) had thrown the gauntlet against the world's super power at that time and preparations were afoot for the battle of Tabuk. This sura calls the Muslims to wage war against the disbelievers and condemns those who, on account of their lack of faith or weakness, shirk their responsibility to participate in the efforts for Allah's cause, and promises Divine help in case the hypocrite Muslims do not come forward to hold the banner of faith aloft. By referring to such Divine help against the enemies of the holy Prophet (PBUH) while the latter was taking refuge in the Cave, Allah made the believers firm in their faith in similar help in future in case they fought for the cause of Islam.

The disappointed polytheists, after their unsuccessful attempt to apprehend the holy Prophet (PBUH), announced a reward of 200 camels for any one who could arrest or assassinate the holy Prophet (PBUH) and his companion, Hazrat Abu Bakr.

After staying in the Cave for three consecutive nights and days, when the polytheists had given up further attempt to trace him, the holy Prophet (PBUH) sent for Abdullah bin Ariqat, the man with the she-camels, to come to the Cave on the fourth day. Hazrat Abu Bakr's daugther, Hazrat Asma brought with her food and ration for the journey but forgot to bring the strapped pouch (Kajawa') in which such articles are loaded and hung on the camel's back. She tore her waist band in two and tied with it the container of food and provisions and hung it on the camel's harness. Since then she was nick-named as the" lady who tore her waist band in two."

In the latter part of the night, the small caravan of two camels, led by Abdullah bin Ariqat left for the destination—Medina—the holy Prophet (PBUH) and Hazrat Abu Bakr each riding a camel with Hazrat Aamir bin Fahira sitting behind Hazrat Abu Bakr on the same camel.

According to Qastlani, this momentous journey of migration commenced on Monday, as the holy Prophet (PBUH) had spent the night of Friday, Saturday and Sunday in the Cave of Thaur. The caravan kept on moving till afternoon of the next day. Hazrat Abu Bakr, finding the comforting shade under a protruding rock laid a carpet under it and suggested to the holy Prophet (PBUH) to rest a while. Hazrat Abu Bakr got some milk from a shepherd boy who was grazing his flock in the nearby pasture and offered it to the holy Prophet (PBUH) to drink. When the sun's heat subsided, they set out on the journey ahead. But, suddenly, when the camels led by Ariqat stepped out of the hilly terrain and came on a plain tract, Hazrat Abu Bakr noticed a horse-rider approaching them.

Hazrat Abu Bakr got worried and spoke:

"O, Messenger of Allah! The pursuer has come quite close."

"May Allah make him fall from horse-back", the holy Prophet (PBUH) prayed. And instantly, the rider fell from the horse, but he again jumped on horse-back and started pursuing. The holy Prophet (PBUH) prayed and the rider's horse sank chest-deep in the sand. Now the rider was evidently perplexed and he drew a lot to ascertain whether his pursuit would be successful. The result was in the negative. This disheartened him completely and he thought to himself that the holy Prophet (PBUH) would succeed in escaping from him. Therefore, he loudly shouted in a trembling voice giving out his name as Suraqa bin Jaasham and swearing that he should be allowed to be heard as he would do no harm. He came near and informed the holy Prophet (PBUH) of the reward for his head announced by the polytheists of Mecca. He apologetically said to the holy Prophet (PBUH):

"O, Messenger of Allah! Kindly command me to do whatever you want me to do. You will find me obedient."

But the holy Prophet (PBUH) only asked him to keep his whereabouts during this journey a guarded secret and to prevent any one from pursuing him.

On Suraqa's request, the holy Prophet (PBUH) asked Aamir bin Fahira to write on a piece of leather that the former had been pardoned and granted protection in future. Thus, it was again a Divine marvel that the man who had come to assassinate the holy Prophet (PBUH) turned into a protector telling others not to go in the direction of his small caravan as he had searched the entire area and there was no trace of the holy Prophet (PBUH).

The holy Prophet (PBUH) kept on journeying toward Medina till the sand dunes of Quwaid became visible an the sun's heat became less oppressive and its rays acquire a yellow hue like that of dried grass, and the shades in the foot-hills grew bigger and bigger. Just in front lay the tent of Umme Maabad where something to refresh the wear travellers could be hoped for. The holy caravan inched forward and reached the tent. What happened there, had already been narrated in the opening part of this book.

The real destination was Medina, at a distance fro Quwaid, where the Ansar (Helpers) and Muhaji (immigrants) were awaiting the arrival of the holy Prophet (PBUH) most impatiently with extreme anxiety about his welfare. Every morning, a group of theirs looked for him on the approaches to Medina and they returned to the homes in the evenings in despair.

But tomorrow was going to be that auspicious day when they will not return in despondency, because who will enter the limits of Medina, on the coming day would belong to them for good.The Ansar and the Muhajirs were figuring out by calculating the normally taken on journey from Mecca to Medina, after arrived at the conclusion that the holy Prophet (PBUH) should have reached by then. Since their expectations had not materialised according to their earthly calculations, they were all visibly worried and over-anxious on account of that person, who was more dear to them than their own children and their personal possessions.

No one should misconstrue their deep devotion to the holy Prophet (PBUH) because they had reposed unswerving belief in his Prohethood, but because they were also enamoured of his personal qualities of head and heart, his spotless character, moral conduct, noble precepts, pious deeds, truthfulness and trust-worthiness, benevolent disposition, kindness to the kindred, sympathy for the oppressed, generosity towards the indigent, distinctive personality, noble temperament and stainless example of human behaviour.

If one scans, the 40-year life of the holy Prophet (PBUH) prior to Prophethood and analyses all the facets of his career from any angle of a biographer, no one would find any blindside in his personality.

You have already read how the holy Prophet's (PBUH) slave, Zaid bin Harise refused to go with his parents and continue to live with the holy Prophet (PBUH) only because he was so charmed by the nobility of his character and personality that he completely ignored his parental love and affection.

Acts and Operations

The holy Prophet's (PBUH) pious life is a practical demonstration of the teachings of the holy Quran. This underlines an extremely important aspect of Islam—it stresses first on practice and action than on mere principles and preachings. The holy Prophet's (PBUH) forty-year career before Prophethood preceded, as a practical example, the maxims and laws of Islam as enunciated in the holy Quran. Therefore, the practicability of this religion remains unchallenged.

Is there a man, in human history, who can stand beside the holy Prophet (PBUH) and can match him in any way from the standpoint of the multitude of persecuted and oppressed persons who stood firm in their faith in his Prophethood and the truth of the words uttered by him and falsehood of the claims of his detractors.

Divine blessing can be attained only through true and perfect love for His last Prophet (PBUH). And, if one were to observe the love, respect and high esteem for the holy Prophet (PBUH) that his followers have for him, one has only to look at the dedication and strong emotional attachment of those devotees who enter the limits of Medina, where the Noblest Prophet (PBUH) rests peacefully.

Appendix

Original Document

Full Text of Charter : English Version

Clause 1

"This is a document from Muhammad (PBUH), The Prophet between the Believers, Muslims of Quraysh and Yathribites, and those who followed them and fought with them. They will form one Ummah to the exclusion of others."

Clause 2

"The Quraysh Muhajireen will pay blood money within themselves according to the present custom."

Clause 3

"They will redeem their prisoners with kindness and justice common among Believers."

Clause 4

"The Banu Auf will pay blood money, within themselves according to the existing custom."

Clause 5

"All parties will redeem their prisoners with kindness and justice according to practice among Believers."

Clause 6

"The Banu Saeeda, The Banu Harith, The Banu Jusham and The Banu Najjar will be governed on the above lines."

Clause 7

"The Banu Amr, Banu Auf, Banu Al-Nabeet, and Banu Al-Ass, will be governed in the same manner."

Clause 8

"Believers will not fail to redeem their prisoners or fail to pay blood money on behalf of one of them."

Clause 9

"The Believers will not make the freedman of another Believer as his ally against the wishes of the other Believer."

Clause 10

"The Believers who fear Allah, will oppose rebellious elements and those that encourage injustice or sin or enmity or lack of co-operation among Believers."

Clause 11

"If anyone is guilty of any such act all the Believers will oppose him even if he is the son of any one of them."

Clause 12

"A Believer will not kill another Believer, for the sake of an un-Believer."

Clause 13

"No Believer will help an un-Believer against a Believer."

Clause 14

"Protection in the name of Allah will be common. The weakest among Believers may give protection and it will be binding on all Believers."

Clause 15

"Believers are all friends to each other to the exclusion of all others."

Clause 16

"Those Jews who follow us will be helped and will be treated with equality."

Clause 17

"No Jew will be wronged."

Clause 18

"The enemies of Jews will not be helped."

Clause 19

"The peace of Believers cannot be divided."

Clause 20

"No separate peace will be made when Believers are fighting in the Path of Allah."

Clause 21

"Conditions must be fair and equitable for all alike."

Clause 22

"On expedition a rider must take another behind him."

Clause 23

"The Believers must avenge the blood of one another when fighting in the Path of Allah."

Clause 24

"The Believers because they fear Allah, they are better in showing steadfastness and as a result receive Guidance."

Clause 25

"No un-Believer will be permitted to take the property of Quraysh under his protection."

Clause 26

"No un-Believer will intervene in favour of a Quraysh."

Clause 27

"If any un-Believer kills a Believer, without good cause, he shall be killed in return, unless the next of kin are satisfied. All Believers shall be against such a wrongdoer. No Believer, if he believes in Allah and the Last Day, will be allowed to shelter such a man who-ever shelters such a man, on him will be punishment of Allah on the Day of Judgement".

Clause 28

"When you differ on anything, the matter shall be referred to Allah and Muhammad (PBUH)."

Clause 29

"The Jews will contribute towards the war when fighting alongside the Believers."

Clause 30

"The Jews of Banu Auf are one community with the Believers. The Jews have their religion and the Muslims have their religion."

Clause 31

"The same applies to the Jews of Bani-al-Najjar, Bani-al-Harith, Bani Saeeda, Bani Jusham, Bani Al Aus, Thaalba, and the Jaffna, a clan of the Bani Thaalba, and the Jaffna, a clan of the Bani Thaalba, and the Bani-al-Shuraiba."

Clause 32

"Loyalty gives protection against treachery."

Clause 33

"The freedman of Thaalba will be offered the same status as Thaalba themselves."

Clause 34

"Those in alliance with the Jews will be given the same treatment as the Jews."

Clause 35

"No one will go to war except with the permission of Muhammad (PBUH). If any wrong has been done to any person or party it may be avenged."

Clause 36

"Any one who kills another without warning amounts to his slaying himself and his household, unless the killing was done due to a wrong being done to him."

Clause 37

"The Jews bear their own expenses and the Muslims bear their own expenses."

Clause 38

"If anyone attacks anyone who is a party to this Charter the others must come to his help."

Clause 39

"They must seek mutual advice and consultation."

Clause 40

"Loyalty gives protection against treachery."

Clause 41

"A man will not be made liable for the misdeeds of his ally."

Clause 42

"Anyone who is wronged must be helped."

Clause 43

"The Jews must pay to the Muslims."

Clause 44

"Yathrib will be sanctuary for the people of the Charter."

Clause 45

"A stranger who has been given protection will be treated as his host while doing no harm and is not committing any crime."

Clause 46

"Woman will be given protection only with the consent of her family."

Clause 47

"In case of any dispute or trouble which may result in trouble, the matter must be referred to Allah and Muhammad (PBUH), the Prophet of Allah. Allah will accept anything in this Document which is for piety and goodness."

Clause 48

"Quraysh and their allies will not be given protection."

Clause 49

"The parties to this Charter are bound to help each other in the event of an attack on Yathrib."

Clause 50

"If they are called upon to make and maintain peace they must do so. If a similar demand is made on the Muslims it must be carried out, except when the Muslims are already engaged in a war in the Path of Allah."

Clause 51

"Every one will have the share in accordance with what party he belongs to."

Clause 52

"The Jews of Al-Aus, including their freedmen, have the same standing as other parties to the Charter, as long as they are loyal to the Charter. Loyalty is a protection against treachery."

Clause 53

"Anyone who acts loyally or otherwise does it for his own good."

Clause 54

"Allah approves this Document."

Clause 55

"This Document will not protect any one who is unjust or commits a crime."

Clause 56

"Whether an individual goes out to fight, or remains in his house, he will be safe unless he has committed a crime or is a sinner."

Clause 57

"Allah is the Protector of the good people and those who fear Allah, and Muhammad (PBUH) is the Messenger of Allah."

Bibliography

Abdul Hamid Siddiqui, *The Life of Muhammad (PBUH).*

Adolphus Slade, *Record of Travels.*

Ali Kattani, *Muslim Minorities in the World.*

Allan Nouvin, *The Gateway to History.*

Andre Beaufre, *General Introduction to Strategy.*

Andre Mauris, *History of England.*

Arnold Toynbee, *The World and the West.*

Arnold, Sir Thomas, *The Caliphate,* London, 1965.

A Short History of Saracens by Amir Ali, London, 1951.

Aspects of Islamic Civilization, Ann Arbor, 1963.

Basham, A. L. ed., *A Cultural History,* Oxford University Press, New Delhi, 1975.

Bhawany, *Revolutionary Study of National Development.*

Carl Bockleman, *History of Islamic Peoples.*

Clafson Fredrick, *Justice and Social Policy.*

Corbett, P.E., *Law and Society in Relation to States.*

Corbin, H., *Avicenna and the Visionary Recital,* New York, 1960.

Cultural Trends in Medieval Period, Bombay, 1968.

Czaplicka, M.A., *The Turks of Central Asia in History*, Amsterdam, 1973.

Dawud, Rahbar, *God of Justice*, Leiden, 1960.

Dinet and Salman, *Life of Muhammad* (PBUH).

Dorothy Vaughan, *Europe and the Turks.*

Doughty, *Travels in Arabia Deserta.*

Drew Pearson and Constantine Brown, *The Diplomatic Game.*

Durrani, F.K.K., *Muhammad (PBUH) The Prophet.*

Earle Meade, *Makers of Modern Strategy.*

Edward Coke, *Paramountcy of Parliament.*

Edward Mortimer, *The Politics of Islam.*

Emil Brunner, *Justice and the Social Order.*

Esme Wingfield, *The Price of Liberty.*

Eton, *Survey of the Empire.*

Faris, Nabith A., *The Book of Knowledge*, Lahore, 1962.

Field, Cland H., *The Alchemy of Happiness*, London, 1910.

Fred Joseph, *International Relations.*

Frykenberg, *Land Control and Social Structure*, Wisconsin, 1969.

Gauba, K.L., *The Prophet of the Desert* (PBUH).

Gibb, H.A.R, *Islamic Society and the West London*, 1960.

Gibbon Edward, *History of the Decline and Fall of Roman Empire.*

Glimpses of Medieval Culture, Bombay, 1959.

Glubb, Major General, *The Great Arab Conquests.*

Glubb, Major General, *The Story of Arab Legion.*

Guiberg Morris, *On Justice and Society.*

Gustav E. von Grunebaum, *Unity and Variety in Muslim Civilization.*

Harley Williams, *The Conquest of Fear.*

Hasan, Ibn, *The Central Structure of the Empire,* New Delhi, 1980.

Hitti Philip, *History of the Arabs,* Macmillan and Company Limited, New York, 1960.

Holt, Lambton and Lewis, *The Cambridge History of Islam,* Cambridge, 1970.

Hussaini, *Constitution of the Arab Empire.*

Ikram, S.M., *Muslim Civilization,* New York.

James Piscarton, *Islam in the World of National States.*

Jamil Jaibi and Qazi A. Qadir, *The Changing World of Islam.*

Kamal A. Faruqui, *Islam Today and Tomorrow.*

Karnest Barker, *National Character.*

Khalifa Abdul Hakim, *The Islamic Ideology.*

Khalifa Abdul Hakim, *The Prophet (PBUH) and His Message.*

Lewis, Bernard, *Islam,* New York, 1974.

Lord Moron, *An Anatomy of Fear.*

Ludwig Renn, *The Relation of War to Society.*

MacClosky, *Pacts for Peace.*

Manzuruddin Ahmad, *Islamic Political System.*

Miller, *Current International Treaties.*

Montgomery Watt, *Muhammad (PBUH) at Madina.*

Montgomery Watt, *The Majesty that was Islam.*

Muhammad Abdullah Enan, *Decisive Moments in the History of Islam.*

Muhammad Ayub, *The Politics of Islamic Revolution.*

Muir, William, *Early Caliphate.*

Muir, William, *Life of Muhammad* (PBUH).

Philips, E.C. ed., *Politics and Society*, London, 1963.

Rizvi, S. A. A., *Muslim Revivalist Movements*, Agra, 1965.

Rosenthal, E.I.J., *Political Thought in Medieval Islam*, Cambridge, 1962.

Sergeant, *Constitution of Madina.*

Sergeant, *The Sunnah Jamia.*

Setalvad, *War and Civil Liberties.*

Sharif, M.M., *A History of Muslim Philosophy*, Wiesbaden.

Shaukat Ali, *Masters of Muslim Thought.*

Shemesh, A.B., *Taxation in Islam*, Leiden, 1958, 1965.

Syed Amir Ali, *The Spirit of Islam.*

Tripathi, R.J., *Some Aspects of Muslim Administration*, Allahabad, 1959.

Tritton, A.S., *The Caliphs and Their non-Mulim Subjects*, Oxford, 1930.

Trueblood Eiton, *Declaration of Freedom.*

Wahed Husain, *Administration of Justice during Muslim Rule*, Delhi, 1977.

Weech, *History of the World.*

Wilfred Seamen Blunt, *The Future of Islam.*

Yeome Yezbeck Haddad, *Islamic Values.*

Index

❑❑❑